CONTRACTING STATES

CONTRACTING STATES

SOVEREIGN TRANSFERS IN INTERNATIONAL RELATIONS

Alexander Cooley and Hendrik Spruyt

PRINCETON UNIVERSITY PRESS   PRINCETON AND OXFORD

Copyright © 2009 by Princeton University Press
Published by Princeton University Press, 41 William Street,
Princeton, New Jersey 08540
In the United Kingdom: Princeton University Press, 6 Oxford Street,
Woodstock, Oxfordshire OX20 1TW

Library of Congress Cataloging-in-Publication Data

Cooley, Alexander, 1972–
Contracting states : sovereign transfers in international relations / Alexander Cooley
p.   cm.
Includes bibliographical references and index.
ISBN 978-0-691-13723-0 (hardcover : alk. paper)
ISBN 978-0-691-13724-7 (pbk. : alk. paper)
1. Sovereignty. 2. Military bases, American—Foreign countries. 3. Military bases,
British—Foreign countries. 4. France—Armed Forces—Foreign countries.
5. Regionalism (International organization) I. Spruyt, Hendrik, 1956– II. Title.
JZ4034.C665 2009
355.7—dc22
2008043873

British Library Cataloging-in-Publication Data is available

This book has been composed in Sabon

Printed on acid-free paper. ∞

press.princeton.edu

Printed in the United States of America

10 9 8 7 6 5 4 3 2 1

For Christine Farnon, inspiration and role model, and Eugenia Katelani Cooley, an icon of many sovereign lands

Contents

Illustrations

Figures

Tables

Preface

LIKE MANY BOOKS, this one takes off from and builds on some of our previous work on the topic of sovereignty. In his earlier books Alex Cooley studied the fragmentation of the USSR and other empires using insights from the business and institutional economics work pioneered by Alfred Chandler and Oliver Williamson. In his most recent work he has turned to the analysis of U.S. overseas military bases, its underlying agreements, and the domestic political problems in host nations engendered by the American military presence. Hendrik Spruyt studied the rise of the early modern territorial state, and most recently the final victory of the principle of territorial sovereignty and the various modalities of "end of empire." Throughout these works we could not help but conclude that territorial fragmentation, state formation, and regional integration all form parts of a dynamic and interrelated process. Over the past few years we have crystallized our thinking about how sovereignty is transferred across these different domains and found many unexpected and intriguing commonalities.

Above all, we were determined to present an analytical framework to recast these sovereign processes. This past decade's research in international relations and comparative politics, as well as contemporary events, underscore how the traditional distinction of anarchic and hierarchical realms is sometimes useful, but more often fails to capture a more complex reality. This book seeks to provide an integrated perspective that illuminates how various governance structures come into being (of which anarchy and hierarchy are but two opposite ends) and why they might dissolve. We certainly would not claim that ours should be the only way to examine these sovereign issues, though we hope these arguments will draw further attention to the topic.

Our argument starts with the recognition that sovereignty consists of a bundle of rights. Some polities maintain most, and perhaps almost all, such rights for themselves. Others, willfully or by force, relinquish considerable rights to external powers. Yet others, as polities in some regional organizations, surrender some sovereign rights to new institutional sites while they retain others for themselves. Like property rights, aspects of sovereignty can be split or shared by states and other international actors. Though often neglected, these mixed sovereignty arrangements are a critical part of the fabric of international governance and often help facilitate international systemic change.

We employ insights from economics and business to shed light on how particular sovereignty arrangements may evolve over time. More specifically we use incomplete contracting theory to analyze diverse empirical cases involving mixed sovereignty arrangements. We examine historical and contemporary cases, and we offer new theoretical explanations for the timing and nature of post-imperial extrication, the evolution of U.S. overseas military basing arrangements, and the varied institutional forms of regional economic integration in Europe and North America. We thus focus on security issues, contracting over specific economic assets, and regional economic integration.

Across these topics, we explore how incomplete contracting and hybrid sovereignty arrangements emerge against the backdrop of relative power imbalances and credibility of commitment problems. Transferring sovereignty can be fraught with political complications, nationalist anxieties, and fears about the future. Yet, we also now observe that states, contra the assumptions of certain theories of international relations theorists, frequently agree to do so despite these risks and their uncertain consequences. States consistently have crafted creative mixed sovereignty arrangements in the form of incomplete contracts. We subsequently examine the downstream consequences of incomplete contracts once they are adopted, particularly with regard to the bargaining leverage of the respective participants, the durability of these agreements, and the dynamics of subsequent renegotiations.

These processes cannot simply be reduced to the relative power differentials between actors. We see many unexpected outcomes: former imperial cores and peripheries have reached agreements in the most difficult of circumstances that ultimately ended bloody conflicts and facilitated imperial disengagement; small states have bargained hard with the United States over military basing rights and many even have expelled the superpower; and a series of very general agreements among Western European countries, seemingly limited in scope initially, generated a supranational entity unique within international relations.

Beyond these main insights we sketch out additional applications in three concluding mini-cases of sovereign transfers. We submit that an incomplete contracting perspective can shed light on the circumstances under which federal bargains in multiethnic states are likely to promote or dampen separatist ethnic antagonism. Moreover, we believe that insights gleaned from the study of decolonization apply to other cases of bilateral territorial disengagement. We examine how institutions that promote joint sovereignty over such site-specific assets as the water resources in Gaza and the West Bank might help facilitate or retard a resolution to the Arab-Israeli conflict. Finally, we explore how incomplete contracting may apply to third-party sovereign transfers by examining the transfer of authority to an international administration and subsequently the Kosovar government. Indeed, the United Nations itself, contra its position during the cold war, no longer regards the sovereignty of member countries as an inviolable right; the international community is now actively assuming the responsibility of sharing sovereign functions and institutions with states that are not deemed capable of governing themselves. Clearly, the frequency of sovereign transfers is not diminishing in this post–cold war or global era.

Throughout this joint endeavor—our very own longstanding incomplete contract—we have incurred many debts, and we are grateful to those who have suffered through our earlier drafts. As is the case with multiyear book projects we run the risk of inadvertently omitting some; we offer our apologies in advance.

We owe a particular debt to Walter Mattli, Philip Roeder, and Katja Weber for reading the manuscript in its entirety and offering many helpful suggestions. We hope we have done justice to their advice. David Lake's own work has inspired ours, and beyond that David has (as always) generously commented on earlier parts of the book in more panels than he cares to remember. Many others have similarly provided critiques and valuable insights. We owe thanks to Karen Alter, Dan Deudney, Lynn Dobson, Yale Ferguson, Ian Hurd, Kim Marten, Dan Nexon, Volker Rittberger, Jack Snyder, and Carolyn Warner for commenting on earlier drafts. Patrick Johnston and Christopher Swarat assisted with the preparation of the manuscript and provided many keen insights. We also thank Chuck Myers and the outstanding staff at Princeton University Press for their assistance with the review and production process.

Hendrik Spruyt would particularly like to express his gratitude to Robert Keohane, Helen Milner, Andrew Moravcsik, and Anne Sartori for their comments and the opportunity to present rudimentary thoughts on the topic at a seminar at Princeton. He is similarly appreciative for the opportunity provided by Charles Lipson and Duncan Snidal and the Pipes seminar at the University of Chicago, as well as the many comments of the group. At Columbia's Institute for War and Peace Studies he had the opportunity to present his thoughts in a workshop sponsored by the Carnegie Corporation and run by Dick Betts, Kim Marten, Tanisha Fazal, and Alex Cooley. Thanks to all those who participated. USC's Center for International Studies provided the forum for a stimulating discussion. Patrick James's invitation and Gerardo Munck's profound insights were of great help in the final stages of this book. He is, furthermore, grateful for the support of the deans of Weinberg College, Provost Daniel Linzer, and President Henry Bienen. The Norman Dwight Harris Chair at Northwestern University has provided a much appreciated and most conducive research base.

Alex Cooley would like to thank the Carnegie Corporation, the German Marshall Fund of the United States, and the Smith Richardson Foundation, without which much of the empirical research and required travel for this project would not have been possible. Various earlier versions of our chapters were presented at annual meetings of the American Political Science Association and the International Studies Association, as well as at seminars held by Northwestern University, the University of Pennsylvania's Browne Center, and the MIT Security Studies Program. Columbia University's seminar titled "Soft Borders and Limited Sovereignty," supported by the Harriman Institute and codirected by Gordon Bardos, was a source of rich discussion, creative ideas, and debate. Finally, Rawi Abdelal, Peter Andreas, Deborah Avant, Mark Blyth, Erik Gartzke, Jonathan Hopkin, Bob Jervis, Robin Varghese, and Susan Woodward all provided excellent suggestions that helped clarify important concepts.

We are both thankful to be part of outstanding research communities in Evanston-Chicago and New York and to have such engaging colleagues and supportive friends. And last but not least, we are of course but the shadow players to our better halves, Lucy and Nicole, who have supported us in more ways than we can mention through this multiyear, multivenue endeavor. This book would not be possible without their understanding and good cheer.

CONTRACTING STATES

Chapter 1

Incomplete Sovereignty and International Relations

Introduction

Territorial sovereignty presents us with a paradox. On the one hand, it forms the key constitutive rule in international relations.[1] In strict terms it denotes that the people within recognized territorial borders are masters of their own fate. No higher juridical authority exists above that of the national government. And all states are equal in international law. Sovereignty is thus highly desired. As we have witnessed in the former Soviet Union and Yugoslavia, and many other parts of the world, nations vie for their own state, and people fight and die for that cause.

Yet on the other hand, the world is replete with instances where sovereignty appears fragile. Some observers claim that the territorial state is obsolete and in the process of being supplanted by other institutional forms.[2] Others see territorial sovereignty solely as a juridical fiction. Although states are equal from an international legal perspective, they fail to capture the continued relevance of power, domination, and hegemony.[3] Indeed, in the wake of American military action in Iraq and elsewhere, some argue that we are witnessing the resurrection of the study of empire and imperialism. Empire, thought to have become obsolete in the decades after World War II, has returned as an international reality.[4] But many cases of sovereign relations do not comfortably fit these categories.

Consider the following two cases. The first involved the evolution of sovereignty within Iraq itself. On June 28th, 2004, the United States transferred sovereignty to an interim government in Iraq, formally concluding a fifteen-month occupation that followed its military campaign to forcibly disarm the country and enact regime change.[5] Even though the Coalition Provisional Authority led by Paul Bremer formally disbanded, the continued presence of over 120,000 American troops in Iraq led many analysts

---

[1] See, for example, Ruggie 1986; Spruyt 1994; Zacher 2001.

[2] Herz (1976) argues this is the case for security reasons, whereas Ohmae (1995) attributes this to economic changes.

[3] See especially Krasner 1999.

[4] For representative examples, see Cox 2004; Johnson 2004. For skeptical analytical responses, see Nexon and Wright 2007; Motyl 2006.

[5] Chandrasekaran 2006; Diamond 2006.

to question whether this handover was practically significant.[6] Four years after the transfer the exact division of sovereignty between Iraq and the United States still remained ill defined and incomplete. The UN mandate authorizing the presence of the U.S.-led coalition mission in Iraq was extended through 2008. However, in 2007 the United States and Iraq agreed to negotiate a bilateral framework to govern critical future sovereign issues after 2008, including the role of U.S. forces, the legal status of military contractors in Iraq, and the future levels of U.S. economic and military assistance to the country. The politically thorny question of the likelihood of a permanent U.S. military basing presence in the country was also brought to the fore. Iraq had regained much of this sovereignty since the 2003 U.S. invasion, but many of these sovereign transfers happened gradually and remain open-ended.

Just one week before the 2004 formal transfer of sovereignty in Iraq, leaders of the (then) twenty-five members of the European Union (EU) agreed to adopt a common constitution that would consolidate previous agreements, clarify voting procedures, expand the role of the European parliament, and unify the foreign policy preferences and decision-making procedures of the member countries. Although leaders were relieved to have actually agreed upon a text for the accord, thereby avoiding the public embarrassment that followed the collapse of negotiations six months earlier, immediate concerns arose as to its future political viability. According to one observer, the accord was the product of "arm-twisting, obfuscation and opt-outs" that had papered over substantive disagreements over the future of the EU.[7] One year later, the rejection of the constitution by the French and Dutch publics in national referenda indicated that the European Commission had not been able to guarantee to these skeptical publics that its authority would be restrained and accountable. It took three more years to allay the resistance among the French and Dutch citizens—at least for a majority—as many of the same provisions were included in the 2007 Lisbon Treaty, but even this accord was rejected by Irish voters in a June 2008 referendum. These rejections show how Europeans remain concerned about the exact future contours of the European project and the scope and momentum of ongoing European integration.

Despite their obviously contrasting regional settings and political processes—the disengagement of Iraq from American control and the continued integration of the EU countries—both of these cases highlight a number of common features and dilemmas surrounding the institution of state sovereignty in contemporary international politics. First, in both cases,

---

[6] For example, see *International Herald Tribune*, June 30, 2004, p. 5.
[7] *The Economist*, June 26, 2004, 42.

the exact apportioning of sovereignty after these agreements, despite weeks of prior speculation and analysis, was unclear. Could Iraq truly claim to be a meaningfully sovereign country—despite the fact that it controlled the functions of twenty-six ministries—if American troops operating under their own command and control remained in the country for an indefinite period of time? Would the position of an EU foreign minister have any credibility or authority when individual member countries dissented from the external policy positions of the EU? In both cases, sovereignty had been reapportioned across political actors, but the exact nature and boundaries of this sovereign authority was difficult to specify.

A second common feature of these agreements was the uncertainty surrounding their exact downstream distributional consequences. How would these accords affect the future relative bargaining power of these states? Would the handover of sovereignty give the Iraqi government real authority or even veto power over the United States and its military decisions? How would the new voting procedures affect the ability of the European "big three" to shape the European Community's policy agenda? After the failed referenda, would the Commission try to "smuggle" in these constitutional changes through other established procedures and European agencies? Thus, not only were the particular contours of sovereign authority unclear, but the future consequences of these particular sovereign arrangements were also uncertain. Yet, even without being able to anticipate future power dynamics and distributional consequences, the various states involved in concluding these agreements had agreed, at least initially, to reapportion and transfer their sovereignty.

Finally, both of these agreements ignited renewed domestic political debates about the acceptability of altering the existing institutional scope of sovereignty. Would the Iraqi public be able to accept the continued presence of so many foreign troops now that they had regained their nominal sovereignty? Would U.S. policymakers call for the withdrawal of U.S. forces now that a major political disengagement had taken place? In the European case, the very ability of a member country to secure public acquiescence to greater integration was thrown into question. Thus, in both cases, new agreements over the scope of sovereign authority exacted a fresh set of domestic political costs and constraints.

These cases are but two examples of a much larger set of instances in which states negotiate about, bundle, or surrender their sovereign prerogatives. To be sure, territorial sovereignty remains a critically important institution in international relations. If it were merely organized hypocrisy, pace Stephen Krasner, how should we understand the desperate pursuit of that goal by so many nations?[8]

[8] Krasner 1999.

But sovereignty is rarely absolute. Rather, sovereignty consists of a bundle of rights and obligations that are dynamically exchanged and transferred between states.[9] For example, decolonization and territorial partition do not always mean that the newly independent states acquire full sovereignty. Instead, nationalist leaders might be content to obtain partial sovereignty if it accelerates the process of imperial withdrawal. In other instances, elites might grant some sovereign rights to another state or international organization because of perceived gains from the transaction.[10] Such forms of hybrid sovereign relations represent mixed forms of organizational governance that are neither purely "anarchical" nor "hierarchical."[11]

In agreeing to such hybrid sovereign relations, leaders are rarely sure about the long-term consequences of the agreements they sign. Few European statesmen foresaw the expansion of the EU and the depth of integration of the Community today. When Algerian nationalists and the French government agreed that France could maintain military bases and oil facilities after Algerian independence, they had no clear view of the durability of that agreement and the credibility of both parties to follow through. Who knows whether American-Iraqi agreements that authorize the presence of American troops in Iraq will stand the test of time?

What is noteworthy from our perspective is that states *frequently* contract with other international actors in both the economic and security spheres, despite the uncertainty and distributional pressures that the anarchic international system generates. As we shall see across the areas of international security and economy, states regularly and voluntarily divide and cede their sovereignty in both bilateral and multilateral settings.

Our book has two key aims. First, we wish to delineate how a particular sovereign governance structure emerges. Second, we will show how choices made at a given point in time have important downstream consequences that may not be readily apparent to the contracting parties at the time of the initial agreement.[12]

We argue that incomplete contracting theory can clarify how and why states choose to bundle and unbundle their sovereignty, what the dynamics will likely be of future renegotiation, why some agreements are more readily achieved than others, and why some of these incomplete contracts

[9] On sovereignty as a bundle of rights, see A. Cooley 2000–2001.

[10] On rulers and their possible interest in ceding sovereignty, see Krasner 1999.

[11] On the anarchy-hierarchy distinction and continuum of sovereign relations, see Lake 1996.

[12] As Kathleen Thelen notes (2004), institutional outcomes do not always follow from initial preferences. Indeed, as she shows from her discussion of labor relations in Germany, opponents and proponents of particular outcomes today occupy diametrically opposite positions from where they stood a century ago.

might unravel. Incomplete contracting theory can shed light on many diverse governance structures, and we will highlight the relevance of our theory by looking in depth at imperial and postcolonial relations, overseas military basing agreements, and regional integration.

The Importance of Incomplete Contracting in International Politics

Agreements such as the end of formal U.S. occupation of Iraq or the European Union's draft constitution are incomplete contracts. Although both agreements transfer significant elements of sovereignty among international actors, many clauses of these treaties and accords remain initially unspecified or are deferred for future negotiation.

Theories of incomplete contracting are particularly instructive for explaining the organizational boundaries of the international system. Kenneth Waltz's seminal work on international politics draws on the concept of market competition as an analogy for state competition,[13] but the international system more closely resembles an imperfect market than a perfect market. In international relations, anarchy generates a tremendous degree of uncertainty and informational asymmetries about the actions and intentions of political actors.[14] The lack of a central governing authority ensures that states must be wary of the long-term distributional consequences of their actions and be hesitant to commit to long-term agreements.[15] Moreover, states cannot take for granted that other international actors will honor agreements, especially when they lack well-established domestic institutions such as constitutions or electoral systems that help establish this credibility.[16] As David Lake notes, "opportunism is ubiquitous in international relations."[17] This imposes significant costs on the actions of political actors. Even when ceding authority to an international institution, states consciously design rules and procedures for international institutions so that they can adapt to changing circumstances.[18]

---

[13] Waltz 1979, 89–91.

[14] Koremenos (2001) notes how contextual uncertainty and confounding variables, which make it difficult for actors to assess contractual outcomes, hamper the ability of states to conclude long-term agreements.

[15] Grieco 1990.

[16] Lipson 2003; Cowhey 1993. On the importance of democratic legislatures for establishing credibility, see Martin 2000. Ikenberry (2001) describes how even powerful states can benefit from strategically restraining themselves through international institutions.

[17] Lake 1999, 52–53.

[18] See Koremenos, Lipson, and Snidal 2001.

In such an environment, incomplete contracts offer two important advantages for states. First, incomplete contracts delineate general principles and broad goals to which states can aspire. Given that actors cannot foresee, anticipate, or describe every possible contingency that may arise, general framing agreements are more likely to be initially accepted than a complete contract, and states will be willing to defer the negotiation of more intricate details to a later stage. Second, contractual renegotiation acts as an important institutional check on the future behavior of actors. As has been argued elsewhere in reference to international regimes, renegotiation increases the iteration among actors and ensures that problems of information and verification that pertain to the initial contract can be identified and resolved and/or redefined.[19] Incomplete contracts also offer states added flexibility to correct for distributional asymmetries that may arise as the result of the initial agreement.[20]

In short, incomplete contracts between states are framework agreements that do not fully apportion sovereignty. Instead, such agreements make the distribution and allocation of sovereign rights a matter of ongoing negotiation between the contracting parties or between those parties and a third party, such as a supranational organization.

Hypocritical Agreements?

Existing theories of international relations are not particularly concerned with explaining the dynamics of such mixed forms of sovereignty and the political uncertainty generated by "incomplete" agreements. The prevailing view among international relations scholars is that such modified forms of sovereignty are largely insignificant and do not alter the fundamental capacities and preferences of states. Stephen Krasner perhaps best summarizes this consensus by arguing that the institution of sovereignty is given lip service by the international community but is consistently violated by powerful political actors.[21] From this perspective, the nominal sovereignty of Iraq is of little practical consequence, as the United States is still able to exert its power and impose its preferences on the country. Similarly, the EU Constitution is relatively insignificant given that it still allows countries to opt out or veto EU decisions, especially in the realm of security policy. For skeptics of international institutions, contractual arrangements are secondary to the national interest and capabilities of the powerful actors entering these arrangements.[22]

---

[19] On regimes and iteration, see Keohane 1984.

[20] We share many of the assumptions that underlie the work of Koremenos 2001, 293–94.

[21] Krasner 1999.

[22] Such is the standard skepticism expressed by neorealist theories of international relations and international institutions. See Mearsheimer 1994–95.

But while sovereignty, at times, may seem like "organized hypocrisy," its mere violation, erosion, or compromise does not necessarily diminish its causal significance. By thinking in the strict binary terms of "full sovereignty" or "violations of sovereignty"—or "autonomy" and "hierarchy"—scholars have neglected the many mixed forms of sovereignty, split property rights, and hybrid governance arrangements that have historically proliferated through the international system. While we agree with the aim of prevailing attempts to explain the dynamics of non-sovereign forms of governance such as supranationalism and empire with organizational theory, especially transaction costs theory and relational contracting, we regard the strict anarchy/hierarchy distinction as unable to capture many of the nuanced forms of sovereignty that are critical for understanding many forms of international organization and governance.[23]

From a practical perspective, understanding the various ways in which sovereignty can be bundled and unbundled underscores how states can potentially develop creative and new non-conflictual institutional solutions to problems that surround their sovereignty such as territorial partition.[24] Often the sovereignty-related underlying sources of conflicts among states—contested assets, territory, borders, and functions—can all be split, shared, and reapportioned in a mutually beneficial manner. States can agree to lease or use an asset or piece of territory for a specified duration or during a transitional period before exclusive sovereignty arrangements are finalized. Delegation of a certain state function to a third-party organization can bind both parties to a common set of principles and procedures. The malleability of sovereignty and partial sovereign arrangements may thus help foster stability and orderly arrangements in international politics. Forms of hybrid sovereignty may provide additional institutional solutions for competing states to avert the high costs of conflict.

Recasting Our Understanding of "Integration" and "Disintegration"

By focusing on the varied modes of contracting employed by states across a broad range of issue areas, we recast our understanding of the twin processes of "integration" and "disintegration" in international relations. Traditionally, scholars have examined integration as the aggregated

[23] Some of the most important works on sovereignty and relational contracting include Lake 1999; Weber 2000; Frieden 1994.

[24] Our emphasis on different governance forms as solutions to intractable conflicts and/or territorial disputes thus differs from scholars who view territoriality and indivisibility in more socially constructed or psychological terms. On social legitimacy and indivisibility, see Goddard 2006; on ideational barriers to territorial disengagement, see Lustick 1993.

transfer of sovereign assets or functions to another actor or organization, while disintegration is viewed as the process by which territories and functions are disengaged from a larger polity. However, our framework suggests that both integration and disintegration in their incompleteness involve the reconfiguration and re-bundling of assets and/or functions from one party to another. We show that all processes of sovereign transfer—including imperialism, supranationalism, decolonization, and overseas military basing agreements—involve the reapportioning of sovereign, rights, functions, and territories from one actor to another.[25] For example, the loss of a state's exclusive sovereignty over an area of economic governance to a regional organization also implies that regional organization's gain of the governance of that same function. Similarly, the collapse of an empire or multinational state implies a transfer in sovereignty from a territorially greater polity to a newly independent state. Thus, both integration and disintegration involve sovereign gains, losses, and reconfigurations of assets and functions for the involved contracting parties. Accordingly, we believe that these different forms of sovereign transfers and their institutional dynamics can and should be studied within a common analytical framework despite their varying issue areas. From our perspective, the direction of these sovereign transfers matters less theoretically than the mode and contractual arrangements that govern their transfer and whether these arrangements are exclusive and complete or hybrid and incomplete.

The Argument in Brief: Incomplete Contracting and the Organizational Dynamics of Sovereignty

The Logic of Incomplete Contracting

The type of contracting employed by political actors during integration and disintegration has observable effects on various aspects of state sovereignty and institutional arrangements. Critical to our account is the distinction between complete contracts and incomplete contracts. Complete contracts describe and specify the full array of responsibilities and obligations of the contracting parties, as well as anticipate every possible future contingency that may arise throughout the course of the exchange agreement.[26] By contrast, incomplete contracts arise from the imperfections and transaction costs generated by the contracting environment that

---

[25] In this sense, this collaborative project is a continuation of our recent individual work on the common institutional dynamics of empire, decolonization and other hierarchical forms of territorial organization (Spruyt 2005; A. Cooley 2005a).

[26] For an overview and discussion, see Hart and Bengt 1987.

prevent actors from specifying complete contracts. Incomplete contracts arise for both "procedural" and "strategic" reasons.

Procedural incompleteness arises when contracting actors are unable to do the following: (1) anticipate the full array of contingencies that may arise in the future; (2) negotiate optimal agreements given the asymmetries of information that characterize the contracting environment; and/or (3) negotiate an agreement that is verifiable or enforceable by the parties themselves or an outside third party, such as a court system or central regime. As a result of these different transaction costs—"uncertainty," "negotiating costs," and "enforcement costs"—states, even if they prefer a complete contract, may not be able to anticipate all the possible transaction costs, exogenous events, and future bargaining positions that might arise throughout the course of an extended exchange.[27]

As a result, contracts will often specify the initial terms of the exchange (as in the complete contract), but will also neglect several contingencies. Consequently, the contract itself will have to make provisions for the process of renegotiation, revision, and adjustment that will likely be needed but cannot be accurately predetermined or specified *ex ante* by both parties—that is, the contract will be "incomplete."[28] Thus, the incomplete contract will provide the starting point but not necessarily the long-term specifics for the exchange relationship. In some extreme cases, such initial contracts that specify common goals and objectives as opposed to plans of action have been described as "framing agreements."[29]

Contracts can also be left incomplete for strategic reasons—*strategic incompleteness*. When actors transact over specific assets, the incompleteness of a contract may arise not only from transaction costs and exogenous shocks but also from the strategic advantage gained by one of the parties from renegotiating the agreement at a later date. When assets are specific and transactions are frequent, the owners of these assets will have increased bargaining leverage or will be in a position to "hold up" the agreement and exchange.[30] As a result, strategic incompleteness

[27] See Hart 1995, especially 23–28.

[28] For an overview of the various debates that have been spawned by the incomplete contracts approach, see Schmitz 2001.

[29] Milgrom and Roberts 1992, 131, as discussed in Doleys 2000, 535–36.

[30] This is the classic hold-up problem described in O. Williamson 1985. We discuss the theory at length in the next chapter. Transaction-specific assets are assets that cannot be easily redeployed to some alternative use. Thus buyer and seller are locked into the transaction to a significant degree (O. Williamson 1985, 52–56). Williamson suggests that asset specificity arises out of site specificity, physical asset specificity, and human asset specificity. We will focus particularly on the site-specific nature of assets, as natural resource ventures and overseas basing, in chapters 3 and 4. Indeed, we will discuss transaction-specific assets almost exclusively in the sense of site specificity.

may be desirable for a party that feels it can extract a greater payoff or rent after renegotiations rather than as part of the agreement *ex ante*. Much as Barbara Koremenos, Charles Lipson, and Duncan Snidal argue about the rational design of institutions in general, states consciously design and incorporate incompleteness in their contracts in order to best pursue their interests.[31]

Analytic Categories of Incomplete Contracting Theory: Allocating Rights, Bargaining Power, Momentum for Integration, and Credibility of Commitment

Over the course of this book, we explore how both procedural and strategic incomplete contracts involve several distinct facets of state sovereignty: the distribution and governance of rights among parties; the relative bargaining power of the contracting members over time; the momentum for sovereign transfer (i.e., the evolution of the incomplete contract); and credibility of commitment. Particularly when transaction-specific assets are at stake, the possibility of hold-up arises. Moreover, since bargaining power shifts to one power as time progresses, the disadvantaged party will require assurances from the other actor. In the following chapter we develop a causal model that incorporates these categories. Here we wish to highlight how these categories serve to differentiate complete from incomplete contracts.

First, incomplete contracts involve the division of property rights over sovereign issues and assets. Intermediary forms of hybrid governance can emerge as stable organizational solutions to contracting problems. Specifically, incomplete contracts allow sovereignty to be unbundled into various rights and then split or shared among contracting parties. Of these property rights, the most important distinction is that between "control rights" and "use rights."[32] Control rights allow a party to make decisions about how to use an asset, such as the right to lease, transfer ownership, or even destroy the asset. Use rights designate the right to incur the costs and reap the benefits from the use of an asset, usually for a finite period of time. By splitting the control rights and use rights of an important sovereign asset—such as a strategic installation or site-specific economic asset—incomplete contracts allow states to divide sovereign assets and territory in nonexclusive ways. Alternatively, states can also share sovereignty over an asset or function by creating joint production agreements,

---

[31] See Koremenos, Lipson, and Snidal 2001.

[32] On various property rights, see Eggertsson 1990, chapters 2 and 4. For a discussion and application to sovereignty, see A. Cooley 2000–2001.

thereby jointly supplying the particular sovereign good.[33] Rather than exclusively apportioning sovereignty to either state, incomplete contracts allow states to both split and share sovereignty over especially sensitive or important assets and functions.

Second, incomplete contracting affects the relative bargaining power of the contracting parties over time. As David Baldwin notes, power in international relations is a relative concept that must be specified in terms of scope and domain.[34] The interactions and relative positions of contracting states change over time, and initial decisions made about contracting modes can have important downstream consequences. Specifically, the apportioning of property rights over a particular asset or territory at a given time t determines the threat point of subsequent renegotiations and bargaining games at $t + 1$.[35]

Complete contracts involve one-time concerns regarding bargaining power. Bargaining asymmetries are clear and static. With incomplete contracts, by contrast, bargaining leverage may change over time and in unforeseen directions. In certain cases of incomplete contracting, such as contracting over natural resource use, the host country tends to gain more leverage as the foreign country (the investor) sinks more transaction-specific assets into such exploitation.[36]

Consequently, renegotiation is a critical juncture at which point relative bargaining power over sovereign issues can shift dramatically and in a way that does not correspond to contracting partners' relative power capabilities.[37] States that hold the residual rights of control over an asset will be empowered to appropriate any surplus rent or revenue stream at renegotiation, even if the other party remains more powerful absolutely.[38] For example, Algerian ownership rights over the Saharan oil reserves gave the Algerian government increasing leverage over the French government and companies that were allowed to exploit such oil after Algerian independence in 1962. Thus, incomplete contracts alter the relative bargaining positions and change the distribution of benefits to contracting parties over time. Most important, the holder of residual rights of control will be able to determine the future allocation of sovereign rights that were not covered in the initial agreement.

[33] These are also known as "horizontal agreements" in the institutional literature.
[34] Baldwin 1989.
[35] See Schmitz 2001; Hart and Moore 1990.
[36] Vernon 1971; Moran 1974.
[37] Arguably, if the exact consequences of renegotiation could be foreseen *ex ante*, then the contract would cease to be incomplete as the renegotiation outcome could be folded into the initial agreement. See Tirole 1999.
[38] This is the main insight of the property rights literature, as developed by Oliver Hart. See Hart 1995; Hart and Moore 1990.

Third, we argue that the particular sovereignty arrangement can affect the momentum for sovereign transfers. Complete contracts do not automatically have consequences for renegotiation and the forward momentum of further (dis)integration. Actors know the terms of the agreement, which is meant to be final and complete. Incomplete contracts, however, are based on the premise that future negotiations will be forthcoming and that the complementarity of assets and incentives for future iterative relations might change.

All other things being equal, actors will prefer to change incomplete contracts to complete ones to reduce the uncertainty that goes with renegotiations. However, an increase in the level of incompleteness of a contract expands the available continuation equilibria, thereby increasing the available ways in which an institutional arrangement can be maintained and, if necessary, amended.[39] Since iteration itself may have positive distributional consequences, rational states may also use strategic incompleteness to continue to capture surpluses during multiple renegotiations.

Whether or not a hybrid sovereignty arrangement unravels will depend on the potential efficiencies and increasing returns from joint production.[40] Further, how such renegotiations proceed will also depend on the availability of alternative contracting parties. Greater gains might be achieved by either party by violating the terms of the incomplete contract and seeking terms with other states. For example, U.S. displacement of the Netherlands as the primary investor in Indonesia greatly increased momentum toward the dismemberment of the incomplete contract between the Dutch and Indonesian governments regarding Dutch fixed assets.

All forms of contracting inevitably raise questions regarding the ability of actors to commit. But complete contracts address the issue in a different manner than do incomplete agreements. Complete contracts that involve transaction specificity increase the possibility of hold-up. Thus, partners to a complete contract will seek noncontingent solutions to the problem. Vertical integration will be the most preferred solution, thereby diminishing the issue of credibility of the contracting parties over time.

In contrast, incomplete contracts split ownership by allocating and dividing control rights and use rights. Given the incentives for actors to renegotiate or expropriate fixed assets, the credibility of the contracting parties will remain a continuous issue, but will fall especially on the shoulders of the party with the residual rights of control. What guarantees does one have that the distribution of rights will remain acceptable to both parties as time passes?

[39] Bernheim and Whinston 1998, 917.
[40] On complementary assets and increasing returns, see Hart 1995, 47–51; Joskow 1985.

TABLE 1.1
Summary Table of Characteristics of Complete and Incomplete Contracts

Sovereignty-Related Issues	Complete Contracts	Incomplete Contracts
Governance of Assets	Absolute and exclusive sovereign rights	Mixed governance arrangements
Effect of Specific Assets	Hold-up potential leads to vertical integration or hierarchy	Split property rights (separation of use rights from control rights)
Bargaining Leverage	Static: transparent at initial agreement	Changes over time in favor of residual rights holder
Possibility of Residual Surplus/Rent	None	Available for capture at time of renegotiation
Momentum for Transfer (Integration or Disintegration)	Limited; specifies complete scope of integration or disintegration	Significant; incompleteness increases continuation pathways
Effect on Renegotiation	No impact; scope of agreement perfectly described *ex ante*	Strategic use of renegotiation by holder of residual rights
Effect of Complementary Assets/Functions	No impact; scope of agreement perfectly described *ex ante*	Increased likelihood of further transfers
Credibility of Commitment	Credibility issues are dealt with by specification in initial contract (self-enforcing; mutual hostage taking; vertical integration)	Credibility issues exist *ex ante* particularly for the actor who wishes to obtain residual rights of control

The Domestic Costs of Contracting for Sovereignty

All of these issues can of course impose domestic political costs for elites. Issues involving state sovereignty are often among the most contentious for state leaders, and bargaining over sovereignty can inflame nationalism and increase demands for intractability over certain sensitive issues. If cast in terms of complete contracts, the options will seem dichotomous and zero-sum. One party will gain full control over the assets at stake, which the other state will have to forego.

Incomplete contracting can mitigate such domestic political pressures in a number of ways. By splitting the property rights of certain sovereign territories, assets, or functions, bargaining states can find acceptable mixed governance arrangements short of exclusive sovereignty than can satisfy the immediate short-term needs of both parties. By specifying a time period and incorporating a renegotiation clause within an agreement about sovereignty, elites can reassure constituents that initial agreements are only temporary and will eventually revert to their desired payoff. For example, the Ukrainian government was able to absorb the domestic political costs and public criticisms of leasing the Crimean harbor facilities to Russia by specifying that the agreement be limited to a period of twenty years, after which it would be subject to renegotiation.[41] Finally, the temporary duration of incomplete contracts can allow key domestic actors to modify their preferences. Assets or functions previously considered indispensable or integral to their operations might become less so at the contract's renegotiation. In short, if actors can credibly commit to such incomplete contracts, this raises the possibility that the hold-up problem can be mitigated or solved, short of assigning exclusive sovereignty to one particular actor.

Scope of This Study

We argue that the principal advantage of our incomplete contracting approach over other institutional accounts of sovereignty lies in our ability to study many different types of political organizations, polities, and processes under a common theoretical framework. While scholars typically study many of these processes as distinct topics—for example, studies of supranational EU integration will rarely invoke the literature on imperialism, territorial disintegration, or overseas basing—we seek to show that their common organizational dynamics can be explained within a single theoretical framework. Nevertheless, there are some im-

[41] See A. Cooley 2000–2001.

portant limits to our study. Most notably, our incomplete contracting framework assumes that states, to some degree, can make voluntary choices about the nature and shape of their organizational boundaries.[42] One might object that states do not always voluntarily choose institutional arrangements, even if they are framed in terms of treaties or contractual obligations. However, even formal empire often required the support of local elites.[43] Moreover, one of the aims of our study is to show how, over time, coercion-based interactions can actually give way to the contractual-based dynamics described by our model. We explore this dynamic further in our empirical investigations of decolonization agreements and the evolution of U.S. military basing agreements. Furthermore, as empire has become highly contested, the contractual dynamics by which states seek to solve issues of asset allocation and reallocation of sovereign rights have become more important.[44]

Finally, since sovereignty has become an ever more entrenched principle of the international system, leaders will be reluctant to engage in complete contracts that fully allocate such rights to one of the parties. Put differently, even if joint production gains might be achieved by allocating authority to one of the contracting parties, each individual government will be reluctant to surrender control over "hot button" items as sovereign control over natural resources, or to yield use rights for some foreign-run military base.[45] An incomplete contracting perspective is thus highly relevant to understanding interstate conduct today.

Chapter 2 lays out our approach in greater detail and compares our incomplete contracting approach with other organizational theories, most notably transaction costs approaches. We specify our theoretical model in greater detail and show how incomplete contracts affect the configuration of ownership rights over specific assets. The particular configuration of rights in turn affects the bargaining leverage of actors, as well as the momentum of integration and disintegration. We further discuss our methodological approach and the rationale behind our case selection. Finally, we offer a set of general hypotheses and propositions that frame the following case chapters. Each of the ensuing empirical chapters further specifies these hypotheses with regard to the cases at hand.

---

[42] We thus follow many of the methodological assumptions of Lake (1999) and Koremenos, Lipson, and Snidal (2001).

[43] Doyle 1986, 135; Nexon and Wright 2007.

[44] See Spruyt 2005.

[45] As will become clear from our discussion in the empirical chapters, natural resources and basing issues tend to generate intense preferences in former subject territories and developing countries. On natural resource debates with regard to foreign ownership and exploitation, see, for example, Krasner 1978; Moran 1974.

Chapters 3–5 apply the incomplete contracting approach to three distinct settings in international relations. In choosing our cases, we have selected topics that encompass both sovereign integration and disintegration, and issues that span the fields of both international security and international political economy as traditionally defined. Thus, like other recent works, we seek to show how organizational logics are common to sovereign transfers involving security and economy.[46] Each of the case chapters examines the theoretical propositions developed in chapters 1 and 2, but also engages with the broader literatures on integration and sovereignty inherent in that particular topic or field.

Chapter 3 examines how hybrid sovereignty arrangements emerged following the decolonization of modern empires. We explore how leasing agreements, joint production arrangements, and other hybrid forms of sovereign governance designated over peripheral military installations and economic assets facilitated the disengagement of core powers in the British, Dutch, French, and Soviet empires. We show how explicitly splitting the control and use rights of key peripheral assets within the framework of incomplete contracts allowed new national elites to overcome domestic opposition and permit foreign agencies and multinational companies to use national assets in exchange for achieving independence. The chapter first clarifies how initial preferences, shifts in the balance of power, and the ability to commit influenced the choice for particular hybrid sovereignty arrangements. We subsequently chart how these agreements were renegotiated and explore how these host countries used the bargaining power afforded by their residual rights of control to secure more beneficial terms. Decolonization thus usually involved bilateral negotiation and the distribution of fixed assets. Bargaining leverage over time was likely to shift to the host country (the newly independent state). Momentum favored further specification of ownership rights in favor of the host country and full sovereignty. Consequently, credibility of the host country *ex ante* became a key issue for the successful conclusion of such incomplete contracts upon independence. Far from being peripheral arrangements, we show how the successful conclusion of such intermediate solutions was critically important to facilitating decolonization and sometimes averting or concluding violent conflict between former imperial metropoles and emerging independent states. Across these cases we observe considerable variation. The incomplete contracts between the Netherlands and Indonesia unraveled in short order, without being replaced. The French agreements with Algeria and Tunisia did not last either, but France continues to maintain a network of hybrid sovereignty arrangements with

---

[46] Lake 1999; Koremenos, Lipson, and Snidal 2001.

its overseas bases, which are not that different in nature from the types of agreements it concluded during the decolonization period. In the former Soviet space, Russia's incomplete contracts with the "Near Abroad" continue to show a remarkable resilience. And, finally, the British, cautious about the bargaining leverage that flows to host countries holding residual rights, have retrenched to bases that they can hold outright without sovereign concessions.

Chapter 4 focuses on the various incomplete contracts that determined the sovereignty of U.S. overseas forward basing and security installations during the cold war. Military basing agreements provide a particularly powerful arena to test our claims, given that security considerations and relative power distributions should be paramount, yet we find that basing agreements were characterized by similar organizational logics as other sovereign transfers governed by incomplete contracts. We describe how the United States organized a network of overseas sites and outline the hold-up problem faced by U.S. planners when securing agreements to govern their important or specific installations. We explore how host countries strategically used their residual rights of control to periodically renegotiate these agreements to extract greater material and political concessions from the United States and restrict the scope of U.S. basing activities and use rights. We present more detailed accounts of the evolution of the agreements governing the use of the Subic Bay and Clark bases in the Philippines and the military installations on the Azores (Portugal). In both cases, we chart how incomplete contracts over these specific assets shifted bargaining strength away from the United States and toward the host countries despite these countries' nominal power differentials and alliances with the United States. Finally, we explore how the U.S. Department of Defense's recent global force restructuring plan is a partial response to the political problems created by the incomplete contracts governing the use of overseas military assets. By decreasing its forward presence in countries where its presence has become politically contentious and emphasizing flexibility and mobility in force posture, the Pentagon hopes to avoid cases of political hold-up and excessive quid pro quo demands by countries hosting overseas military assets. This chapter thus deals with bilateral negotiations in which states choose to bundle fixed assets.

Chapter 5 explores whether an incomplete contracting approach can shed light on the formation and deepening of regional economic integration, even if we relax our assumption of transaction specificity of assets, which we employed in chapters 3 and 4. It examines the institutional consequences of the incomplete contracting that governed European integration from the outset and compares this to the nature of contracting that governed the North American Free Trade Agreement (NAFTA). The chapter focuses specifically on the formation of the European Coal and

Steel Community (ECSC) in 1951 and the European Economic Community (EEC) in 1957. The institutional choices made during that formative phase influenced the subsequent evolution of the European Union. We highlight how the European Commission and the European Court of Justice used their bargaining power and the control rights that were delegated to them to extend their jurisdiction over complementary issue areas and functions. We then contrast the incomplete contracting that has characterized European integration with the relatively complete contracts that typified NAFTA. Furthermore, we show how variations in the type of contracting correlated with differences in initial preferences, relative distribution of power, and ability to credibly commit. The variation in initial contracting subsequently affected the bargaining power of the international institutions that were created in these two cases of regional integration, as well as the momentum toward further integration. Finally, we argue that despite widespread discussion of the impending onset of economic regionalism, other regional organizations are unlikely to achieve the level of integration in the EU, especially as they continue to adopt a complete contracting approach to their negotiations.

In chapter 6, we recapitulate our central theoretical arguments and offer suggestions for further research. In addition to assessing the organizational boundaries of integration and contraction in the international system, we argue that the incomplete contracting/property rights model potentially offers new theoretical insights on many additional issues such as why federal arrangements may encourage stability in some multinational states more so than in others, how hybrid forms of governance over fixed assets has impacted Arab-Israeli peace negotiations, and what the logic of incomplete contracting suggests for international transitional administration in post-conflict territories such as Kosovo.

A Theory of Incomplete Contracting and State Sovereignty

Introduction

What determines the organizational boundaries of states? When and how do states cede control over their sovereign assets and functions to an external actor? Can seemingly disparate patterns of sovereign integration and contraction be explained by a common logic?

This chapter develops a theory of incomplete contracting and the transfer of state sovereignty. Complete contracts are agreements that aim to specify and proscribe behaviors for the contracting parties in such a way that covers every contingency. Incomplete contracts, as we argued in the previous chapter, leave terms to be specified because of procedural and strategic uncertainty. In the following chapters we will show how international agreements in which one actor cedes particular sovereign rights to another actor often take the form of incomplete contracts. We will explore how the modes of contracting undertaken by international actors affect the development of hybrid institutional forms. Specifically, we argue that incomplete contracts generate endogenous momentum for the expansion of organizational boundaries, shift bargaining power to the holder of residual rights, and lead states to adopt certain types of governance arrangements over other alternatives in order to mitigate credibility problems. This logic holds equally in broad types of sovereign transfers and reconfigurations, including instances of integration and disintegration.

Our theory of the political economy of sovereign transfers draws on theoretical developments in the field of institutional economics. As economists and, increasingly, political scientists have noted, institutions arise when actors cannot independently reach cooperative arrangements.[1] To date, the most influential approach to the topic has been the transaction cost analysis of vertical integration developed by Oliver Williamson. His work must be considered a starting point for any institutional-based analysis. In the following section, we review and critique the Williamsonian theory of vertical integration. Next, we present an alternative theory of integration that focuses on the importance of incomplete

[1] Keohane 1984; Eggertsson 1990; North 1990; Ostrom 2005.

contracts and property rights arrangements for creating hybrid sovereign configurations. We then discuss the implications of this model for understanding integration and the dynamics of institutional formation in the international system. After presenting our hypotheses, we summarize how our case studies will investigate these dynamics and theoretical expectations.

Oliver Williamson, Specific Assets, and Vertical Integration

In his groundbreaking work on the origins of vertical integration, Oliver Williamson examines the conditions under which firms choose to conduct transactions within the firm as opposed to the market. Williamson's well-known analysis posits that the frequency of transactions and the nature of the assets involved determine the level and mode of governance.[2] Specifically, when transactions are frequent and assets are idiosyncratic or "specific," vertical governance or hierarchy will result.[3] Williamson reasons that hierarchical organizational forms alleviate the hold-up problems generated by relationally specific exchanges in a manner that cannot be guaranteed by comparable independent actors involved in market-based exchanges.

Applications to International Relations

Applications of the Williamsonian model to various aspects of international relations have yielded significant conceptual breakthroughs and promising initial empirical results. Market exchange in this understanding resembles relations between polities that maintain distinct, sovereign authority structures. Vertical integration parallels the merging of sovereignties under a new and unified authority structure, that is, hierarchy. Robert Keohane's theory of international regimes observes that governments create formal governance structures, with rules, norms, and procedures, to regulate interstate relations that are frequent and that involve transaction-specific assets.[4] Jeffry Frieden applies the transaction costs model to argue that colonial powers with many site-specific investments, such as mines

---

[2] O. Williamson 1985. Many of these ideas are extensions of the reasoning presented in O. Williamson 1975.

[3] Various types of specificity include site-specific investments, physical asset specificity, human specificity, and dedicated assets. O. Williamson 1985, 95–96.

[4] Keohane (1984) focuses less on transaction specificity and more on how international institutions mitigate transaction costs.

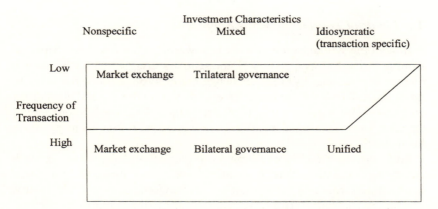

2.1. Williamson's Governance Model of Contractual Relations.
Source: Williamson 1985.

or plantations, were more likely to opt for direct control and empire, rather than other powers with investors who held more mobile assets such as monetary debt.[5] Charles Lipson's earlier work built less explicitly on Williamson's views, but in noting the differential effects of direct investments (as in natural resource exploitation), versus other types of investments, his work shows considerable affinity to Frieden's analysis.[6]

David Lake has employed the model to explain variation in the degree of unilateralism and alliance patterns in U.S. foreign policy.[7] Beth Yarbrough and Robert Yarbrough have used elements of the model to explain historical variation in patterns of trade liberalization.[8] Katja Weber creatively utilizes a transaction costs approach to explain why firms in the EU would prefer integration and vertical control. She then extrapolates from these firm preferences to state behavior.[9] Finally, Celeste Wallander has employed the approach to explain patterns of institutional persistence and adjustments in the holdings and strategies of the NATO alliance after the end of the cold war.[10] These and other approaches within the political science discipline clearly testify to the predictive power and cross-issue applicability of Williamson's theory of vertical integration.

[5] Frieden 1994.

[6] Lipson 1985, 29.

[7] Lake 1999. For further applications of the argument to Soviet and post-Soviet imperial dynamics, see Lake 1997.

[8] Yarbrough and Yarbrough 1992.

[9] Weber 2000; see also Weber and Hallerberg 2001.

[10] Wallander 2000.

The Limits of Transaction Costs Approaches

Although the Williamsonian theory is powerful, it has also been criticized from a variety of perspectives. Some scholars disagree with his analysis of firm contracting.[11] Others challenge the extrapolation of his work to international relations and disagree with the analytic parallel of firms and states. While acknowledging the relevance of his work to our understanding of international relations, we extend and hope to improve on his insights.

First, the stark dichotomy between hierarchy and the market insufficiently describes the variety of organizational arrangements and relational contracting forms that fall somewhere in between these poles. In reality, several intermediary forms of relational contracting can provide alternatives to the market/hierarchy dichotomy, as Williamson himself concedes.[12] Some alternate hybrid governance arrangements include reciprocity arrangements, franchising, joint ventures, binding arbitration, and quasi-vertical integration.[13] For example, within certain environments, binding arbitration can suffice to prevent defection, an institutional arrangement far short of formal hierarchy and one that is increasingly prevalent in international business transactions.[14] In short, there is nothing inherent in the Williamsonian framework that prevents us from exploring the dynamics that typify relations in the intermediate range between market exchange and hierarchical authority.

Second, some scholars have argued that Williamson ignores issues of relative power and vulnerability and that transaction specificity and frequency of interaction, by themselves, may not determine whether and how governance structures emerge.[15] Williamson assumes that the distribution of asset-specific goods favors one actor over another. Consequently, the actor who might be vulnerable to hold-up by the possessor of the transaction-specific assets will seek vertical integration. However, if both contracting actors have shared assets with equal vulnerability (i.e., mutual vulnerability), then the likelihood of hold-up may well decrease. Both actors will have strong incentives to keep the status quo relation going and will construct contracts short of hierarchy that should mitigate opportunism by either party. That is, relationally specific transactions can just as easily create mutual dependence (as opposed to opportunism) that

[11] For a critical view of Williamsonian theory from a business and economic perspective, see Kay 1995.

[12] O. Williamson 1985, 83.

[13] For an overview, see Dow 1987.

[14] See Mattli 2001; Van Harten 2007.

[15] Dow 1987.

lead to orderly market transactions characterized by special governance arrangements.[16] Furthermore, the ability to engage in iterative games will also diminish the need to fully integrate, as the "shadow of the future" may bring about a stable institutional arrangement based on reciprocity.[17] The contracting parties may further engage in issue linkage and mutual hostage taking—diminishing the need for vertical governance structures since neither party will have incentives to defect.

The analytic parallel in our cases is that of hybrid sovereignty arrangements involving transaction-specific assets. Although the parties involved would prefer full sovereign control over these assets, a stable hybrid sovereignty arrangement might emerge if joint gains are available and few alternative contracting parties exist (see chapters 3 and 4).

Third, the adoption of vertical integration and formal governance does not necessarily solve the opportunism problem as standard principal-agent models and theories of delegation reveal.[18] Even if transactions are brought within a common governance structure, incentive incompatibilities and opportunistic behavior will still arise from the very process that delegation engenders. Unless appropriate monitoring mechanisms can be designed to minimize shirking, vertical integration in and of itself will not mitigate opportunistic behavior.

Fourth, the Williamsonian model assumes that actors know what their desired relation is going to be and what types of assets will be involved in the future. Although Williamson often highlights frequency and asset specificity, a third determinative factor, uncertainty, remains poorly specified. In reality, most contracting environments are characterized by a strong degree of uncertainty and potential exogenous shocks that might prevent contracting parties from undertaking costly long-term integration. If this is problematic for the understanding of economic interactions, it is doubly so for states in the international realm. The anarchical international realm poses greater uncertainty and greater risks than a rule-based market environment, and, consequently, political elites will also insist on exit options in any agreement, even while recognizing the benefits of vertical integration. As the time horizon of agreements lengthens, actors will likely refrain from engaging in potentially costly vertical integration if the future is uncertain and where gains may be distributed asymmetrically. At the least, they will design mechanisms for contractual renegotiation to redress unintended distributional asymmetries caused by the initial agreement.[19]

[16] Kay 1992, 322–23. As Kay analogizes, this logic is akin to that of mutual assured destruction.

[17] Axelrod 1984.

[18] Eisenhardt 1989; Miller 1992; Zeckhauser and Pratt 1985.

[19] Koremenos 2001.

Finally, the extrapolation of Williamsonian contracting to international relations and political integration also runs into several obstacles. Unlike firms, political elites do not merely seek to maximize their economic benefits for their states.[20] Governments have many reasons to desire to retain their sovereignty. Even if regional integration might yield significant economic gains, governments will fear usurpation by other more powerful states. National culture and self-identification also form important ingredients of politicians' legitimacy of rule.[21] Moreover, strategic politicians will fear a loss of office or diminishing autonomy.[22] Efficiency gains are thus only one aspect of a politician's considerations or utility.

None of these criticisms is necessarily fatal to the theory. However, they do suggest that the Williamsonian model should be considered an analytical starting point, as opposed to a definitive model, for building a more nuanced theory of sovereign integration. Specifically, two theoretical issues frame our modification of the model: first, we identify a number of hybrid governance arrangements and organizational forms in corporate governance and in the international system that lie somewhere between the anarchy/hierarchy continuum emphasized by Williamson. Second, we seek to explain how power relations partially determine the institutional choices of negotiating actors and to clarify the subsequent endogenous bargaining processes. Fortunately, we can find theoretical guidance on both these issues of organizational forms and bargaining processes from an alternate theory of firm organization—Oliver Hart's model of vertical and lateral integration.

An Incomplete Contracting Theory of Integration

In a series of recent works, institutional economists, in particular Oliver Hart, have developed an alternate way of thinking about the organizational boundaries of the firm and the processes through which governance

---

[20] Katja Weber thus translates European firm preferences for integration into political preferences. Weber 2000; Weber and Hallerberg 2001. Political elites, however, may have divergent preference sets (depending on their constituencies' interests) and they might be concerned about their loss of autonomy. This is not to say that her argument is incorrect, but merely to suggest that their preferences need not be homogeneous.

[21] See Abdelal 2001.

[22] Krasner 1999, for example, argues that decisions about sovereignty should be modeled by the interests of political rulers rather than by the interests of states. Also see Bueno de Mesquita et al. 2003 and their theory of political survival and the selectorate. Domestic institutions may also influence whether politicians have key incentives to provide public goods and focus on efficiency and welfare for the populace as a whole, or whether they are more concerned with providing private goods to narrower constituencies. See particularly Lukauskas 1997.

arrangements emerge.[23] The Hart model builds upon several insights provided by neoclassical theories of the firm, agency theory, and Williamsonian transaction costs economics, and adds the concepts of incomplete contracting and property rights. Theories like the Hart approach explain the sources of bargaining power that various configurations of property rights afford to contracting parties and how these configurations affect incentives for the expansion or contraction of organizational forms. Although we do not provide a full description or technical rendition of the model, we discuss the key central concepts of incomplete contracting and property rights as a prelude to demonstrating their applicability to international relations.

Complete vs. Incomplete Contracting

No standard definition of incomplete contracting is accepted, but the concept is rooted in standard principles of institutional economic theory that assume that actors are boundedly rational, that is they pursue their utility to the best of their ability given market uncertainty, imperfect information, transaction costs, and cognitive processing limitations. To a great extent, the distinction between complete contracts and incomplete contracts reflects the standard distinctions drawn between neoclassical rationality and bounded rationality.

Under neoclassical assumptions of rationality, agents choose the best complete contract that is available from a number of readily identifiable alternatives. Suppose that two economic agents—Firm B (the buyer) and Firm S (the seller)—decide to contract over the provision of some product or economic function W. In a neoclassical world, both parties could carefully craft an optimal contract that would explicitly specify the rights and obligations each party would assume in the relationship. Presumably, the contract would detail what is to be produced and how much is to be produced by what time and at what price.

In addition, a truly "complete" contract would also have to specify certain provisions in anticipation of the circumstances or contingencies that might arise to alter the terms specified above. Firm B, after a certain period of time, might discover that it needs a dramatically different quantity of W, a level that Firm S is unable or unwilling to provide under the initial terms. Conversely, Firm S may find that it has misjudged its production capacities and/or is unable to adjust its activities to accommodate the changes sought by Firm B. Up to a certain point, parties could presumably anticipate the routine events or circumstances that might affect the terms of their initial agreement. These contingencies and potential

---

[23] Hart 1995; Hart and Moore 1990; Grossman and Hart 1986.

remedies (i.e., price adjustments, arbitration, etc.) would also be included in the initial contract.

By contrast, the incomplete contracting approach assumes that in long-term relationships, the imperfections of the marketplace will force the parties to renegotiate many aspects of the initial contract. The process of long-term contracting is itself costly and fraught with different types of transaction costs that actors cannot foresee or specify in advance.[24] First, contracting environments are characterized by a great deal of uncertainty. In a changing and unpredictable world, it is difficult for parties to think of the types of unforeseen contingencies that might arise in the future. Second, it is difficult and costly for parties to negotiate, given the asymmetries of information that might characterize the negotiating environment. Third, even if the parties can successfully negotiate a contract, they must do so in a manner that is readily verifiable to an outside observer or a third-party enforcer such as a court or external arbitrator. These three transaction costs—uncertainty, negotiating costs, and enforcement costs—might prevent the parties from writing an optimal complete contract. These are the procedural sources of incompleteness.

In addition to these routine transaction costs, an unpredictable exogenous event might make the fulfillment of the contract impossible on its initial terms. A fire might damage the production capacity of Firm S, leaving it unable to complete its order. A new piece of government regulation or legislation might dictate that the production of W adheres to new standards of manufacturing or quality control. Firm B might unilaterally decide that W did not meet the requirements specified in the contract and might withhold payment until the terms of the relationship were changed.

As both Williamson and Hart point out, even in the most routine circumstances it is often not possible to write a contract that anticipates all the possible transaction costs, exogenous events, and future bargaining positions that might arise throughout the course of an exchange. The final contract written by the parties will delineate the initial terms of the exchange, but it will neglect several contingencies. Most important, the contract itself will have to make provisions for subsequent renegotiations and adjustment procedures that are impossible to specify *ex ante*. Thus, the resulting "incomplete contract" will provide the starting point but not necessarily the long-term specifics for the relationship between Firm B and Firm S.

Incomplete Contracts and Relationally Specific Assets

The above transaction costs would be manageable in most real-world situations where the contracting parties could readily find alternate trad-

---

[24] Hart 1995, 24–27.

ing partners or their exchange was a one-off. That is, the frequency of interaction over time would be low. Any attempt by either Firm B or Firm S to unilaterally change the terms of the contract or engage in other types of opportunistic behavior would drive the other party to terminate the relationship and seek an alternate exchange partner.

In situations, however, where transactions are frequent and the transaction involves an idiosyncratic asset or relationship, the omissions, uncertainty, and ambiguities inherent in an incomplete contract might exacerbate the potential Williamsonian hold-up problem. At the period of renegotiation, Firm B might demand additional quantities of W at a greatly reduced cost or Firm S might hold out for exactly the opposite. Without alternative partners for exchange and/or given high levels of initial investment, either party might be reluctant to continue investing in the relationship. Moreover, in the case that either of the parties could not guarantee *ex ante* that such renegotiations could successfully take place, then both would be reluctant to make relationally specific investments in the first place and might forgo the potential benefits of specialization so as to defer the potential costs of entering into an incomplete contract.

In order to understand these situational bargaining processes and the full range of institutional solutions to the hold-up problem, we need to introduce our second key concept—the notion of property rights and ownership.

Property Rights and the Allocation of Control

Although we are accustomed to thinking about property as embodying exclusive ownership arrangements, the Hart model unbundles the various property rights that govern the ownership of assets. A key insight of the property rights approach is distinguishing formal ownership from de facto control or "use" value. In general, the property rights inherent to any asset can be disaggregated into two sets of rights: *control rights* and *use rights*.[25] Control rights allocate the power to make decisions on how to use an asset, such as the ability to sell, lease, transfer, or even destroy an asset. Control rights also grant the right to transfer any of these formal rights to another party. Use rights, on the other hand, specify the rights to receive the benefits and to incur the costs from the deployment of an asset. In economic settings, such rights are usually monetary and are known as "cash-flow" rights.[26]

In an incomplete contract, the control rights of an asset are particularly important as they govern the residual rights of control to the asset: that is the right to use the asset in any manner beyond what is specified in

---

[25] For a useful discussion, see Boycko, Shleiffer, and Vishny 1995.
[26] For a discussion, see A. Cooley 2000–2001.

the initial contract. Thus, control rights within an incomplete contract delineate the potential relational power over an asset. In our example, if Firm B and Firm S are independent organizations, Firm S will possess the residual rights of control over the production of W beyond the terms specified by the contract. That is, S could decide to sell additional W at the same price, demand an increased price, or not sell the additional W at all. However, if Firm S were integrated into Firm B as a subsidiary, then Firm B would retain the residual rights of control over the assets of Firm S and would determine decisions over W. Thus, even though Firm B and Firm S might be conducting the exact same exchange under both governance structures, the residual rights of control would change depending on the organizational status of Firm S.

In turn, residual rights of control are critical in insofar as they alter the bargaining power or threat point of renegotiating parties over the appropriation of *ex post* surpluses. If the two firms were separate, then Firm S would retain the residual rights of control and the status quo bargaining point would be that Firm S would not supply any more of W. In practice, that would offer Firm S the power to set the terms of renegotiations at time $t + 1$ so that it appropriates nearly the entire anticipated surplus. However, if Firm B owned Firm S, the status quo bargaining point would be that Firm S produces the uncontracted-for supply. In this case, Firm B would be in the position to appropriate the $t + 1$ surplus. Thus, when contracts are incomplete, the organizational boundaries of the two parties will dramatically affect both the bargaining power and divisions of the *ex post* surplus in the relationship.

The GM-Fisher Case

An often-cited historical example—that of General Motors (GM) and the automobile body manufacturer Fisher—helps illustrate these dynamics in practice.[27] Assume that GM enters into an initial contract in which Fisher agrees to supply a certain number of car bodies every week. Now suppose that the demand for cars rises (as it did in the mid-1920s) and that GM wishes to increase its total output, but the initial contract does not specify this possibility. If Fisher is a separate company, then it will hold the residual rights of control in any renegotiation to provide extra car bodies. The threat point or status quo in any contractual renegotiation will be that Fisher does not supply additional car bodies. Alternately, if GM owned Fisher (either as a subsidiary or a subdivision), then GM would retain the residual rights of control over Fisher's factory and production line. If Fisher refused to supply GM with extra bodies, GM could presumably

---

[27] Hart 1995, 6–8; Klein 1988.

fire Fisher management and hire someone else to follow these new directives. In this case, the status quo point for a renegotiation will be that Fisher must acquiesce to supply additional car bodies. Unless Fisher management was itself specific to the point of being indispensable, Fisher's bargaining power in any renegotiation would be significantly diminished.

In the actual historical case, Fisher—operating autonomously under a long-term ten-year contract to supply GM—effectively held up GM. When demand for cars rose during the middle of the contract, Fisher agreed to supply additional bodies on previous contractual terms, but refused to implement measures that could have reduced the costs that, under the terms of the old contract, it was passing on to GM. Fisher management did not adopt new more efficient technologies and declined to relocate its production nearer GM in order to maintain the high profit upcharge on its high labor and transportation costs.[28] Holding the residual rights of control in the transaction-specific relationship, Fisher squeezed GM for the *ex post* surplus that was generated by the follow-up contract.

Anticipating these differences in bargaining power and the division of the *ex post* surplus, the incentives of GM and Fisher to make specific investments in their relationship would vary greatly depending upon whether the two companies are separate or not. GM would be much more likely to invest in specialized machinery that is specific to Fisher car bodies if it owned Fisher than if Fisher were a separate company, since the hold-up and expropriation threat would be reduced. Conversely, the incentives for Fisher would be exactly the opposite. Fisher management would be much more likely to innovate and invest in cost-saving physical assets if Fisher were an independent firm rather than a division of GM. As an independent entity it would receive a more favorable division of a surplus and return on its investments whereas if GM owned it, its surplus value would be expropriated. For Hart and other theorists of the property rights approach, these incentives represent both the costs and benefits of integration.

The issues that confront GM and Fisher are essentially the same as those confronting states and their cross-border deployment of fixed assets. When deploying fixed assets such as military bases overseas, states ideally would prefer sovereign hierarchy so that they could use these assets in any manner that they saw fit. For example, Britain's deployment to bases that it can hold directly as sovereign territories (such as Diego Garcia, which is part of the British Indian Ocean Territory) is the analytic equivalent of GM incorporating Fisher. However, in most cases of over-

---

[28] See Klein 1988.

seas base rights, sending countries must sign a contract with a sovereign host country to guarantee access. The terms of these basing agreements delineate what the base is for, how sovereignty is to be apportioned, and what, if any, payment is to be provided to the host in exchange for providing basing rights. Because host countries retain the rights of residual control, they can delimit the activities or "use rights" to the base to what is specified in the actual basing rights contract and, if need be, drive a harder bargain during a renegotiation of an initial accord. Algeria's actions vis-à-vis French bases on its territory or those of the Philippines when renegotiating base rights with the United States are similar to an independent Fisher exercising its bargaining leverage over GM.

Theoretical Summary

In many real-world situations, parties that cannot foresee or specify contingencies must write an incomplete contract that they agree to renegotiate at a later point. In a relationally specific investment, the dynamics of such renegotiations will be determined by which party holds the residual rights of control as opposed to the use rights or cash flow rights of the asset. Ownership of these control rights will depend on whether the two parties are independent or integrated within a single organizational entity. Realizations about such variations in *ex post* bargaining power and surplus divisions will affect each party's incentives when entering long-term relationally specific investments. These dynamics and incentives help determine the organizational boundaries of the firm.

Explaining the Boundaries of State Sovereignty and Its Transfer

Assumptions and Limitations

The described model has important applications for the study of international relations. But in order to precisely identify the model's theoretical "value added" and specify concrete hypotheses, we need to be conscientious of both the similarities and differences between economic and political analysis. As David Epstein and Sharyn O'Halloran point out, politics "has no equivalent of the free-market or price-system in economics" and the "correct baseline" for our analysis must be "political efficiencies," not economic ones.[29] In addition, the types of transaction costs involved in certain types of contracts in international relations might be distinctly political, with no obvious economic analogy. For instance, political elites' decisions on integration and decolonization are inevitably influenced by

---

[29] Epstein and O'Halloran 1999, 44.

public opinion and the strength of nationalism,[30] geostrategic calculations, susceptibility to electoral pressures and rival political elites,[31] institutional divisions within government and asymmetrically distributed information,[32] and sensitivities to systemic externalities and concerns about relative gains.[33] As we develop our theory and case studies, we pay careful attention to noting the goals and preferences of political actors.

Nevertheless, while we acknowledge certain differences between the dynamics of firms and political actors, we argue that both share three common features that justify the application of the incomplete contracting/property rights approach. First, despite the possible variations in their baseline preferences, both firms and political actors share an important structural similarity—they are types of organizations. Both political and economic organizations must organize and perform certain functions and routines that are structurally necessary for the overall operations of their governance structures. Like firms, political actors such as states or international organizations are characterized by both vertical and horizontal boundaries on their activities and functions.[34] Horizontal boundaries delimit the types of activities that organizations engage in, as well as the differentiation between these functions. Vertical boundaries denote the overall scope of authority for any given function, and the point at which institutional authority is limited in any given issue. As with firms, we regard the actual vertical and horizontal boundaries of international political actors as fluctuating and amenable to both expansion and contraction.

Second, we assume that bounded rationality characterizes the actions of both economic and political organizations. Like their economic counterparts, political actors must make decisions and pursue goals within the constraints of environmental uncertainty, imperfect flows of information, cognitive limitations, and transaction costs. These features are particularly characteristic of the anarchic international system in which no overall governing authority can guarantee orderly exchange. Indeed, information and uncertainty problems will be virulent given that states, in comparison with firms, are more likely to pursue relative gains rather than absolute gains.[35]

Finally, we regard institutional choice as a feature common to both economic and political organizations. That is, just as firms in the private

---

[30] Abdelal 2001.
[31] Snyder 2000.
[32] Milner 1997.
[33] See Grieco 1990.
[34] See A. Cooley 2005a.
[35] See the discussions in Baldwin 1993.

sector choose from a number of possible governance arrangements, international actors also tend to choose institutional arrangements—in this case various modes of integration and governance—because they represent the best political option from a restricted set of institutional alternatives. While we must always be careful when importing an analysis developed from a different discipline, we believe that the organizational similarities shared by firms and political actors justify the use of the incomplete contracts/property rights approach.

Our approach shares much in common with Barbara Koremenos, Charles Lipson, and Duncan Snidal's "Rational Design of International Institutions." They focus on institutions, defined as "explicit arrangements, negotiated among international actors, that prescribe, proscribe, and/or authorize behavior."[36] Similarly, we concentrate on explicit agreements motivated by rational actors, and like their project we address issues of distribution, the number of actors, enforcement problems, and the uncertainty of future conditions. However, we emphasize the particular allocation of property rights and the downstream effects of such allocation, both in terms of original contract design as well as the durability of the original contract.

Residual Rights and Third Parties

Although we seek to uncover the common organizational processes across different types of integration and disintegration, the logic of incomplete contracting plays out differently across these institutional settings. In cases of territorial partition and overseas basing the question revolves around which state in a bilateral interaction will get the residual rights of control. In the case of regional integration the question is rather how much authority third parties, that is, international institutions, should receive. Should these institutions gain significant residual rights they in effect might become supranational entities. Conversely, if the contracting parties retain the residual rights of control, these institutions are more accurately understood as agents acting on behalf of the principals (the contracting states).

The distinction has important practical implications. Take, for example, the distinction between a currency union and a dollarized economy. In a currency union, such as the Eurozone or the East Caribbean Currency Union, member countries agree to pool their monetary functions and devolve control over money matters to a common and supranational banking authority, such as the European Central Bank, according to a mutually established set of institutions and governance procedures. By contrast, in

---

[36] Koremenos, Lipson, and Snidal 2001, 762.

a dollarized economy one country replaces its territorial currency with that of another country (such as the use of the U.S. dollar in Panama), thereby effectively subordinating its monetary policy to the national central bank that issues the circulating currency (regardless of whether it is the dollar or not).[37] Thus, even though both types of currency integration involve the merging of sovereign functions and assets, the existence of a supranational authority imbues it with the residual rights of control over that function and differentiates the currency union from the hierarchical process of dollarization. In the former the residual rights of control reside with the third party. In the latter, the residual rights in effect reside with the state that issues the circulating currency.

Similarly, the different allocation of residual rights in the formative phases of the EEC and NAFTA has had profound consequences for their subsequent development. As we will show in chapter 5, by giving residual rights of control to a third party, the bargaining leverage and momentum in the European case shifted to EEC-level institutions. In short, the transfer of residual rights to another state or states or, conversely, to a supranational authority has important implications for how hybrid sovereignty arrangements will evolve.

General Propositions on Incomplete Contracting

Having presented the theoretical foundations of the incomplete contracting approach, compared them with the transaction cost approach, and specified the similarities and differences that characterize contracting in economic and political environments, we are now in position to present the model's general expectations regarding the choice for a particular governance structure as well as to generate more specific hypotheses regarding bargaining leverage, momentum, and credibility of commitment.

Complete vs. Incomplete Contracting

G1: *When the political transaction costs of sovereign integration or disintegration are high, incomplete contracts allow states to create hybrid governance arrangements rather than opt for formal hierarchy or anarchy.*

This proposition restates the general problem of contracting in the international system. Formal integration in the realm of international politics (empire) is often not possible given the long-term uncertainty of the

---

[37] For more on the organizational distinctions between these types of currency integration, see Cohen 2003, especially 33–66; Helleiner 2002; J. Williamson 2003.

international system, international norms against hierarchy or occupation, and political concerns over ceding sovereignty. Incomplete contracts allow intermediate institutional arrangements to emerge that are politically preferable to allocating exclusive sovereignty over an asset or function to a single political actor.[38]

The most common way that incomplete contracting splits sovereignty is through the separation and allocation of property rights to different parties. Usually, sovereignty can be divided into "control rights," the formal ownership and right to transfer or sell an asset, and "use rights," the right to derive the benefits and incur the costs from using the asset. By dividing the "control rights" and "use rights" of an asset or territory, states can reach stable mixed governance arrangements, such as a leasing agreement, short of exclusive hierarchy. In this book we draw attention to the contracts that allow a host country to grant residual rights of control to a foreign power or, conversely, allow the host country to maintain these residual rights for itself (allocation with national residual rights). Additionally, states can transfer decision-making or judicial authority to a third party or supranational body. International arbitration also potentially fits this category, as the form of such arbitration may itself vary and can range from a private ad hoc arbitrator to a permanent supranational body or legislative authority.[39]

G2: Incomplete contracting allows hybrid governance arrangements short of hierarchy to emerge over specific assets.

While mixed governance arrangements can help states overcome high transaction costs, the presence of relationally specific assets will especially necessitate that states adopt hybrid governance structures. In addition to their strategic and possible commercial value, fixed assets such as canals (Panama, Suez) and access ways, mines and oil wells, and basing installations have a high political and/or national symbolic value. Under strict Williamsonian logic, vertical integration and hierarchy will be required to govern these assets.

---

[38] Intermediate arrangements among firms include split property rights arrangements (leasing or other forms of temporal division) and shared property rights arrangements (joint production and horizontal agreements). On the organizational logic of the joint venture and its advantages in mitigating transaction costs, see Kogut 1988, 319–22. Similarly, states can share or pool their sovereignty through joint production agreements or joint ventures with other states or economic actors. Under such "horizontal agreements," states or other organizations jointly own the residual rights and incur the costs and benefits of using the asset.

[39] Mattli 2001; Van Harten 2007. Furthermore, states are increasingly sharing sovereignty by agreeing to binding arbitration over commercial and/or even border disputes. See Simmons 2002.

In the realm of international politics, however, their exclusive owner-ship by one contracting country would impose significant, and in some cases unacceptable, political costs on the other contracting party or even third parties. Think, for example, of the consequences of Egyptian nation-alization of the Suez Canal, and the American reaction in 1956 to Britain, France, and Israel's attempts to reverse this by force. By splitting or shar-ing sovereignty, states can avoid exclusively assigning specific sovereign assets to one party and, in certain contentious cases, can even avoid con-flict. Although exclusive sovereignty may emerge in the long run, usually after multiple renegotiations between the contracting parties, we expect such hybrid arrangements to emerge, particularly in cases of territorial disintegration and partition. Indeed, such arrangements may actually hold the key to successfully concluding new sovereign arrangements such as federal unions and basing access. This will particularly be the case when neither side can unilaterally force the other party to surrender all claims to sovereign control over the assets in question. We articulate this more fully in the next chapter.

Bargaining Leverage among Contracting States

B1: Upon renegotiation of an incomplete contract at t + 1, *the holder of the residual rights of control will have leverage and will bargain for re-newed contractual terms that will appropriate any available* ex post *sur-plus and sovereign authority.*

This more specific hypothesis restates the central insight about contrac-tual renegotiation and the allocation of property rights. Incomplete con-tracts generate potential rents and surpluses that can be appropriated by actors who hold the residual rights of control to an asset. International actors who own the residual rights of control will use the full extent of the bargaining power afforded to them. Accordingly, residual owners will tend to set the terms of the $t + 1$ bargain at or close to the maximum level acceptable to the actor with use rights, while appropriating the rest of the available surplus or rent.

In bilateral settings, such as decolonization negotiations or military basing agreements, we expect that this bargaining leverage may even be more important than the relative power capabilities of the contracting parties. Thus, even though a country may possess significant military capabilities, it will still be at a disadvantage in negotiations if it lacks these residual rights. This was the situation in which many former colo-nial powers found themselves when initial decolonization agreements were revisited, and this dynamic has also characterized base negotiations between the United States and many of its considerably weaker military base hosts.

We do not argue that relative power asymmetries are insignificant. Indeed, if joint gains of production exist and power asymmetries are severe, then the dominant actor might unilaterally assert full control over the assets in question, as in the case of empire. Moreover, even if empire is not feasible, the level of asymmetry might influence the type of incomplete contract that the actors conclude, and determine whether the foreign power acquires residual rights or whether the national (host) country retains them.

We maintain, however, that in complete contracts power asymmetries are dealt with by careful specification of the actual terms of the agreement. With incomplete contracts, the holder of residual rights will have the bargaining advantage even if the distribution of power does not change over time. Thus, the *ex post* bargaining power that flows to the holder of residual rights has an independent and significant effect on the contours of the renegotiated settlement.

These bargaining dynamics will play out in a different manner in regional integration. In bilateral settings, involving relationally specific assets, the weaker party can maintain and increase its bargaining power by holding the residual rights of control. Regional integration, however, does not revolve around the control of relational specific assets as much as it does revolve around agreements on internal and external tariffs, subsidies, competition policy, even accords on the movement of people, and monetary union. Thus, in subsequent renegotiations the more powerful states will yield few of their rights while trying to get the smaller states to surrender some of theirs. With incomplete contracts the more powerful states will thus seek to reinterpret and redraft the initial terms to their advantage. Weak states that agree to the incomplete contract at time $t + 0$ must fear subsequent defection and increased leverage of the more powerful state at time $t + 1$.

Nevertheless, the more powerful states cannot indiscriminately capitalize on their bargaining power during (re)negotiations because of the credible commitment problem. In order for a stronger power to get weaker members to contract, it must either agree to a complete contract or agree to credibly bind its authority in a reassuring fashion. The larger states, consequently, might acquiesce to such institutions to signal credible commitment. Without the ability to credibly commit, they too will be unable to achieve the level of integration they prefer in order to capitalize on gains of trade and investment.

With incomplete contracts, supranational bodies with residual rights subsequently will attempt to codify and institutionalize these rights. For example, Simon Hix's explanation for the adoption of the Maastricht Treaty shows that the European Parliament exercised its "discretion through rule-interpretation" to shape the incomplete contract of the constitutional negotiations, thereby managing to delineate and increase its own power vis-à-vis member states, well beyond what many of the states originally intended.[40] In other words, with the transfer of residual rights to a third party, that entity acquires enhanced bargaining leverage as time progresses.

The Momentum for Sovereign Transfers

M1: In both bilateral and multilateral settings, renegotiation of an incomplete contract at t + 1 *will more explicitly delineate, specify, and codify the governance arrangements of an asset or function. All else being equal, incomplete contracts tend to completeness.*

M2: Incomplete contracts will be maintained as long as (a) joint supply gains are institutionalized and/or (b) states lack alternative contracting partners.

When and under what circumstances do incomplete contracts remain stable and when do they tend to become complete contracts? As we have argued, because of its unspecified nature and built-in renegotiations, incompleteness also affects the momentum for continuing further sovereign transfers and the bundling and unbundling of assets and functions. All else being equal, contracts that are incomplete must eventually be renegotiated, clarified, and adjusted. This general proposition describes the result of the learning processes that contracting actors will experience between the initial contract $t = 0$ and bargaining point $t + 1$. Upon renegotiation, parties will have improved information about the distributional consequences of the initial agreement as well as a better understanding of previous omissions or contingencies that are critical to the continuation of the institution. In cases of third-party delegation or supranationalism, actors will use their discretionary authority delegated at $t = 0$ to institutionally codify their jurisdiction and make it permanent at $t + 1$. Thus, over time, previously incomplete provisions will become increasingly more specified (or complete) and develop the necessary institutional apparatus in order to do so. When sovereign rights among bilateral contracting parties are split into control rights and use rights, this learning should allow the party with the residual control rights to further constrict the scope of the use rights of an agreement (ceteris paribus).

As stated above, in bilateral settings where ownership rights and use rights are divided, the bargaining advantage over time tends to reside with the owner of residual rights. The owner will thus prefer to bundle these rights as time progresses or at least renegotiate the rents obtained from

---

[40] Hix 2002.

the user. However, as long as the user (the home country) can offer particular rents or other goods desired by the owner (the host country), the incomplete contract can be maintained.

ALTERNATIVE CONTRACTING PARTIES

This natural momentum toward completeness will be enhanced, and thus hybrid sovereignty arrangements will unravel, if alternative contracting parties become available. This logic holds for either of the two parties to the agreement. The foreign power will be less willing to pay for the use rights it is given by the host country if it sees a cheaper alternative or substitute. But this logic holds a fortiori for the owner of residual rights. In this case, the leverage of the owner of the residual rights will increase even further to the detriment of the possessor of use rights. The entrance of alternative potential partners will allow the owner of residual rights to operate in a competitive market with multiple "consumers" of the good. The residual rights holder will thus ratchet up its demands and, if possible, try to gain exclusive sovereignty over the governance of the asset or function. For example, prior to the expulsion of the United States from its military base in Uzbekistan in July 2005, Russia signaled that it was willing to enter into a security relationship that would be less intrusive in the internal affairs of Uzbekistan, thereby making its terms more preferable to the authoritarian regime in Tashkent than the mixed messages that had been sent by the United States.[41] Conversely, a lack of alternate contracting partners for the residual rights owner will make continuation of the incomplete contract more likely and the institutionalization of joint gains under such hybrid arrangements a stronger possibility.

JOINT GAINS

Absent alternative contracting partners, incomplete contracts should endure as long as they produce joint gains for the contracting parties. A further intuitive implication of the Hart model is that assets that exhibit a high degree of complementarity should be governed under the same organizational form.[42] By definition, highly complementary assets generate increasing returns to scale when used together.[43] Thus, at any renegotiation of an incomplete contract, highly complementary assets not specified for integration at $t = 0$ will delineate the minimum size and scope of

---

[41] See A. Cooley 2005b; *New York Times*, July 31, 2005.

[42] Hart 1995, 50–53. For a classic example involving coal mines and electric generating plants, see Joskow 1985.

[43] On increasing returns and institutional formation, see Pierson 2000.

the organizational boundaries of integration at $t + 1$. The inverse of this insight should also hold: independent assets and functions will not generate momentum for subsequent integration at $t + 1$. In the absence of increasing returns and related lock-in effects, the integration of noncomplementary sovereign assets will provide no additional benefits while it will still incur costs for the contracting parties.

However, we reiterate an important point made earlier in chapter 1. Although highly complementary assets might provide for greater efficiency and lead to integration among firms, this need not be the case among independent polities. States also have a strong preference for autonomy. If there are gains to be had from joint production of security or from the exchange of rights in the economic realm, and full integration under one authority (i.e., empire) is impossible, joint gains will be pursued through incomplete contracts and division of control and use rights.

Credibility of Commitment Problems

Given that incomplete contracts are subject to future renegotiations, all parties will be concerned with the subsequent distribution of rights and assets (at $t + 1$). From the discussion above it should be clear that all contracting actors will face credibility problems given the concerns about bargaining leverage and the forward momentum of the agreement. In bilateral negotiations, such as in decolonization and overseas basing arrangements, the credibility problems will particularly arise for the actor who holds the residual rights. This will be particularly pronounced in cases where the holder of residual rights has ownership over transaction-specific assets but grants use rights to the other actor. The foreign investor of the relationally specific asset, or the state that is placing fixed assets in forward bases, will want institutional assurances that the holder of the residual rights (the host) will not renege and engage in hold-up. This leads to the following general propositions.

C1: Incomplete contracts will be easier to conclude when the parties can credibly commit through institutional or reputational mechanisms.

C2: The burden of credible commitment falls particularly on the holder of residual rights of control.

Toward a Causal Model of Governance Structures

This book has two theoretical objectives. First, we wish to clarify why actors opt for a particular governance structure and demonstrate how a variety of hybrid sovereignty arrangements might emerge in different

TABLE 2.1
Summary of General Propositions

Governance of Sovereign Rights and Asset Allocation

G1: When the political transaction costs of sovereign integration or disintegration are high, incomplete contracts allow states to create hybrid governance arrangements rather than opt for formal hierarchy or anarchy.

G2: Incomplete contracting allows hybrid governance arrangements short of hierarchy to emerge over specific assets.

Bargaining Leverage among Contracting States

B1: Upon renegotiation of an incomplete contract at *t + 1*, the holder of the residual rights of control will have leverage and will bargain for renewed contractual terms that will appropriate any available ex post surplus and sovereign authority.

The Momentum for Sovereign Transfers

M1. In both bilateral and multilateral settings, renegotiation of an incomplete contract at *t + 1* will more explicitly delineate, specify and codify the governance arrangements of an asset or function. All else being equal, incomplete contracts tend to completeness.

M2: Incomplete contracts will be maintained as long as: a). joint supply gains are institutionalized; and/or b). states lack alternate contracting partners.

Credibility of Commitment Problems

C1: Incomplete contracts will be easier to conclude when the parties can credibly commit through institutional or reputational mechanisms.

C2: The burden of credible commitment falls particularly on the holder of residual rights of control.

---

contexts. Second, we analyze how the particular choice of the initial hybrid sovereignty arrangement or incomplete contract then has downstream consequences for the contracting parties.

Incomplete Contracting as a Dependent Variable: The Choice of Governance Structures

At one extreme the sovereign rights of one state might be completely usurped by another, as in the case of empire. At the other end of the spectrum, a state might be in full possession of all control and use rights within its territorial borders. This is the basic principle associated with Westphalian sovereignty. Between formal empire and full independence lies a wide range of possible intermediary forms of governance. Which form emerges will largely depend on three factors: the preferences and goals of the states involved; the relative distribution of power; and the ability of contracting parties to credibly commit. Thus the pursuit of preferences will be tempered by structural conditions.

We readily admit that the factors that influence actor preferences are largely exogenous to our model. Whether states wish to pursue empire, grant independence, or agree to some hybrid governance form between these two will depend on myriad contextual factors. Preferences will be influenced by changes in geostrategy; the availability of alliance partners; and even technological transformations.[44] Thus, while we trace actor preferences, we inevitably must rely on inductive observations of the historical record and use structured focused comparison and process tracing to substantiate our findings.[45] This does not mean we turn our back on deductive theorizing. To the contrary, like the analytic narrative approach, we combine theoretical tools that are commonly employed in political science and economics, with historical narration.[46]

The states in question will thus engage in calculation of the relative merits of different governance arrangements as suggested by our general proposition (G1). Although preferences are difficult to stipulate *ex ante*, we may expect that in the case of transaction-specific assets, as with territorial partition issues and overseas basing, that each of the parties will prefer to hold the maximum amount of control and use rights (vertical integration).

However, the relative distribution of power will set material constraints on what is feasible. If we are dealing with a declining great power and ascending nationalist movement, the symmetry of power will make it very costly to impose a colonial solution. For example, the French attempt to hold Algeria against its will was prohibitively more costly than, say, Britain's desire to hold on to Diego Garcia.

Finally, the creation of a particular governance structure will be influenced by the ability of the respective parties to commit. Where reputational or institutional mechanisms exist to counteract the likely consequences of shifts in bargaining leverage and momentum, an incomplete contract will be more readily concluded. The parties to such agreements, of course, will realize where the leverage and momentum of a future contract will trend. As suggested above, in cases of territorial partition and overseas basing the holder of residual rights, usually the host country, will want the contract to trend to completeness, or at the very least the host

---

[44] To give but one example of how technology affects the pursuit of empire: the shift from sail to coal required the Royal Navy to obtain re-coaling stations, and thus overseas bases around the globe.

[45] A. George 1979.

[46] Bates et al. 1998, 10.

country will wish to capture higher rents and threaten to renege. With this in mind the party most likely to suffer the consequences of such behavior will want to see the credible commitment up front. That is, without credibility of commitment *ex ante* a hybrid governance structure is unlikely to emerge.

Incomplete Contracting as an Independent Variable: Downstream Consequences of Hybrid Sovereignty Arrangements

From the propositions above, it will also be clear in which direction hybrid sovereignty is likely to develop (ceteris paribus). Even without significant shift in relative power, the holder of residual rights will gradually expand its authority. In decolonization and basing agreements, the holder of residual rights will seek to gain more control rights and higher rents. Leverage and momentum will be on its side. Thus the incomplete contract will become an obsolescing bargain as time progresses. The unbundled sovereign rights of the host country in the incomplete contract will evolve toward unified holding.

However, this need not occur if both parties still see joint gains from the hybrid sovereignty arrangement and few alternate contracting parties are available. If states perceive continued joint gains from pooling their security assets, or when they continue to reap benefits from mixing their economic resources, the agreement need not unravel. Given that the temptation to undo the agreement exists particularly on the side of the party that holds the residual rights of control, its perceptions of whether there are such gains and a lack of alternative parties will be particularly crucial.

Formulating Hypotheses and the Logic of Case Selection

Above we delineated general expectations regarding patterns of hybrid governance. In subsequent chapters we illustrate these propositions in greater detail and test them against the empirical evidence in cases of territorial partition (decolonization), overseas basing, and regional integration.

Incomplete Contracts over Sovereign Rights and Pseudo-Contracts

It is important to realize that our analysis focuses on "real" contracts. Parties sign these agreements because they expect that they will govern their relations for some time in the future. These agreements proscribe and authorize particular behavior, and are not merely "window-dressing." In this sense they might be distinguished from "pseudo-contracts."[47] In the latter case, political elites might sign contracts even though they have grave doubts that the contract will be durable or that the parties will adhere to the contract. They might, nevertheless, conclude such contracts if domestic audiences matter and such an audience might be led to believe that the contract will be a durable and meaningful agreement. For example, if the French government knew the agreement with the Algerian government on French bases and resource exploitation would be fleeting, one might conjecture it signed merely to mislead domestic audiences. And even when domestic audiences do not weigh in, one might conjecture a government would sign such an agreement to save its international reputation.

We focus, however, on "real" rather than "pseudo" contracts. Consequently, as we demonstrate in our empirical discussions, the political elites who signed such incomplete contracts could rationally come to the conclusion that the agreement would hold for some time. While the contracting parties understood that bargaining leverage would flow to the holder of the residual rights (the host country that had residual rights of control over the military bases or natural resources), the foreign power (the holder of use rights) could reasonably conclude that the host country would adhere long enough to the agreement so that the foreign power could reap some of the envisioned joint gains. Consequently, our chapters focus on cases where former imperial powers assigned residual rights to the host, and we discuss why they could expect the host to adhere to the specified terms.

It is, furthermore, important to understand the domain of incomplete contracts in which we are interested. We limit our analysis of incomplete contracts to agreements about rights that are usually bundled under the rubric of sovereignty—rights based on the principle that the government of a territory with internationally recognized borders is the highest authority in that territory. The rights of the sovereign state thus extend over that territory, and that state's government is juridically supreme.[48] We focus on cases in which governments have yielded some of these sovereign rights to other governments, either by granting the other actor particular use rights to the host's territorial space or by recognizing that the state's jurisdictional powers are not supreme (as in the European Union).

---

[47] We are indebted to Robert Keohane for drawing our attention to this distinction as well as for suggestions on how one might discern whether contracts do indeed constrain behavior or are merely meant to deceive domestic or international audiences.

[48] Janis 1993, 182. States may also have rights extending from that territory, for example, rights to the air space above its territory and to the territory's adjoining seas.

We recognize that states may sign incomplete agreements that do not impinge on their sovereign authority. For example, states may contract to exchange certain goods, or perform certain joint tasks, depending on the continued performance of the other actors.[49] However, we limit our analysis of incomplete contracts to cases in which the contracting arrangements blur the distinction between anarchy and hierarchy, that is, where some sovereignty is surrendered.

Case Selection and Methodology

We assess the plausibility of our theoretical observations across a variety of political settings, issue areas, and contracting environments. In choosing cases, we focused on what we considered "big issues" and topics in the areas of both international political economy and international security.

One might be concerned that we have sometimes selected cases that are instances of incomplete contracting rather than comparing cases that demonstrate complete contracting dynamics with cases evincing incomplete contracting.[50] For example, in the next chapter (on decolonization) we focus on cases in which the retreating imperial power is granted certain use rights by the former subject territory, which holds national residual rights of control. Have we thus selected on the dependent variable and consequently tested our theory with cases from which the theory was inferred?

This concern is unfounded. First, our theory presents deductive propositions, which are not derived from mere observations of the empirical data. This a priori approach allows us to test these propositions against empirical cases, with theory and observations independent from one another. Second, our aim is to clarify the *consequences* of complete versus incomplete contracting and to analyze why certain incomplete contracts proved more durable than others. Thus, focusing on the downstream consequences of hybrid sovereignty in decolonization (chapter 3), we observe considerable variation in the durability of some incomplete contracts versus others, thus demonstrating variation on the dependent variable. Moreover, in chapter 5 we discuss why North American regional agreements ended up looking like complete contracts, while the European states opted for incomplete contracting with strong third-party institutions—again evincing variation on the dependent variable.

---

[49] We are thankful to Helen Milner for her observations on this point.

[50] For the latter logic of cross case comparison, see King, Keohane, and Verba 1994, 21–23, 46, 141. For a discussion of Mill's logic of comparison by difference, see Lijphart 1971. The question might arise in chapters 3 and 4. In chapter 5 we more explicitly contrast a complete contract (NAFTA) with an incomplete contract (the European Economic Community treaty). For a perspective different from King, Keohane, and Verba, see Van Evera 1997.

We have also chosen cases (in chapters 3 and 4) that all clearly involve transaction (site)-specific assets. In picking cases that focus on military bases and on mineral and resource exploitation, we can squarely engage the Williamsonian expectation that joint gains should lead to vertical integration (full sovereignty) and contrast that with our incomplete contracting approach.

Our cases also allow for a measure of control, across cases and across time, for power differentials. For example, France and Britain were both declining Great Powers, and the distribution of power vis-à-vis their colonies was more or less similar. Yet French agreements and British bassing arrangements showed considerable variation. The unraveling of French agreements with some of the North African states resembled the transience of Dutch agreements with Indonesia, even though the French could still claim to be a major power, while the Dutch clearly could not. Moreover, diachronically and within cases, bargaining leverage sometimes shifted in favor of the host country, even when the relative power on the part of the home country had not changed—thus allowing us to test the significance of power differentials versus causal explanations based on the nature of the contract. Thus, even a superpower like the United States has been confronted by hard bargaining of host countries when it came to renegotiation of its basing rights—demonstrating dynamics inherent to the contract, rather than merely the consequences of power distributions.

We also engage the existing international relations literature across the case chapters, specifically realist and constructivist accounts, and ask how our theory adds or differs from those. While we recognize both have considerable relevance, we maintain that an analysis of the particular logic of contracting exerts an important independent effect. In some cases, such as chapter 5 (on regional integration), we also discuss the robust literature on delegation and regional institutions and demonstrate the model's utility for understanding other cases of regional integration.

Overall, we present what we hope is a rich set of historical cases and issues to show the importance of incomplete contracting theory to the study of international relations. Thus, we submit that an incomplete contracting perspective shows its explanatory power across four very different historical European empires. Our interpretation of the organization of U.S. basing contracts is wholly new and distinct, and seeks to explain a category of sovereign transfers that have so far received little attention from organizational theorists and scholars of international security.

In chapter 3 we examine the agreements that governed imperial disengagement across a number of decolonization settings. We explore how incomplete contracting allowed colonial metropoles to acquiesce to disengagement (proposition G1), and show how splitting and sharing the specific assets located in colonial peripheries, especially site-specific economic assets and military installations, facilitated imperial disengagement (G2). Furthermore, we discuss how these initial accords were subsequently renegotiated on terms favorable to the ex-colonies (M1) who, as owners of residual control rights, were in more powerful bargaining positions to change initial contractual terms (B1). However, this prospect raised significant credibility problems for host countries that sought to gain control rights (C1 and C2). Our discussion reveals that such hybrid institutional arrangements played a critical role in facilitating decolonization that might otherwise have been politically difficult or even conflictual. These effects exerted by incomplete contracts operated independently of the relative power capabilities that still characterized the former metropole and host countries.

Chapter 4 applies the insights of the theory to cold war cases of U.S. overseas basing agreements. It demonstrates how splitting the sovereignty of overseas military installations has been critical in finding politically acceptable and stable institutional arrangements to govern the U.S. military presence abroad (G1). Moreover, it shows how certain military installations and assets whose specificity to the U.S. basing network were high (G2), such as Clark and Subic in the Philippines, became the objects of contentious hard bargaining and strategic renegotiation by basing hosts (B1). Over time, host countries were able to use their residual rights to demand increased political and economic concessions from the United States and to restrict further the use rights of the superpower in each renegotiation; host countries intentionally demanded shorter agreements so as to increase the frequency of these renegotiation payoffs (M1). This raised credibility problems (C1 and C2) for host countries. For its part, the United States calculated the relative costs of paying compensation to host countries with moving or replacing these installations, tried to maintain and consolidate various complementary functions within these agreements, and steadily shed nonessential installations that were proving to be too costly (M2). Finally, we interpret the Pentagon's recent global force restructuring agreement as an attempt to temper the hold-up problems and disruptive political consequences of these incomplete contracts and reduce its reliance on large, specific, forward deployments.

In chapter 5, we explore the general effects of incomplete contracting on the formation of supranational institutions such as *ex post* legislation, arbitration, and joint production agreements (G1), as well as examine the process through which incomplete agreements become codified at subsequent renegotiations (M1). We examine how the strong powers within the EU often have had to subordinate authority to supranational institutions in order to signal their credible commitment to weaker powers over the direction of integration. Finally, we compare and contrast how the incompleteness of EU agreements combined with the transfer of residual rights to supranational third parties has generated momentum for additional integration in a manner that the complete contract of NAFTA has not.

Severing the Ties That Bind: Sovereign Transfers in the Shadow of Empire

Introduction

In the preceding chapters we argued that hybrid sovereignty agreements constitute incomplete contracts. In this chapter we examine how such incomplete contracts can help facilitate orderly and peaceful transfers of state sovereignty in cases of territorial disengagement. We apply our theoretical insights to several cases of twentieth-century decolonization in which parties concluded hybrid sovereignty agreements involving site-specific assets following what previously had been hierarchical governance. In other words, following the retreat of empire, two independent sovereign entities emerged—a new nation-state and a reduced former imperial state. However, new sovereign rights were rarely allocated in their entirety at the moment of formal decolonization. Portions of previously bundled sovereign rights were transferred to distinct parties through incomplete contracting.

Transitions from one form of governance to another are often fraught with conflict. Such transitions become particularly contested when both rival parties lay claim to site-specific assets within a periphery, especially assets that had been previously critical to the imperial state. Assets such as military bases, canals, oil and gas resources, plantations, mines, and water are thus natural sites of contention between emerging independent states and imperial powers (the metropole or central government). The imperial power will usually prefer the *status quo ante*. Continued control through hierarchy provides it with strategic military assets and economic benefits. For similar reasons, the secessionist (nationalist) group will prefer to fully control these assets itself and will want to emphasize the symbolic value of claiming sovereignty over these assets. The status of such specific assets can delay or complicate decolonization. Historically, the process of transferring sovereignty during decolonization was as challenging for the early European colonial powers as it was for Russia during the more recent dissolution of the USSR.[1]

---

[1] Such contested sovereign transfers continue to this day. How, for example, might Israel design a hybrid sovereignty agreement with the Palestinian Authority, as mandated by the Oslo I and II agreements, specifically with regard to the West Bank's water supplies? (We broach this issue in chapter 6.)

The Variety of Decolonization Outcomes

The presence of lingering specific assets can generate several different political outcomes during the decolonization process. At one extreme, the imperial state will try to retain control rights as well as use rights by force. This is the standard (neo-)imperial solution and the political equivalent of the Williamsonian model of vertical integration. At the other end, the secessionists will aim to oust the imperial power and thereby gain full control rights and use rights for the newly independent state. In this case, full sovereignty would accompany nationalization of foreign assets and bases. Both of these outcomes may be regarded as examples of complete contracts, given that they settle sovereign prerogatives, both control rights and use rights, with one of the two parties, and do so without intent to reallocate sovereign assets in the future. There are no outstanding issues regarding the shift in bargaining leverage—the scope of the agreements is perfectly understood—and there is no momentum for renegotiation or specification. Sovereign transfers would be carried out completely in the nationalization scenario or not at all in the neo-imperial case.

Such complete allocation of rights, however, might not be politically feasible. When secessionist struggles yield no clear victor, or when parties cannot agree on a peaceful transfer of all rights, alternative intermediate solutions might emerge. Specifically, by dividing the control rights and the use rights of a contested asset, the competing states can reapportion sovereign rights in a hybrid fashion and facilitate a more orderly disengagement. In one outcome, the former imperial power might yield control rights to the nationalists while it retains use rights. Bases may thus be assigned legally to the newly independent state (the host country), while the former imperial center (the foreign country) retains the ability to use those bases for a fixed period of time at a given cost or for some otherwise specified quid pro quo. We define this outcome as *allocation with national residual rights*. The residual rights of decision making will reside with the host, the newly independent state, even while the former imperial state is allowed to use the asset.

Conversely, the former imperial state may retain ownership and property rights but yield to the host country use rights such as a share of the proceeds of rent. Thus the metropolitan government might retain ownership of assets but allow the periphery to partially enjoy the fruits of that asset. This constitutes *allocation with foreign residual rights*, in that the former imperial power retains ownership rights but cannot reap the full benefits of that ownership. Residual rights remain with the foreign country. Short of the specified rent and quid pro quo for the host, this arrangement will transfer surplus rents to the metropole.

These latter two outcomes contravene the assumption that the control of transaction-specific assets necessarily correlates with vertical control.[2] Solely based on a Williamsonian perspective one would expect transaction specificity and frequency to determine the pattern of governance. The incomplete contracting approach explains a range of intermediate outcomes that is not fully captured by relational contracting approaches.

Implications: Incomplete Contracts and Orderly Disengagement

This typology of decolonization arrangements denotes a range of outcomes rather than a strict two-by-two matrix. In many instances actual agreements might straddle the ideal types at the ends of the spectrum. For example, in some instances the sovereignty allocation with foreign residual rights might come close to outright imperialism as, for example, some of the nineteenth-century agreements that the European powers signed with local African powerbrokers. As we show in chapter 6, in the cases where a third party such as an international administrative power supervises territorial disengagement, the outside governing body may initially assume complete sovereign powers (neo-imperialism) but soon after may agree to foreign residual rights as it prepares the territory for full independence (see lower-left quadrant of figure 3.1). These outcomes are fluid and can evolve even within the same case.

This perspective contains significant policy and theoretical implications. From a practical perspective, if metropoles and their peripheries can more readily conclude such "mixed" agreements, the likelihood of conflict to settle rival claims to sovereignty decreases. Territorial partition might occur through negotiated contracting rather than through zero-sum contests in which the imperial power seeks to maintain its holdings by force while separatists seek to acquire all of the assets possessed by the metropole.

Theoretically, this chapter focuses on two key questions. First, why did the parties agree on a hybrid governance structure? In this sense we take governance structure initially (at $t = 0$) as our dependent variable. Second, what were the downstream political consequences of these incomplete contracts? More specifically, how did the subsequent bargaining leverage and momentum of such hybrid sovereignty arrangements contribute to

---

[2] For an early argument that explores the relevance of transaction specificity to empire, see Frieden 1994. See also Lake 1997, 1999. Some of this line of reasoning is foreshadowed in Lipson's discussion (1985) of Britain and the informal empires of the United States in Central and Latin America.

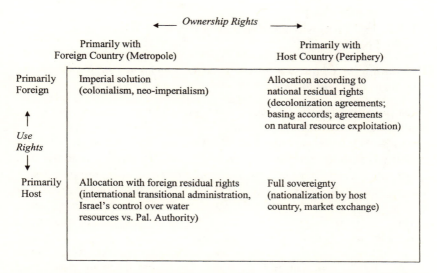

3.1. Configurations of Property Rights over Specific Assets during Decolonization.

their unraveling in some cases whereas others proved more durable? Thus, we examine how, over time, the initially chosen governance structure operates as the independent variable (at $t + 1$) and assess their outcomes down the line.

We focus on several cases of decolonization in the Western maritime empires. We offer evidence from the British, French, and Dutch cases, all of which had certain historical and cultural particularities, yet across which the logic of our approach still holds. In our fourth case, we argue that the same logic of inquiry can shed light on the partitioning of fixed assets in the wake of the more recent breakup of the USSR. Incomplete contracting theory does not provide a full articulation of causal sequences in all their elements. Some of the factors that determine whether given parties will agree to hybrid sovereignty arrangements are admittedly exogenous to our model. The preferences of actors will hinge on alliance partners, geostrategic calculations, technological shifts, and other factors that are idiosyncratic to the case at hand. Process tracing and induction play an important part in our analysis. However, an incomplete contracting approach provides insights into which causal factors will be particularly salient and it provides *ex ante* expectations regarding the preferences of the actors. Moreover, this approach provides a framework to examine the downstream consequences of hybrid sovereignty agreements.

Theoretical Propositions Regarding Bilateral Bargaining over Fixed Assets

Explaining the Choice for Sovereignty Arrangements: Preferences, Power, and Commitment

The options confronting the contracting governments run the gamut from unified hierarchy to the full extension of sovereignty to the erstwhile periphery—a decisive parting of ways. In the latter situation, in structural realist terms, both entities become sovereign states under anarchy. Both claim full authority within their own borders and lay no claims to jurisdiction or particular rights in the other state. The adoption of a hybrid sovereignty arrangement will depend on three factors: the preferences of the actors, the distribution in power, and the ability of the residual rights holder to credibly commit to the agreement.

As said, ceteris paribus, the foreign government, or metropole, will prefer to retain all control and use rights. Transaction-specific assets, and particularly site-specific assets, are by nature vulnerable to hold-up, seizure, destruction, or sabotage by the subject territory. If this option is not feasible or governance is too costly, then the center might relinquish ownership but maintain claims to use rights of particular assets—allocation with residual rights for the new nation. Or the imperial power might try to retain the ownership of fixed assets in the host country but yield on use rights and pay the host a percentage of the proceeds—foreign allocation of residual rights. In both of the latter instances, nationalist entrepreneurs or opposition elites might challenge the newly independent government of the host country and criticize subjection to the metropole, demanding full control over the proceeds. The imperial power will thus prefer unified hierarchy over the uncertainties of hybrid sovereignty contracts, as one would expect from a Williamsonian perspective.[3]

Conversely, the periphery, or host country, also has reasons to distrust the erstwhile imperial power. If it relinquishes use rights to the former central government, it risks inviting a reassertion of imperial control. For example, the Newly Independent States of the USSR had to remain fearful of Russian neo-imperialism, and to this day Russian influence remains high in many of these states. Similarly, if the periphery grants the center control rights and has to rely on rents or sharing in the proceeds, it might be vulnerable to exploitation. For example, African colonial rulers concluded agreements with European mining firms that were supposed to hold for fifty years or more and that unquestionably favored metropolitan

---

[3] Raymond Vernon (1971, 46) aptly described the process of increasing demands by host governments on foreign multinationals as an "obsolescing bargain."

profit-seeking rather than peripheral development.[4] The secessionists (nationalists) will thus see full sovereignty over specific assets as their first preference. Granting use rights to a foreign power (the top-right quadrant in figure 3.1) would be less preferable but still better than an outcome in which the foreign power maintained residual rights of control (the bottom left quadrant). A neo-imperial outcome with very few rights for the subject territory would be of course worst of all.

In addition to initial preferences, the outcome will be determined by the distribution of power among the actors. Implicit in our hypothesis (and in our general theory of incomplete contracting) is the assumption that under certain conditions, complete contracting, as in full hierarchy (neo-imperialism) or anarchy (full separation of previously integrated territories), is unfeasible because of the relative configuration of power.[5] Thus, even though mixed arrangements are not the first preference of either actor, a more symmetrical distribution of power may force the hybrid option. Thus, our first thesis, as stated in chapter 2, has two corollaries.

G1a: If the distribution of power is highly asymmetric in favor of the metropole, the center will prefer a neo-imperial solution to incomplete contracting.

G1b: If the distribution of power is highly asymmetric in favor of the host country, the latter will opt for full sovereignty.

Large asymmetries will compromise the willingness of the actors to enter into an incomplete contract since the more powerful actor will have the ability to renege or renegotiate to its advantage at any time. When neither the metropole nor the periphery can force the other's hand, and a definite settlement (complete contract) regarding the separation of fixed assets is too costly, actors seek hybrid governance structures (G2).

Finally, the type of governance structure that emerges will depend on credibility of commitment. As suggested by our theoretical discussion, the party that holds the residual rights of control will face considerable commitment problems (C1). This commitment problem will be particularly acute when the holder of residual rights controls relationally specific assets. That party will be inclined to demand increased benefits and security and thus shift to expropriation in the case of national allocation of residual rights, whereas the foreign allocation of residual rights will entice

---

[4] In one case, "the lease given to the Firestone Company by the Liberian government in 1926 was to run for 99 years and covered one million acres of land" (Smith and Wells 1975, 566n13).

[5] As David Lake points out, hierarchy and coercion will likely result in resistance by the local population, thus increasing governance costs. The greater the likelihood that such resistance will be successful, that is, when power distribution is relatively symmetric, the more likely it is that the subject area will try to secede. See Lake 1997, 41.

the former imperial power to pursue an increasingly neo-imperial solution. The holder of such residual rights of control needs to signal credibility either by its institutional design or by reputation. In the following discussion we clarify how actors dealt with downstream credibility problems during decolonization, specifically, how domestic institutions affected the credibility of the holder of residual rights.[6]

But previous behavior can also enhance credibility and make cooperative solutions using incomplete contracts more feasible at $t = 0$.[7] For the former imperial powers, particularly those that could engage in piecemeal decolonization, such a reputation could be established by earlier concessions in other peripheries. Thus, arguably Britain could more readily conclude deals with its colonies given its reputation for adhering to previous agreements with the Dominions in the nineteenth century and concessions to some of the colonies in the interwar period.

For nationalist movements such reputation was more difficult to establish. These were, after all, newly emerging regimes. Although difficult, this was not impossible. Thus nationalist elites might enhance credibility by choosing political regimes that were more in line with the retreating empire's preferences. Often this would involve domestic political costs. For example, by declining a political alliance with the communists in Indochina and clamping down on the indigenous left, Indonesian nationalists signaled to Dutch politicians and business elites that a compromise solution could be achieved. We thus restate the two propositions with regard to credibility at $t = 0$ that governed decolonization cases.

C1: *Incomplete contracts will be easier to conclude when the parties can credibly commit through institutional or reputational mechanisms.*

C2: *The burden of credible commitment falls particularly on the holder of residual rights of control.*

Downstream Consequences of Incomplete Contracting

Equally important to our discussion of the historical cases is assessing the downstream consequences (at $t + 1$) of adopting incomplete contracts as part of the initial decolonization bargain. Specifically, incomplete contracting theory helps us identify changes in bargaining leverage and the likelihood of further contractual specification and/or contractual renegotiation.

---

[6] Cowhey 1993; Martin 2000; Lipson 2003.

[7] Axelrod (1984) notes how previous cooperative behavior tends to elicit similar responses in a tit-for-tat manner. Thus long-term cooperation might be feasible. Sartori (2005) discusses how a reputation for honesty and acquiescence is strategically rational.

BARGAINING LEVERAGE

According to our general hypothesis on bargaining leverage, the owner of residual rights in decolonization agreements has incentives to bargain hard for the appropriation of surplus as time progresses (B1). This incentive to bargain hard, along with the host's ownership rights, will give it considerable leverage at $t + 1$. The bargaining leverage for the actor with residual rights of control will be particularly high in the case of transaction-specific assets, as they give the actor with control rights over such assets leverage over the actor who only possesses use rights.

A key insight of our argument is that bargaining leverage is not just a function of initial transaction specificity (as Williamsonian models predict) but a logical consequence of the design of the incomplete contract. The residual rights of control give the holder the ability to allocate and claim rights in new issue areas as they emerge. The incomplete agreement does not merely confer to the residual rights holder the right to decide over the specific asset allocation as agreed in the initial contract; it gives the holder the ability to claim assets and rights that are not covered in the original contract. In other words, it resembles the subsidiarity principle: any rights not covered in the initial agreement reside with the actor to whom residual rights of control were allocated.

As we have seen, short of outright hierarchical control, the imperial power will prefer foreign allocation of residual rights over national allocation to the former periphery. It will opt for ownership rights while granting use rights to the former subject territory. Conversely, the former colony will prefer national allocation of residual rights if it cannot obtain its first preference for full national sovereignty.

Our conjectures regarding the trend in bargaining leverage over hybrid sovereignty arrangements—as time progresses—lead to two extensions.

B1a: With foreign allocation of residual rights, the formerly dominant polity will seek greater certainty through neo-imperial policies.

B1b: If residual rights are allocated to the former subject territory, the latter will seek to change the outcome to full sovereign control.

MOMENTUM

Incomplete contracts generate a momentum for further specification. Each side will have incentives to appropriate a greater surplus from the asset if possible, to clarify uncertain terms, and to resolve outstanding issues (proposition M1 in chapter 2). Indeed, the very nature of incomplete contracting anticipates that actors will engage in such renegotiations. In particular, we expect this to occur in empirical cases where actors cannot foresee how the larger military and economic context might value or devalue the holding of transaction-specific assets.

We further expect that the contracting parties will seek to renegotiate the incomplete contract and move toward complete contracting and increased specificity if the benefits of joint supply are low. The contracting parties will prefer to shift from allocation with national residual rights to full sovereignty (complete contracts and market exchange). Conversely, the former colonial power, which still maintains residual rights of control, will seek to reestablish a neo-imperial governance structure if at all possible. Thus an incomplete contract will trend toward completeness.

Contracts will retain incomplete allocation of sovereign rights only when there are continued benefits of joint production and when few alternative contracting parties are available. If alternative contracting parties are available, the specific identity of the supplier and consumer (in Williamsonian terms) recedes. The exchange relationship takes on the characteristics of market exchange. Imagine, for example, that the need for overseas bases by a great power can be fulfilled by multiple suppliers. The United States might be indifferent as to whether it has bases in Ethiopia or Eritrea as long as it can project power in the Horn of Africa. Conversely, there might be situations where multiple great powers (consumers) vie for access to one supplier. For example, during the 1956 Suez Crisis, the government of Libya rejected British requests to use its basing facilities—a request premised upon the basing rights granted by the Anglo-Libyan Treaty of July 1953—to project force in Egypt, as it considered Egypt and the Soviet Union as alternative suppliers of security and patronage.[8] The availability of alternative contracting parties for any one of the two actors, therefore, diminishes the likelihood that the terms of the agreement will be honored. Defection will be less costly and thus more likely. Contracts will become more complete with single ownership asserted by the owner of residual rights (proposition M2).

Similarly, if former colonies grant the erstwhile metropole use rights, they will only do so as long as the colonial power can compensate the newly independent state or give it some other needed quid pro quo. If not, nationalist elites will rescind the agreement. Over the longer term, joint production will be unattractive. These various downstream consequences are presented in figure 3.2.

Empirical Cases

In the sections that follow we discuss four instances of territorial partition and decolonization involving France, the Netherlands, Great Britain, and

---

[8] See Worrall 2007.

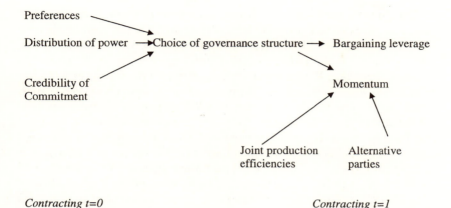

Preferences

Distribution of power → Choice of governance structure → Bargaining leverage

Credibility of
Commitment   Momentum

                                        Joint production   Alternative
                                        efficiencies   parties

Contracting t=0   *Contracting t=1*

3.2. Causal Dynamics in the Creation of Hybrid Sovereignty and Its Downstream
Consequences.

the Soviet Union. Overseas military bases and economic fixed investments
have traditionally been sources of contention. Imperial powers are loathe
to relinquish such specific assets, even as they acquiesce to a decolonization settlement. Military installations entail significant outlays in terms of
docks, landing strips, barracks, and so on, which cannot easily be redeployed. Moreover, often the location of these bases will have been chosen
initially for their geostrategic importance, not just to control the former
periphery. In these situations, there are few countries that can provide the
desired bases or natural resources. Similarly, in many instances there will
only be a limited number of states that can project force overseas and that
require distant bases. These are not perfect market-like exchanges. These
different cases of decolonization arrangements illustrate the various path-
ways and contractual dynamics that we have identified; some of these
hybrid agreements quickly unraveled after their formal adoption, whereas
others remained relatively stable.

We begin with a discussion of the French-Algerian conflict and the
Evian agreement. Although France granted Algeria independence in the
1962 accord, it maintained several bases and preferential oil concessions
in Algerian territory. The agreements on French use rights of bases and oil
exploration, however, quickly unraveled. Similarly, the Dutch-Indonesian
conflict (1945–49) led to an agreement whereby the Netherlands yielded
sovereign control but maintained an economic foothold until 1957. However, the accords started to unravel well before the actual nationalization
of Dutch facilities. Both cases thus involved incomplete contracts that
emerged after protracted struggles. And both incomplete contracts proved
unstable.

We contrast these cases with two decolonization processes that had different outcomes. Britain withdrew from its imperial holdings gradually. Well before World War II, it had granted the Dominions considerable autonomy but had retained extensive holdings in those areas, as well as close military ties. Retreat from empire started in earnest from 1945 onward. However, it maintained many naval bases, which had been cornerstones of empire, for decades thereafter. We focus next on the dissolution of the Soviet Empire. The ability to reach agreements between Russia and the former Union Republics on the fixed assets in what Russia described as its "Near Abroad" enabled the dissolution to proceed quickly without significant bloodshed. For the most part, these agreements have remained stable for well over a decade after their initial adoption. Both the British and USSR cases demonstrate instances in which incomplete contracts emerged without significant conflict between the former imperial center and the host country. Moreover, some of these agreements proved relatively durable.

France's Hybrid Sovereignty Arrangements in Northern Africa

France lost most of the territories it acquired in its first imperial phase in the Seven Years' War (1756–63) and the Napoleonic Wars. However, it acquired significant new areas, particularly in North Africa and Southeast Asia, in the second imperial period from 1830 onward. Like the other western maritime empires, it relinquished virtually all of its colonies and overseas territories in the post–World War II era but some of these only after brutal conflict.

We focus on French relations in North Africa, particularly Algeria. Considered part of France proper, Algeria was administered by the Ministry of the Interior, not the Ministry of Overseas Territories. It had very close economic ties with France, and more than a million French had settled there. It should come as no surprise then that France tried to maintain these connections first through empire then by hybrid governance arrangements. Nevertheless, it failed in these attempts. We first explain how a hybrid sovereignty arrangement emerged and then why it unraveled.

Algeria and the Evian Accords as an Incomplete Contract

The Evian Accords of 1962 brought eight years of bloody war with Algeria to a close. Although Algerian nationalism had first erupted in the Sétif uprising (launched on V-E Day in 1945), the Algerian war proper started in 1954. It gradually escalated such that France deployed more than

400,000 troops at its peak. By 1958 its forces started to gain the upper hand but the large military deployment proved increasingly costly to sustain and the number of casualties continued to rise. In the end, French casualties numbered about 25,000 military personnel, and hundreds of thousands of Algerians perished.[9] Many Algerians died in the conflict with the French, while others died in the internecine battles among the Front de Libération Nationale (FLN) and pro-French Algerians; there was also bloodletting among the nationalists themselves. France itself was several times brought to the brink of civil war, and multiple attempts were made on President de Gaulle's life.[10]

France's reticence to yield Algeria had many causes. The military, the local colonial administration, and particularly the large settler population proved to be the most ardent supporters of a French Algeria. The armed forces perceived its colonial mission threatened, while the million settlers feared a loss of property and privileged status.

The conflict was also complicated by French desire to retain access to the Saharan oil and gas reserves of southern Algeria, which were just coming on line by the 1950s, and to retain a military foothold in northern Africa.[11] Economically, the Saharan reserves were deemed so important that the Evian talks originally failed in June 1961 because an agreement could not be reached with regard to these resources. Virtually every major party (except for the Communists) argued that control over Saharan oil was critical for the French economy. The Christian Democrats noted in one of their manifestos that "the petrol riches of the Sahara . . . will liberate us from the economic servitude of foreigners."[12] Militarily, the Mediterranean fleet, not the Atlantic deployments, had strategic primacy for Paris. Thus, the military installations in Algeria, and to lesser extent Tunisia, were deemed critical for France's overall security.

Despite these obstacles, the French and Algerians successfully concluded the Evian talks in 1962. The accords granted France particular use rights over these specific assets in exchange for Algerian independence. The accords were signed in March of that year and went into effect in July after a referendum. The accords provided Algeria full internal and external sovereignty.[13] Paris in turn committed itself to providing "techni-

---

[9] Clayton 1988, 189.

[10] For an overview of French politics in the period, see Berstein 1993. De Gaulle's perspectives are captured in his memoirs; see de Gaulle 1971.

[11] The Reggane center in the Sahara served as the testing facility for the French nuclear program, and it was here that France exploded its first nuclear device. Kohl 1971, 103.

[12] Harrison 1983, 82.

[13] Accords d'Evian, Déclaration Générale, chapter 2, section AI. See also Vial 2002, 270; Delaporte 2002, 324–27. Available at http://www.tlfq.ulaval.ca/AXL/AFRIQUE/algerie-accords_d'Evian.htm.

cal and cultural assistance for its [Algeria's] economic and social development and privileged financial aid."[14]

The treaty specifically discussed cooperation on subsoil resource development. The agreement granted Algeria control rights but committed it
to technical cooperation with France in Saharan oil exploration. It declared that French companies would be allowed to bid on an equal basis
with other companies for permits for exploiting the Saharan wealth.[15] The
importance of this agreement is highlighted in the special section "Declaration of principles regarding economic and financial cooperation."
France agreed to provide economic and financial aid to Algeria for three
years, which could be renewed (title 1, article 1). In articles 14–17, Algeria
recognized French mining or transport companies' rights to search for,
exploit, and transport liquid or gas hydrocarbons or other mineral sub-
stances. The accords provided another special declaration on "the Principles for cooperation to improve the value of the Saharan sub-soil," and
it established joint institutions for this purpose.[16] International arbitration
was called for (title 4) should disputes arise.

Despite the bitterness of the French-Algerian war, the combatants
reached agreement on the nature of France's military presence as well.
Most prominently, Algeria conceded the use of the naval base at Mers-el-
Kébir for fifteen years, which could be renewed. France also retained some
other airstrips and military installations.[17] Mers-el-Kébir, destroyed during the war by the British, had been designated a first rank strategic base
on par with Brest and Dakar. Indeed, in 1948 the French government had
allocated more than 630 million francs to the base, trailing Brest (785
million) but more than double that of Toulon (308 million). Brest and
Mers-el-Kébir got almost 60 percent of the basing budget.[18] The base retained its importance through the decades after the war, with the aerial
and army components increasing in significance. The French government's commitment in financial terms remained very high, and it constructed important facilities that could withstand atomic attack.[19]

The details of the agreement were worked out in the "Declaration of
principles regarding military questions." In article 1, France recognized
that Mers-el-Kébir was Algerian soil. While the naval base was granted
for fifteen years, such lesser establishments as the airfields Lartigue, l'Ar-

---

[14] Accords d'Evian, Déclaration Générale, chapter 2, section B. Algeria would also remain part of the Franc zone.
[15] Accords d'Evian, Déclaration Générale, chapter 2, section B, no. 2. See also Gray 1962.
[16] Accords d'Evian, Déclaration Générale, section C, title III, no. 14.
[17] Accords d'Evian, Déclaration Générale, chapter 3.
[18] Delaporte 2002, 317.
[19] Vial (2002, 283) argues the outlay was equivalent to the cost of two aircraft carriers.

bal, and Bou-Sfer could be used by France for three more years. Yet other installations could be used by France for five years (articles 4 and 5). Regarding criminal jurisdiction, individuals who violated the law and jeopardized the order within the boundaries of these bases would be remanded to the Algerian authorities (article 5 annex), unless the infractions did not pertain to Algerian interests, in which case the French military jurisdiction applied (article 26 annex).

Algeria thus gained control rights over military installations and subsoil mineral assets. The agreement constituted an allocation according to national residual rights. Although France retained some of its bases and was allowed to continue exploration of the oil and gas reserves in the Sahara, Algeria gained formal sovereign ownership. The French, in turn, while not committing themselves to leasing its facilities, engaged in a quid pro quo, particularly with regard to oil and gas development.

INITIAL INTRANSIGENCE AND HOSTILITY TO A HYBRID ARRANGEMENT

Why did a negotiated solution and a hybrid sovereignty compromise not come about earlier? And perhaps more startling, what explains these Algerian concessions in 1962?

Prior to de Gaulle's accession to office in 1958, Paris had shown little interest in negotiating any division of sovereignty. In the immediate postwar period and through the early 1950s, France's relative decline was not apparent to French decision makers.[20] Instead, empire was considered a sine qua non for great power standing with fears of becoming "Greece" or "Portugal" without such holdings. Indeed, metropolitan defense hinged on the availability of overseas contingents. North Africa in particular was considered vital for France's home defense.[21] Moreover, with the deployment of conscripts, starting in 1956, and the use of Challe's special counterguerilla strategy, the military situation in Algeria had started to shift in France's favor. The Parisian government thus believed it could still unilaterally impose its will.[22] It opted for continuing imperial rule.

The nationalists in Algeria, however, believed that French power was declining. The defeat in Vietnam in 1954 was thus clearly a contributing factor to the outbreak of violence in Algeria. The debacle at Suez (1956) similarly indicated the weakness of the colonial powers. They believed, therefore, that the distribution of power was shifting in their favor.

While France saw Algeria as critical for its strategic and economic interest, the Algerian nationalists believed that severing ties with France would

[20] Girault 1986, 64.
[21] For this myth of empire, see Kupchan 1994; Clayton 1988, 154.
[22] The best historical narrative remains Horne 1978.

not be too costly. The nationalists received support from fellow North African states (Tunisia and Morocco) and from Egypt. They thought that perhaps even Soviet support might be forthcoming, as Nasser had started to enjoy. With alternative contracting parties potentially available, and with no joint economies of scale, the nationalists preferred to seek full sovereignty that denied concessions to the French.

Both sides also lacked the ability to credibly commit. Although conventional literature usually sees divided government as having an advantage in signaling credibility, this was not the case for the French Fourth Republic. While divided government with multiple veto opportunities usually provides for policy stability and thus irreversibility on the state's prior commitments, it impedes the ability to credibly *initiate* proposals. The home country, France, lacked the ability to alter its previous colonial policy because of the high degree of fragmentation of its legislature and the commensurate weakness of the executive.[23]

The nationalists were also divided. Regional commands fought with the center and among themselves. Algerian resistance leaders clashed with leaders of the movement in exile. Ethnic, regional, and tribal differences mattered as well.[24] An agreement brokered with one segment of the elite had no bearing on what some of the others might do. Thus, the lack of Algerian credibility greatly hindered the prospects of a compromise, an incomplete contract, at this time. There was no rational reason for Paris to expect that an incomplete contract would be durable.

In short, both sides believed the balance of power tipped in their favor. And, lacking the ability to credibly commit, they pursued their first (and opposite) preferences. Neither side could envision a solution based on some form of hybrid sovereignty.

REACHING THE HYBRID SOLUTION

What changed to produce the Evian Accords of 1962? The Suez Crisis, although a military success in its initial phase, demonstrated French and British vulnerability. Washington's withdrawal of financial support and the subsequent withdrawal from Suez by France and Britain demonstrated that London and Paris were not masters of their own fate.[25] The war in Algeria also proved prohibitively costly in economic and military terms. The governance costs of empire thus started to mount while French ability to exercise military force abroad declined. True, the French forces

---

[23] This is discussed more extensively in Spruyt 2005.

[24] Horne notes that "throughout the war internal dissent and personal animosities were the F.L.N.'s single greatest enemy" (1978, 128).

[25] Lloyd 1978.

had proved adept at integrating new military technology (as the helicopter), but they could not pacify the remote hinterlands, and even some of the cities remained hotbeds of nationalist resistance. Rather than reimposing hierarchy and imperial control, a military stalemate ensued.[26]

The nationalists also became more amenable to compromise. As said, French counterinsurgency tactics had met with considerable success and inflicted significant casualties. Moreover, after Paris had granted Tunisia and Morocco independence, as well as all of West and Central Africa, the Algerian nationalists, paradoxically, were on their own. Even though they received political support, militarily they remained isolated. The level of Egyptian support from Nasser, and indeed from the Arab League as a whole, proved minimal despite French assertions to the contrary. Support from the Eastern Bloc was marginal as well as a result of FLN dominance and control over the Algerian Communist Party (PCA).[27]

The immediate and full granting of sovereignty to Algeria thus seemed more remote than nationalists had thought in the middle of the 1950s. In the theoretical parlance of our earlier chapters, the political and economic costs of full integration (neo-imperialism) or full disintegration (complete sovereignty) were high, thus making hybrid governance more attractive.

Both sides had also improved in their ability to make credible commitments. The French Fifth Republic passed a new constitution, giving vastly expanded powers to the president. De Gaulle could then implement new policy initiatives on the Algerian question without having to rely on the unstable majorities within the legislature. On the Algerian side, the FLN gained the upper hand. The opposition was quelled, jailed, or killed. As a result, both the French executive and the Algerian nationalists could initiate new policy directions while controlling the lower echelons of authority, thus credibly committing their followers to any accord the two governments might reach.

The realization that the distribution of power favored neither side in particular, combined with convergence in preferences and improved credibility to commit, thus led to an agreement allocating residual rights of control to Algeria. The parties granted control rights to Algeria, with concessions to the French on use rights for military bases for a fixed period of time and cooperation on mineral exploitation of the Sahara.

---

[26] De Gaulle also had dramatically different visions of how France could retain (or perhaps regain) its great power standing. Nuclear weapons rather than colonial manpower or possessions were critical (see Kohl 1971). Thus, the overseas bases were deemed of lesser importance as long as these overseas territories did not fall to the Soviet orbit. The decline in relative power and a changed strategic assessment of the value of these bases therefore underlay Paris's posture at this point.

[27] Harrison 1983, 85.

It is important to note that the agreement was not simply window-dressing—an agreement signed for domestic consumption with no expectation that it would be honored. Delaporte argues that the government, military, and engineers believed that retaining Mers-el-Kébir was a realistic objective, despite eight years of war.[28] Raymond Aron thought that the agreement had accomplished much more than initially thought possible. While the long-term success was not assured, neither was its failure. ("Ce success n'est pas assuré, l'échec non plus.")[29] Given the close economic ties and joint benefits of production of Algeria's natural resources, the participants to the accord had reason to believe that cooperation in the future and thus the hybrid sovereignty arrangements could have a chance of success.

The Evian Accords Unravel

The Evian agreement, however, started to fall apart quicker than anticipated. The French presence at Mers-el-Kébir lasted till 1967, only five years beyond the transferral and well short of the fifteen years to which the parties had agreed. By 1968, the last of the French troops left Algeria.[30]

While the relative power constellation between the countries did not shift in any dramatic fashion, both sides had changed their minds about the benefits of joint production, while at the same time alternate contracting parties became available. The momentum, in other words, swung against hybrid sovereignty arrangements. Algeria subsequently used its bargaining leverage to gain full control over its natural resources.

For France, its military posture had shifted from its Mediterranean focus. As far as the military was concerned the need for a North African deployment had decreased as France moved toward nuclear deterrence. Consequently, the importance of the Mediterranean fleet had declined whereas Atlantic ports such as Brest and the Polynesian facilities that formed the location for France's nuclear testing grew in importance.[31] The closing of the Suez Canal following the Six-Day War reinforced the perspective that France's geostrategic orientation needed a dramatic overhaul.[32] France sought alternative contracting partners and bases. Whereas

---

[28] Delaporte 2002, 326.

[29] Quoted in Ageron 1992, 14. Ageron himself lays considerable blame for the subsequent failure not on the nature of the agreement but on French extremists who terrorized the settler population to return to France, thus eroding the multicultural aspects of French-Algerian cooperation.

[30] Alexander and Keiger 2002, xvii.

[31] The strategic calculations regarding the value of overseas bases had started to shift by 1956 following Suez, the fall of Indochina, and nuclear development. Vial 2002, 259–64.

[32] Balencie 1991/92; Delaporte 2002, 330.

Polynesia received virtually nothing in the first two decades after the war, the French nuclear shift allowed it to command a quarter of the infrastructural budget by 1966.[33]

The prospects for long-term economic interaction had also changed. Initially, in the 1950s, the French thought that the Algerians would continue to lack the expertise to find and develop oil and gas resources themselves. Granting French access for technical know-how and development would thus provide both parties joint benefits of production. The French needed the natural resources, whereas the Algerians needed French capital and development. Moreover, the French expected the Algerian government to fit within the francophone network of associated states, linked by mutual trade and financial aid. De Gaulle's referendum in the West African states had led most of these states to opt for independence, but all except one, Guinea, had simultaneously chosen to maintain ties with Paris.

Alternative contracting parties were also not readily available as the United States continued to concentrate on the Middle East, so Algeria could not turn to them to gain their capital and know-how. Conversely, French oil companies were not competitive with American and British firms in the Middle East, which minimized French ability to seek non-Algerian supply sources. But by the same token, as long as those companies concentrated on the Middle East and other markets, the French could hope for a privileged position in Algeria. Thus, the Evian Accords sought to establish use rights in exchange for technological and economic aid. Indeed, in 1963 there were still 21,000 French personnel involved with such exchanges in Algeria.[34]

But this situation deteriorated rapidly with the rise to power of Houari Boumedienne and as Algeria began to capitalize on its bargaining leverage. Boumedienne came to power by backing a coalition that ousted Ahmed Ben Bella in 1965. His strategy for development called for diminishing the neocolonial dependence on France and an explicitly economic nationalist strategy. Thus, during the 1960s the Algerian state started to take control of trade, manufacturing, and natural resource production. By 1971 Boumedienne assumed control of French-owned petroleum extraction facilities, energy firms, and pipelines.[35] After the Algerian takeover, French oil companies could hold only a minority stake in the state-run oil and gas firms. Even as Paris threatened a boycott of Algerian products, it simultaneously sought to renegotiate continued economic ties with its former colony.[36]

[33] Delaporte 2002, 329.
[34] Naylor 2000.
[35] Akre 1992, 75.
[36] Naylor 1992, 218.

France's leverage over the Algerian government was also decisively eroded by the latter's ability to turn to alternative economic partners. The French estimation, going into the Evian negotiations, had been wrong. Algeria was less vulnerable to discontinuing ties with the former metropole than Paris imagined. Other European oil producers (Italian interests among others) and particularly American firms could step in. In 1962 the United States received less than 1 percent of Algerian exports. By 1978 it received 55 percent.[37] Indeed, the whole idea of linking the Algerian national oil and gas company, Sonatrach, with foreign firms was modeled on the firm's 1968 agreement with Getty Oil: "Sonatrach acquired 51 percent of Getty's operations in Algeria and Getty provided the capital for further exploration and production in return for a percentage of profits."[38] Moreover, the oil sector agreements paved the way for agreements with other countries, particularly in the natural gas field. The Algerian government signed contracts with, among others, Italy's ENI and Belgium's Distrigaz.[39] Since then, the move to privatization after Boumedienne and the shift from heavy-handed state intervention has opened the market even further. For example, Britain's BP signed oil cooperation agreements in 1992.[40]

Consequently, as expected, in the economic realm the leverage in bargaining had shifted to Algeria. The nationalist leadership had changed its mind about the benefits of joint production. It did not need to continue the relationship with France, as Algeria itself obtained technical know-how and assistance. Moreover, the presence of alternate contracting parties decisively reduced the incentives to maintain the incomplete contract. As Akre notes, "because Algeria was able to carve out new relationships with the United States and others, the hold of France on Algeria's economy was substantially loosened."[41]

France and Tunisia

Before France granted Algeria independence, the Parisian government had brokered a deal with the Tunisian government of Habib Bourguiba. As was later the case with Algeria, France brokered a hybrid sovereignty agreement with Tunisia giving the latter residual rights of control. France and Tunisia signed two treaties: in the first, the parties settled the juridical

[37] Akre 1992, 87.
[38] Ibid., 88.
[39] Naylor 1992, 219, 223.
[40] Pfeifer 1992, 112.
[41] Akre 1992, 84.

situation in a convention on "interior autonomy" (June 1955). In the second, in March 1956, France granted "principles of political autonomy" to Tunisia. The French would withdraw their troops from Tunisia, except from a key base in Bizerta and six other bases of lesser importance. It would also maintain a presence in the southern zone, which was disputed territory because the borders with Libya and Algeria had not been fixed.[42] France would lease the facilities at Bizerta, but the ultimate status of the base was left open-ended.[43]

The hybrid sovereignty arrangement in this case proved highly unstable. The different interpretation of the two treaties and different views on which agreement took precedence quickly became a source of contention. In an exchange of letters following the 1955 and 1956 pacts, both sides agreed that France would withdraw its troops in 1958, with Bizerta to be dealt with in subsequent negotiations. However, these negotiations never occurred because the Tunisian government wanted to bundle the Bizerta question with a resolution that granted Tunisia access to the Sahara. Based on the 1958 agreement, however, the Tunisians expected a phased withdrawal by France.[44] France, however, wanted to decouple the Saharan issue from Bizerta. By early 1961 the question had not been resolved and in the summer of that year fighting broke out. The number of casualties probably numbered in the hundreds (particularly on the Tunisian side), although estimates range into the thousands.[45] French troops not only continued to hold the Bizerta base but occupied territory beyond it as well.

Shortly after the conclusion of the Evian agreement with Algeria, Paris and Tunis ceased their hostilities. The French then swiftly abandoned Bizerta. By October 1963, France had withdrawn from Tunisia altogether.

Why did the parties conclude a hybrid sovereignty agreement and why was this arrangement unstable from the start? Although France had achieved successes against Tunisian troops, it was clear that Paris did not want to see the conflict escalate, particularly as the demands placed on its armed forces increased in the conflict with Algeria.[46] Moreover, the UN General Assembly had come out against France and had recognized the "sovereign right of Tunisia to call for the withdrawal of all French

---

[42] The authors gratefully acknowledge the aid of Pascal Venier for this section.

[43] Ruf 1971.

[44] Woodliffe 1992, 76.

[45] Ruf 1971, 209. Daniel A. Gordon mentions about 700 Tunisians dead and 24 French in three days of fighting (2000, 2).

[46] De Gaulle indicates in his memoirs that French calculations vis-à-vis Tunisia were inextricably linked with events in Algeria (1971, 117–19).

armed troops on its territory without its consent."[47] Pursuing a neo-imperial solution would thus be very costly for France, while outright sovereignty might be difficult to achieve for Tunisia. The quick agreement that established national residual rights with Tunisia thus made strategic sense.

However, unlike Algeria, Tunisia and France were less intertwined. Algeria was far more important in economic terms than Tunisia.[48] Moreover, given its lack of natural resources, Tunisia depended less on foreign capital and know-how for the exploitation of such assets, as was the case in Algeria. There were thus few perceived joint gains. As France recognized, the bargaining leverage over time would shift to Tunisia.

Moreover, from a security perspective the Evian agreement had given France access to Mers-el-Kébir, a far more important installation than Bizerta. And, as said earlier, its overall geostrategic posture started to shift away from the Mediterranean. Paris thus had alternative contracting parties through which to pursue its geostrategic interests. If Paris started to have second thoughts about the need to keep Mers-el-Kébir, this held a fortiori for a base like Bizerta.

From the Tunisian side, Bourguiba pursued pro-Western, anti-communist policies. In doing so he explicitly appealed to U.S. support. Thus, politically and economically Tunisia looked for alternative partners as well. The incomplete contract between France and Tunisia was thus quickly terminated with Tunisia gaining full sovereignty.

In short, the conclusion and ultimate unraveling of the French-Tunisian accord conforms to our theoretical expectations. In 1955 France was already committed to a hard military campaign in Algeria. Even though it had a sizable number of troops deployed in Tunisia it preferred not to enforce an imperial solution. Tunisia, on its side, preferred to gain autonomy swiftly and without great cost. For both parties, then, hybrid sovereignty with allocation of national residual rights was a rational course of action.

However, several years into the agreement, conforming to our propositions regarding bargaining leverage and momentum, the nationalists favored a complete contract that would grant full control and use rights to the Tunisian government. With receding joint gains (France still planned to hold its Algerian bases, and it was moving toward an extra-Mediterranean posture), the former imperial center conceded exclusive sovereignty to Tunis.

[47] Quoted in Woodliffe 1992, 77.
[48] Marseille 1976, 1984. In 1954 France enjoyed a positive trade balance of 57 milliard francs with Algeria, 26 milliard francs with Morocco, and 13 milliard francs with Tunisia. By contrast, it had a negative trade balance of 79 milliard francs with the United States (Harrison 1983, 76n3).

The Netherlands in Indonesia

The Dutch empire differed from the British and French empires in its limited geographic extension. Although it had holdings in the Americas, Surinam, and several Caribbean islands, Indonesia was far more important for the Dutch economy than its other colonies. Indeed, in the middle of the nineteenth century it contributed more than a third of Dutch national income. Unlike the case for the great powers, for the Netherlands empire constituted an economic asset rather than a grand strategic military means. For the French and British, overseas bases projected military might in far-flung areas while providing local manpower reserves. The Netherlands' bases in Indonesia, however, served merely to defend the colony and to maintain control.

Prior to World War II the Dutch had managed to stifle nationalist sentiments by force. Japanese occupation, however, dramatically altered this situation. The Japanese swiftly defeated the Dutch colonial army and navy in early 1942. As its defeat drew closer Japan aided Indonesian nationalists under Sukarno and Hatta, who proclaimed an independent Indonesian Republic.[49] Nevertheless, as the Dutch had already indicated during the war, they envisioned if not full formal empire then certainly a system that still left the Dutch East Indies and the Netherlands "virtually a single national state" after the Japanese were defeated.[50]

Four years of turmoil and conflict ensued, culminating in two police actions in July 1947 and December 1948 that sought explicitly to retake site-specific assets such as mines, plantations, and oil-producing regions. Tellingly, the most important component of the first action was dubbed "Operation Product." The Hague believed, prodded by business interests, that a nationalist takeover would jeopardize transaction-specific assets. In the course of trying to quell the rebellion, roughly 5,000 Dutch troops and perhaps 100,000 Indonesians died. Due to Allied pressure, the Dutch ultimately had to relinquish control.[51]

The 1949 Round Table Agreement

Whereas French and British handovers involved disputes about the transfer of sovereignty over military bases, the Dutch reallocation of sovereignty revolved around its fixed economic assets in Indonesia. After several months of negotiations in the fall of 1949 (the Round Table

[49] For an overview of these developments, see van den Doel 1996.
[50] Kennedy, Holland, and Yung-ying 1943, 216.
[51] See van Doorn 1990, 1995.

Conference) it agreed to shift sovereignty rights to the Indonesian Republic by the end of the year.[52] Indonesia was to become a federated state, in part to avoid domination of the other islands by Java. The republic (essentially Java) would be incorporated into a union with fifteen other states.[53] While Indonesia was granted independence, technically it remained in a union with the Dutch crown. The Indonesian government also took over the debt burden of the Netherlands East Indies (the colonial name for the territory). The Hague argued that since the colony had been administered on a separate account, and since by their calculations the colonial administration owed public debt to the motherland, the new independent state would have to take over this financial obligation. Finally, the Round Table Conference yielded an agreement that allowed Dutch firms to retain control over their assets as stated by article 1.

> In respect of the recognition and restoration of the rights, concessions, and licenses properly granted under the law of the Netherlands East Indies . . . the Republic of the United States of Indonesia will adhere to the basic principle of recognizing such rights.[54]

Initially then residual rights of control would remain in hands of these firms.[55] Expropriation and nationalization were possible, but only "exclusively for the public benefit," and such expropriations would require repayment to the owners "at the real value of the object involved," as stated in article 3.[56]

Why the Dutch agreed to transfer substantial rights to Indonesia can readily be explained by the relative decline of Dutch power. Although it had been relatively successful in its military campaigns, its gains could easily be negated by sabotage. The colonial army maintained control over the urban areas but the nationalists could impose great costs using typical guerrilla tactics. The relative decline and high costs of governance made The Hague more amenable to a solution with hybrid governance structures rather than one in which neo-imperialism was pursued.

The nationalists, on the other hand, sought to control Dutch assets outright but they realized they did not have the means to exploit their natural resources effectively. Reflecting on why the anticolonial national-

---

[52] For some of the deliberations on the Dutch side, see *Officiële Bescheiden Betreffende de Nederlands-Indonesische Betrekkingen 1945<n>1950*, vol. 19 ('s-Gravenhage: Instituut voor Nederlandse Geschiedenis), docs. 323, 358, and particularly 339 (hereafter *NIB*).

[53] Glassburner 1971, 83.

[54] Ibid., 78.

[55] Cribb and Brown 1995, 24, 32.

[56] Glassburner 1971, 79. The Dutch government and firms estimated at that time that the Netherlands had about 3 billion guilders (about $900 million U.S.) invested in Indonesia. *NIB*, vol. 19, doc. 372.

ists would acquiesce to the Netherlands' demands, Bruce Glassburner suggests that the "Indonesian leaders felt that they could not eliminate the Dutch owners and their administrative staffs because they had little or nothing to put in their place. There were no funds with which to compensate the nationalized owners; and there were no Indonesian experts to operate the firms."[57] Under those conditions the nationalists were content to allow foreigners to yield residual rights, as long as this led to a retreat of direct Dutch political authority.

However, the inability of both sides to make credible commitments to a negotiated solution complicated the shift to a hybrid governance structure. The Dutch proved unreliable in negotiations. At several junctures, as when they in effect repealed the Linggadjati Agreement in 1947, which had been reached the previous fall, The Hague's dissension within the government proved that an accord might be unilaterally altered or reneged. In 1948 the Dutch, arguing that the Indonesians had violated the terms of the Renville Agreement, launched the second police action. The United Nations, despite Dutch protests, concluded that the Netherlands and not the republic were the transgressors.

The Indonesian nationalists also lacked credibility to commit. Dutch companies proved reluctant to make concessions because they feared communist elements within the Indonesian nationalist camp. Indeed, Ho Chi Minh had argued for collaboration between the nationalists in Indochina and Indonesia.[58]

This changed when the nationalists ousted communist elements in the cleansing following the Madiun revolt in the fall of 1948. Consequently, the fear of a communist regime in Indonesia subsided. The U.S. State Department concluded that "the Republican Government was the only government in the whole Far East which had met and disposed of an all-out Communist offensive."[59]

Moreover, as it gradually became clear that the United States and Britain would pressure the Dutch to relinquish control, Dutch business interests began to look for compromise solutions that would allow them continued long-term access to Indonesia. As in the British case, amenable local elites seemed like the best guarantee for Dutch economic interests. Although the Indonesian government lacked strong democratic institutions, it seemed poised for multiparty government, and was thus more credible than a hard-line nationalist or communist government.

[57] Glassburner 1971, 95.

[58] Further complicating matters, some nationalists (including Sukarno and Hatta) had collaborated with the Japanese during World War II and thus were deemed noncredible by the Dutch.

[59] Quoted in van den Doel 1996, 290.

The developments surrounding the Billiton tin concern demonstrate these dynamics. Billiton had a virtual monopoly on tin exploitation in Indonesia thanks to its joint venture agreement with the Dutch government in Indonesia. The government held 62.5 percent of the shares and Billiton 37.5 percent, with operational control and direction flowing to Billiton.[60] Indonesia, just prior to the war, was the second-largest tin producer in the world, and the commodity accounted for 7–9 percent of Indonesia's export earnings in the 1950s.

Indonesian independence did not immediately worry Billiton. The firm simply saw its joint venture partner switch from the Dutch government to the Indonesian one. The company maintained operational control, and virtually all the higher personnel and technical positions were staffed by its employees. Moreover, much of the processing of the ore was done in the Netherlands.[61] Its calculations proved correct, and for five years the company conducted business as it had prior to independence.

Thus, initially the nationalists accepted limits to their country's sovereignty. Indonesia assumed the debt burden of the colony and left considerable residual rights in the hands of the Dutch government and firms. The Dutch even retained full control over Western New Guinea until 1963, since multinational companies envisioned oil and mining possibilities in that region.[62]

The End of the Round Table Agreement

Parts of the agreement soon unraveled. After the transfer of power in December 1949, the Indonesian Republic annulled the federalist clause within months. However, the economic aspects of the agreement showed considerable resiliency. Indeed, by 1953, "70% of the estates on Java and Sumatra were back in foreign hands."[63] This is not to say that the Indonesian government did nothing. It assumed control of the Bank of Indonesia as well as some public utilities. It also favored Indonesian export firms over Dutch and tried to funnel funds to select enterprises. However, as Robison observes, "the development of state enterprises did not represent a concerted move toward socialization, or indeed even nationalization, of the economy."[64] The Harahap cabinet abrogated the Round Table Agreement only by March 1956. It canceled its debt service to the

---

[60] Van de Kerkhof 2005, 127–28.
[61] Ibid., 128, 132, 138.
[62] *NIB*, vol. 19, doc. 359.
[63] Robison 1986, 42.
[64] Ibid., 41.

Netherlands, and the Indonesian government nationalized the Dutch holdings shortly thereafter.[65]

What led to the ultimate unraveling of the Round Table Agreement? In the first year of independence, both sides perceived joint gains in allowing Dutch firms to continue operating in Indonesia. Moreover, while economic and political ties with the United States had become far more important, any expropriation of Dutch investments would jeopardize American support, thereby diminishing the probability of inserting the United States as an alternative contracting partner. In the short run, the lack of substitutes for Dutch firms limited the ability of Djakarta to capitalize on this advantage.

But from approximately 1954 onward, the Indonesian cabinets had started to shift from fostering domestic capitalism with foreign investment to a top-down, state-led development strategy.[66] This required rapid capital mobilization. Expropriation helped satisfy nationalist sentiment while acquiring easy capital. This involved the nationalization of 90 percent of plantation output, as well as the output of 246 factories and enterprises.[67] Indonesia, as the host country, thus decided to capitalize on its bargaining leverage and move toward full control rights.

Alternative contracting partners were also becoming available for Djakarta.[68] Bargaining momentum had shifted in Indonesia's favor. The government did not seek to prohibit foreign access completely; instead it changed the nature of contractual obligations. Rather than attracting foreign capital by granting residual rights of control, the government shifted to production-sharing agreements and intergovernmental loans. Such arrangements were first worked out in the oil sector, and gradually extended to mining, the timber industry, and agriculture as well.[69] Foreign enterprises were thus granted use rights while the Indonesian government increasingly took over the ownership rights. Agreements with American and Japanese firms were based on national residual rights and replaced contracts based on foreign residual rights. Indonesia's relations with the

[65] Nationalization was extended to British and U.S. investments as well in 1963–65, partially in reaction to Britain's support for Malaysia. Cribb and Brown 1995, 66, 72, 80, 85; Robison 1986, 79; Glassburner 1971, 89–92.

[66] As is often the case with late modernization, the military greatly expanded its economic role and vision. The military's influence increased particularly after the introduction of martial law in 1957. One-third of cabinet ministers had to be appointed from the military. Robison 1986, 36–37, 63, 70, 67n50.

[67] Robison 1986, 72–73.

[68] The Dutch position had already declined sharply in the interwar period. In 1913 more than a third of Indonesia's imports came from the Netherlands. By 1935 that had declined to 15 percent, whereas Japan's position had gone from 2 percent to 30 percent. Maddison 1990; van den Doel 1996, 234.

[69] Robison 1986, 79.

Netherlands changed to complete contracting—international agreements between two fully sovereign states.[70]

The assertion of national residual rights was not without costs. Foreign capital was hesitant to invest in Indonesia.[71] However, with the retreat of ardent nationalism and the squelching of the last communist influences with the Suharto takeover in 1965, foreign direct investments returned. Between 1967 and 1976 the Netherlands still engaged in direct investments of $186 million. But this dwarfed into comparison with the United States ($1 billion), Japan ($2.5 billion), and even Hong Kong ($605 million).[72] The Dutch-Indonesian interdependence had receded into the distant background.

Britain: An Empire in Continuous Retreat

It has been observed that the British Empire, despite all its resources and vast extension, constituted an empire in continuous retreat. Even as it expanded its territorial holdings in Asia and Africa, its power diminished relative to that of the United States. Similarly, as it reached its largest territorial extension, shortly after World War I (by gaining Turkish and German territories), it had to grant some of the Dominions considerable autonomy. The far-flung British Empire thus had to match limits to its power with the need to gain local support for its network of military bases around the globe. Britain employed a variety of contracting arrangements to secure its basing network. In some cases it did so by reaching hybrid arrangements in exchange for granting sovereign concessions, such as independence, to host countries. Unlike France in North Africa, these hybrid arrangements proved to be stable given the continuing joint security benefits offered by the enduring British presence and the lack of alternative contracting parties. But Britain also established a number of absolute and neo-imperial sovereign bases, which have endured into the twenty-first century.

Imperial Basing during Pax Britannica

After the Napoleonic Wars, control of the seas formed the foundation of British policy.[73] The Royal Navy's first task was to defend Britain from

---

[70] Following the rise of nationalist pressure in 1954 some of the Dutch multinationals had started to proactively disengage from Indonesia. Billiton, for example, had shifted some of its mining to Rhodesia and had diversified into other industrial sectors. Van de Kerkhof 2005, 143.

[71] Van der Kroef 1955, 20.

[72] Panglaykim 1978, 252–53.

[73] For a broad overview of the Royal Navy's history, see Hill 1995.

invasion. Then came the defense of the empire and the inter-empire movement of forces. Defense of maritime trade ranked third, with offensive operations finalizing the list of priorities. Control of the seas thus required bases to guarantee safe ports for repairs, food supplies, and refueling. Overseas naval bases also gave the fleet the ability to project force abroad and defend the empire and its communication routes.

British naval strategy revolved around several spheres of operation. The Home Fleet was critical for the defense of Britain proper. Hence, these ships were kept in English and Scottish ports. Next in priority came bases deemed critical to guarantee access to India and the rest of Asia, such as Gibraltar, Malta, and Suez. In the North Atlantic the British relied on bases in Halifax (Nova Scotia) and in the North Pacific on their assets in British Columbia. The naval base at Simonstown in South Africa was the key for control of the South Atlantic and the passage around the Cape.

At all times, however, Whitehall was keenly aware that empire required trade-offs. At what cost did the pursuit of empire come in terms of manpower, financial resources, and commitment of the fleet to distant waters?[74]

At the end of the nineteenth century, London's primary focus shifted to Germany's blue water fleet. The Dreadnought race that ensued after British introduction of the eponymous class of advanced battleships raised the real possibility of British defeat on the high seas. Following the Fisher doctrine, Britain concluded that dominance of the seas would revolve around a struggle for control over the North Sea. Whoever won that contest would control all other maritime lanes.

Consequently, the government wished to roll over some of the costs of imperial defense to the Dominions while reallocating some of its naval resources closer to Britain. Indian defense already was posted to the Indian budget. Now Whitehall wanted greater contributions from the Dominions for basing support, manpower, and funds for warships. To gain Dominion support, London had to make political concessions.

Hence, London turned over Halifax to Canada in return for Canadian contributions. Australia and New Zealand contributed considerable resources for naval expansion as well, and each agreed to provide funds for a battleship and secondary ships.[75] In exchange, Britain gave the Dominions considerable autonomy regarding how these new resources for the empire would be used. Special legislation was also passed in the House of Commons, as the Dominion countries were not considered sovereign states and yet purchased warships as if they were. These sets of arrangements between imperial metropole and periphery clearly constituted devi-

---

[74] Friedberg (1988) discusses these issues as they existed at the turn of the century.

[75] The relationship between Britain and the Dominions is well captured by D. C. Gordon (1965).

ations from pure imperial hierarchy without granting the former colonies full sovereignty.

The incentives for Britain to grant the Dominions considerable latitude, exemplified by the handover of control rights to the Canadians of the Halifax base, are relatively straightforward. Britain's relative power on the seas was declining. This made Whitehall more amenable to concessions to the Dominions and at the same time increased the leverage of Canada and the Antipodal states. At the same time the bases in question were also deemed of lesser strategic importance given the expectation of a North Sea showdown. London would not have to rely on Halifax, or Australian ports, as Germany was considered the primary danger and the Japanese threat had been neutralized after the Anglo-Japanese understanding. The bargaining leverage of the Dominions, while considerable, thus had important limitations.

The incentives for the Dominions to take over these bases and accept a heavier financial burden for imperial maintenance are perhaps less obvious. Why did the Dominions accept a greater share of the burden, while linking their security needs with those of Britain?[76] For one, contributing to imperial defense gave the Dominions greater say in how imperial resources would be distributed. Thus, the Australians and New Zealanders were assured that their contributions would be used for naval deployments in the Pacific theater and Hong Kong. They shared a similar geostrategic outlook and similar objectives in providing security to Britain and the Dominions, which were linked militarily, economically, and culturally.[77] The Dominions and Britain thus perceived joint economies of scale in providing defense, and Britain used issue linkages, such as preferential trade arrangements, to maintain this homogeneity of preferences.

Both sides could also credibly commit. Britain's credibility was aided by its incremental granting of autonomy and self-governance in the Dominions. By iteratively engaging in such agreements, Whitehall's reputation for credibility was enhanced. Moreover, its democratic system aided transparency. Likewise, on the side of the Dominions, democratic governments, modeled after Westminster, aided transparency while reducing the likelihood that leaders could easily retreat from publicly made commit-

[76] Cultural aspects in decision making cannot be overlooked. This was still the empire of "kith and kin" and ties of motherland and white settler colonies. It would take another half century before a non-white colony would gain independence, and even then India's entry into the Commonwealth met with strenuous opposition from South Africa and others.

[77] As Fieldhouse (1999, 100) notes, 13.2 percent of UK imports came from the Dominions, while they took 17.5 percent of its exports in 1913. The Dominions saw themselves so intertwined with Britain that their military personnel contributions during World War I equaled that of India, despite the fact that the latter had a population base that was twenty times larger. Darwin 1999, 67.

ments. Audience costs would constrain democratically elected officials in the Dominions from reneging.[78]

These agreements were quite stable. Few alternative contracting parties existed for the Dominions. The United States remained largely isolationist. Even though the Washington Naval Treaty enshrined it as a naval power of the first rank, its willingness to play the role of a global power remained untested. Britain, moreover, still controlled a vast network of bases, which limited the bargaining leverage for any individual country. If any particular Dominion pushed too hard, Britain might simply relocate its assets elsewhere with benefits flowing to the new host. Thus, conforming to our propositions, with continued gains from joint production of security, and with few alternatives available, the Dominions exerted only minimal pressure on Britain. These hybrid sovereignty arrangements thus remained intact.

The Interwar Period

Britain founded its early imperial basing strategy on direct control. It only granted host countries sovereignty rights in the Dominions that were linked to Britain through economic and cultural ties and replicated the democratic institutions of the motherland. This strategy continued during the interwar period, although the Dominions became less complacent in their obligations to Britain.

After World War I, the Asian theater became the critical area of concern for Britain. Following considerable internal debate, the government decided not to renew the Anglo-Japanese agreement, in part to accommodate the United States. This had several consequences. First, the British had to build a new base that was far enough from the immediate theater so as not to come under enemy attack but geographically proximate enough to send forces to the Indian and Pacific oceans. This ruled out Hong Kong, which was already considered vulnerable to air and sea attack, and turned Britain's focus to Singapore, which was chosen as the site on which to build a massive naval base in 1921.[79]

In addition, Australia and New Zealand were not going to be as forthcoming as they had been in the run-up to World War I. Contrary to earlier British assurances, the British government had diverted their imperial defense contributions to the European theater. Consequently, Australia and New Zealand sought to oversee their imperial contributions more closely than before. They reasoned that their own defense might hinge on their

---

[78] See Fearon 1994.

[79] Interestingly, debates were already taking place as to whether the base was strategically sound and defensible. Buesst 1932.

resources rather than those of the empire. In other words, the benefits of joint gains were no longer so obvious.[80]

Nevertheless, relatively little change occurred during this period. Britain did not transfer more control rights to parts of the empire. The bases in its formal colonies remained under full British sovereign control, constituting examples of traditional imperialism. Despite Indian grumblings, Whitehall had no intention of transferring control over British bases on the subcontinent. Important bases, such as Bombay and Trincomalee (on Ceylon), remained under direct British control (the imperial solution), as did all the critical bases on the Britain-India route via the Mediterranean and Suez. In the Dominions it had already ceded control rights while maintaining use rights.

Although Britain's relative power decline continued, it had little incentive to negotiate hybrid sovereignty arrangements for its overseas bases outside of the Dominions and still managed to retain control over many of its colonies. Governance costs were low in key staging areas such as Gibraltar, Malta, Suez, and Cyprus. These could all be held without significant costs of repelling nationalist agitation or foreign encroachment.

Most of the Dominions shared British views of the external threat, even if South African affinity with Germany was a source of concern.[81] Britain and its empire united in opposition to the threats posed by the German-Japanese-Italian alliance. The Dominions had close ties with Britain and enjoyed special trading privileges. The worldwide recession of the 1930s and the turn to imperial preference schemes only fortified such connections.[82] The tendency of the Dominions to rely less on the United Kingdom, which was evident in the 1920s, was reversed.[83] Issue linkages and shared perceptions of the external threat thus gave London assurances that the Dominions would capitalize on their bargaining leverage only to a limited extent. The Dominions and Britain perceived joint economies of scale in their pursuit of security.

Retreat from Empire

British overseas basing strategy reached its final test in the retreat from empire after World War II. India had been granted independence in 1947 as a result of the Cripps commission's agreement with Indian nationalists

---

[80] Clayton 1999. James (1994, chapter 9) captures the tension between the Dominions and Britain over wartime strategy.

[81] Australia and New Zealand were keen supporters of building up Singapore. Buesst 1932, 309.

[82] For the economic ties with imperial preferences, see Rooth 1992, 29–33; Fieldhouse 1999, 100–103.

[83] See James 1994, 456.

in March 1942. Britain, however, still retained many important bases around the globe. Although Prime Minister Clement Attlee argued for an Atlantic arc rather than a global posture shortly after the war, he lost out to combined opposition of the joint chiefs and his own ministers. Britain's retreat from empire would thus take several decades.[84]

In these decades of gradual retreat, Britain maintained some bases and full control and use rights, whereas in other instances it brokered hybrid sovereignty accords that were similar to the agreements with the Dominions in the years before World War II. Today, however, the most important British overseas bases are located in areas that are not independent states, except for Belize and Brunei, both of which gained independence in the 1980s. That is, contemporary British basing agreements do not constitute hybrid sovereignty but are versions of direct rule and governance.

The postwar British overseas bases held different strategic values. The United Kingdom retained "main support areas" that were far from immediate danger zones and could support all aspects of docking, repair, and supply. Sydney and Esquimalt in Canada, for example, were kept for this purpose. These bases in the former Dominions, now part of the Commonwealth, granted Britain use rights while Australia and Canada maintained residual rights of control. "Operational naval bases" were closer to the area of operations and offered most of the support functions as well. In the Indian Ocean this included Bombay, Colombo, Karachi, Kilindini, Fremantle, and Trincomalee on Ceylon, all of which gave Britain use rights. In other areas, such as Aden, Britain maintained an imperial posture, keeping both control and use rights, until the end of 1967 when the retreat from points East of Suez became policy.[85] In the South Atlantic, the South African Simonstown base was still considered a key asset for safeguarding the passage around Africa. Here Britain maintained residual rights of control and paid rent to the South African government. In the Pacific theater, Britain had a sovereignty agreement that granted it use rights in Auckland and Brisbane. And in Hong Kong (until 1997) and Singapore (until 1971) it maintained both control and use rights. "Advanced naval bases" such as Port Darwin and Bahrain were only meant to be utilized in times of warfare and forward positions. British use rights were ad hoc, as their exercise would be determined by the particular conflict that called for naval deployment. Mediterranean access through the Suez Canal meant that Gibraltar, Cyprus, Malta, and Suez remained vital for several decades after 1945. Here Britain opted for full control even

---

[84] Hyam 1992, part III, docs. 276, 277, 283, 284. Also see Clayton 1999, 294.

[85] Murfett 1995, 3. For a discussion of the critical retrenchment from points east of Suez, see Darby 1973.

after independence was granted to Cyprus (1960) and Malta (1964).[86] Only the Suez debacle would lead it to reconsider its position there. With Indian independence, the Colonial Office put Kenya forward as a replacement for strategic army and air force needs, but the armed forces were far more reluctant to see East Africa as a viable substitute.[87]

Thus, whatever the strategic importance of the base, Britain employed a variety of governance forms depending on political circumstances. Where it still could exert significant power and where local opposition was low, Whitehall favored well-worn imperialism. If direct rule was difficult, it would settle for use rights and grant the host country residual rights of control. Indeed, of all of the imperial powers discussed here, Britain seems to have understood best the downstream political consequences of adopting these various governance arrangements.

Two Examples of the Durability of Britain's Incomplete Contracts: Singapore and Simonstown

In some of its key staging areas, the British government could reasonably expect that these incomplete contracts would be quite durable. The negotiations surrounding the Simonstown and Singapore bases are particularly illustrative in this regard. Both were critical for overall British global positioning and both had sizable fixed assets, thus apparently giving the host countries considerable leverage over the United Kingdom.

In the initial postwar decades, London still emphasized the importance of Singapore as the linchpin of the British position in the Pacific and of Simonstown for its control over the South Atlantic. Singapore gave Britain control over the Straits of Malacca and access to the proximate Sunda Straits. With Australia in command of its own waters, the Royal Navy strategists believed they could block any eastern access to the Indian Ocean. Through Singapore Britain could control the Pacific-Indian ocean corridor. Simonstown played a similar role. From here the navy could control the access points between the Atlantic and Indian oceans. Both bases were thus critical to Britain but were located in areas that were already independent (South Africa) or would become independent in the near future (Malaysia). Strategic reassessment by Whitehall also led to careful calibration as to which parts of the globe could or should rea-

---

[86] The British base on Malta was returned in 1979. The two sovereign bases (ninety-nine square miles on Cyprus, Dhekelia, and Akrotiri) remain exclusively sovereign British territory. See Woodliffe 1992. The Gibraltar issues continue to linger to this day. See Gold 2004.

[87] Hargreaves 1996, 94. For the discussions in the government, see Hyam 1992, part III, docs. 337–40.

sonably be kept as dependencies and which were likely candidates for independence.[88]

Given Britain's declining power and the bargaining leverage flowing to the host countries, why would the latter not capitalize on their leverage? That is, why did Britain expect that the Singaporean and South African governments would not renege on these agreements?

Whitehall had various reasons for believing that granting independence to Malaya would not jeopardize its key bases in East Asia. First, the Malayan emergency during the 1950s raised the specter of a communist regime. Consequently, Britain feared that any handover of the Singaporean facilities would put them ultimately within the Soviet or Chinese sphere of influence and thus jeopardize the stability of East Asia. With instability in Indochina (and initially in Indonesia, which stabilized after the military eradicated the communists from power in 1948), British grand strategy thus required a successful conclusion to the emergency before independence could be granted to Malaya in 1957. With the successful end to the campaign, which lasted from 1948 to 1960, British forces in the area became a potential asset to the local non-communist political elites.[89]

Second, when the Malaysian federation (which Singapore had joined in 1963) fractured in 1965, the tensions between the Malaysian government and Singapore meant that a British presence would help guarantee Singapore's independence: "Had British forces not been in Singapore, direct intervention [by Malaysia] might well have been tried with unthinkable consequences."[90] Moreover, the British government allocated significant funds directly to the base, with total expenditure contributing to 25 percent of Singapore's GNP by the mid-1960s.[91] Joint production of security was thus desirable for both sides.

Consequently, the decision to withdraw was primarily driven by imperial decline rather than Singaporean pressure to renegotiate the agreement. The cost of Britain's "East of Suez" policy proved to be too much to bear. In 1966 this policy cost the government around £330 million a year. Of this Malaysia and Singapore received £255 million, with far less funds going to Aden, Bahrain, and Hong Kong.[92] Stationing costs for East Asia surpassed those of the British Army in Germany. By 1967, the pound had to be devalued again. The cost of overseas bases was

---

[88] The Duncan Sandys White Paper of 1957, following the Suez Crisis, played an important role in Britain's strategic reassessment in subsequent years. See Nailor 1996; Navias 1996.

[89] For a discussion of the economic incentives for the British government to defeat the Malayan Communist Party, see White 1998.

[90] Hawkins 1969, 553.

[91] Hanning 1966, 257.

[92] Ibid., 253. Howard (1966, 180) notes an expenditure of £317 million.

reassessed, and Whitehall made the decision to withdraw from points east of Suez. This meant the withdrawal of forces from Singapore by 1971. By then Britain had become more oriented toward its European role and sought alternative contracting parties to provide for its security.[93] The benefits of joint supply of security had diminished for Britain.

Nevertheless, while the incentive to pull out of Singapore was primarily instigated by the British government, Malaysia and Singapore, to some extent, also tried to capitalize on their bargaining leverage. Thus, under the defense treaty with Malaya in 1957, Britain was only allowed to use its bases for out-of-area operations with the consent of the Malayan government. With Singapore joining Malaya in the Malaysian federation, the "bases in Singapore became subject to the same restrictions as those applying in Malaya."[94] Prominent politicians in Singapore also opposed the South East Asia Treaty Organization.

Consequently, with imperial decline and some uncertainty about Singapore's long-term commitment, British planners and pundits started to think of alternatives that could be held more securely and cheaply. Some suggested that a new base might be created in Australia, partially funded by Australia and the United States.[95] Instead, Britain resorted to an island staging post strategy: "Britain . . . set up a new colony, the British Indian Ocean Territory" (BIOT).[96] It did so by carving BIOT from its Mauritius colony in exchange for granting the island territory its independence. BIOT included the coral atoll Diego Garcia, which the United Kingdom transferred on a fifty-year lease to the U.S. Department of Defense in 1966.[97]

In short, the joint production of security with Singapore had declined. Britain saw alternative arrangements as more desirable. It preferred full direct control rather than hybrid sovereignty arrangements. Against that backdrop full sovereignty was handed over to the Singaporean government and Britain withdrew in 1971.

The transfer of the Simonstown facility (1955–57) showed similar dynamics.[98] Whitehall was willing to transfer the control rights over Simonstown, which Britain had held for over a century and a half, to the South African government. However, in exchange it wanted guarantees that Britain would be allowed to use the facilities in a conflict—even if South

---

[93] For an account of Britain's overall strategic assessments, see Carver 1992.

[94] Hawkins 1969, 549, 561. Thus Hawkins, while acknowledging that British reassessment was the key factor, also sees Malaysian and Singaporean pressure as partially to blame.

[95] Howard 1966, 183.

[96] Hanning 1966, 259.

[97] Woodliffe 1992, 89–90.

[98] Du Plessis 1979; Henshaw 1992.

Africa remained neutral, as it threatened to do in World War II. Although the South African government initially balked at the British demands, it ultimately conceded to a lopsided agreement in which it agreed to pay £750,000 for the British assets and took on the burden of running the dockyard at a cost of about £600,000 a year.[99] The agreement, consisting of an exchange of letters, included the transfer of the base as well as an agreement to jointly defend the sea routes round the Cape. In addition the United Kingdom would sell South Africa frigates, minesweepers, and other ships.[100]

Given Britain's relative power decline, Whitehall's decision to surrender its control rights in exchange for use rights seems straightforward. But why did South Africa not capitalize on its bargaining leverage? Why did it sign such unfavorable terms and why did the agreement last as long as it did? Indeed, the Simonstown arrangements would not be terminated until 1975.[101]

First, London and Pretoria had similar strategic preferences and they benefited from a joint production of security. The South African government was concerned with the pace of decolonization and the rise of leftist governments in Africa, as was Whitehall. Both stood to gain from keeping a British naval presence in the South Atlantic to safeguard the Cape route. And, as mentioned, Britain provided South Africa with much-needed military hardware. Moreover, largely because of its apartheid regime, Pretoria found itself isolated internationally. It had few alternative contracting parties.

Consequently, Britain and South Africa had incentives to jointly pursue security in the region. With Pretoria having few alternatives it could not capitalize on its bargaining leverage, thus making hybrid sovereignty a stable solution in this case.[102] It was Britain, not South Africa, that terminated the agreement, largely because of domestic pressures against the apartheid regime.

Thus, in situations in which Britain and its erstwhile colonies continued to have common security concerns or economic ties, and where the basing countries lacked alternative partners, hybrid sovereignty arrangements proved relatively durable. London maintained bases with use rights, and the host country held residual rights of control. However, where White-

[99] Henshaw 1992, 436.

[100] Woodliffe 1971, 754.

[101] Henshaw 1992, 440. The agreement was terminated by mutual consent and formal exchange of letters. Woodliffe 1992, 290.

[102] Ironically, Pretoria engaged in hybrid sovereignty arrangements with a colonial flavor of its own. Although Namibia gained independence in 1990, Pretoria maintained significant military installations at Walvis Bay and regarded it as an integral part of the Republic of South Africa. Evans 1990, 559.

hall recognized the potential instability of such arrangements, given that bargaining leverage and momentum might flow to the host country, Britain shifted to basing areas that it could keep under its direct control. Empire died hard.

Russian Assets in the Near Abroad

Rising nationalist tensions in the USSR during the late 1980s seemed to be a disaster in the making. Although the Soviet system arguably repressed Russians and non-Russians alike, many of the Union Republics bristled at Russian domination. Indeed, many of the USSR's components had been acquired by force, starting with Russian expansion in the sixteenth century and continuing in the aftermath of World War II. Pent-up nationalist fervor and strategic incentives for titular elites to seek full sovereignty put them on a collision course with hard-line elements who wished to retain central control through the Communist Party and the armed forces.[103]

The problem was exacerbated by the high degree of concentration of the Soviet economy in huge enterprises and the distribution of the Soviet military and military industrial complex throughout various regions. The centrally planned Soviet economy concentrated the production of goods and sectors only in certain locations across the different republics.[104] In turn, the numerous Soviet ministries in Moscow vertically integrated and controlled this production. Ron Suny suggests that almost 77 percent of Soviet products originated from single factories that produced a particular good for the entire union.[105] For example, a torpedo assembly plant in Kyrgyzstan supplied the Soviet military as a whole and was not tied to regional developmental needs.[106] And although Russia produced vast quantities of natural resources in its own right, its interest in the oil and gas reserves in the Caucasus and Central Asia, combined with the latter's need for Russian know-how and transportation facilities, inextricably linked the various regions through a union-wide infrastructural grid.

But the strategic importance of the defense installations of the powerful Soviet military that were scattered throughout the union complicated matters perhaps the most. The need for maritime bases outside of Russia proper, due to the inaccessibility of many Russian ports in winter, led to

---

[103] On nationalist movements and the Soviet collapse, see Beissinger 2002; Roeder 1991.

[104] On the organizational logic and structure of the Soviet economy, see Gregory and Stuart 1994; Kornai 1992.

[105] Suny 1997, 490.

[106] See A. Cooley 2005a, 80–88; Rumer 1990.

major deployments in the Baltic, the Black Sea, Murmansk, and the Sea of Okhotsk. The latter two would remain in Russian hands, but the first two could become matters of serious contention. Air bases, early radar warning posts, missile sites, testing ranges, and other key facilities likewise were scattered throughout the union.

All this might have led to neo-imperial responses by proponents of continued central control, especially within the Russian military establishment. Indeed, some clashes erupted between Soviet hard-liners and nationalists in the Baltics. Communist Party members favored a strong Union, or at the very least a tight commonwealth. Host country nationalists, by contrast, pushed for full independence, favoring the complete expropriation of Soviet economic and military facilities and full sovereignty for the former Union Republics as independent states. In short, the distribution of transaction-specific assets across the former Soviet space could have greatly complicated the dissolution.[107]

Nevertheless, the union dissolved swiftly and without full-blown conflicts between Russia and its former republics.[108] A weak Commonwealth of Independent States, which included only a subset of the former Union Republics, replaced it in 1991.[109] That this dismemberment took place without considerable violence or significant bloodshed can be partially explained by the ability of Russia, the former territorial core of the union, to broker hybrid sovereignty arrangements with the Newly Independent States (NIS).

National and Foreign Residual Rights Agreements in the Post-Soviet Era

The Russian agreements with the NIS, which Russians described as the "Near Abroad," in some instances allocated residual rights of control to Russia and in other instances to the new states. Russia, or Russian firms, often insisted on control rights over economic assets. With regard to its military facilities, these arrangements usually took the form of allocation with national residual rights. That is, Russia relinquished claims to ownership of those facilities in favor of the new governments. In exchange, it retained use rights for which it paid the NIS a specified rent or wrote off

---

[107] On the prospect of the Russian Empire being reconstituted to govern these transaction-specific assets, see Lake 1997.

[108] On the dynamics of this dissolution, especially in comparison with Yugoslavia, see Bunce 1999. It should be noted that several ethnic conflicts erupted within former Soviet republics—including in Moldova, Georgia, and Tajikistan—in which elements of the Russian military played a pivotal role. See Rubin and Snyder 1998.

[109] For analyses of these events, see Dunlop (1993) and Matlock (1995).

bilateral debt and committed itself to renegotiation at a particular time. Key facilities in Kazakhstan, the Baltics, and Ukraine were negotiated in those terms in the mid-1990s.[110]

HYBRID SOVEREIGNTY ARRANGEMENTS OVER DEFENSE-RELATED ASSETS

For example, Kazakhstan contained key missile and space facilities. Foremost among these was the Baikonur space facility, which served as the launching platform for military and civilian spacecraft. Clearly this constituted a key specific asset with fixed installations and few alternatives. In July 1994, the Russian government brokered an agreement by which it would lease Baikonur from the Kazakh government for twenty years. Moscow furthermore committed itself to paying $115 million annually to Kazakhstan. A similar agreement was reached for continued use of the missile installation at Saryshagan and Emba, but for a shorter duration (ten years) and a lower rent ($26.5 million). By 2000, Russia had transferred these testing functions to an alternate range on Russian territory at Kapustin Yar.

The Russians also reached agreements with Belarus, which hosted important installations for Russia's early warning radar and submarine communications. The agreement was to last for twenty-five years in exchange for which Russia committed itself to providing Belarus with technical assistance. Moscow even reached agreement with Latvia, one of the recalcitrant Baltic States during the last years of the USSR, regarding the Skrunda radar installation. The agreement, in which Russia took on $5 million in annual payments, however, was only for four years but facilitated Russia's extrication.

The strategy of brokered disengagement revolved around the linchpin of the Black Sea Fleet installations at Sevastopol, Ukraine, located on the Crimean peninsula. The Black Sea Fleet, a critical component of the former Soviet Navy, had significant military value. Matters were further complicated by the nationalist tensions surrounding the Crimea in general. Crimea had only been transferred to the Ukraine in 1954, and thus by the late 1980s a slight majority of its population remained ethnically Russian. Hard-liners in the Russian Duma refused to countenance any agreement with Kiev over the sovereign status of the fleet and its port city, instead preferring to revoke the 1954 transfer and call for bringing the Crimea

---

[110] This section builds on A. Cooley 2000–2001. A useful overview of Russia's contracts with the NIS over its fixed assets within the context of a discussion of Russian economic coercion can be found in Drezner 1999, 153–230.

back into Russia. Conversely, Ukrainian nationalists resisted Russian neo-imperialism and saw an opportunity to lay sovereign claim over the fleet.

Despite these difficulties, in 1997 Russia and Ukraine negotiated the Partition Agreement, a classic hybrid sovereignty arrangement. Kiev and Moscow agreed to divide the fleet, with Moscow buying several ships from the Ukrainian government. They concluded a leasing agreement for the harbor facilities in Sevastopol in which Moscow pledged a payment of almost $100 million a year. Control rights, that is, legal sovereignty over the Crimea, unambiguously came to reside with Ukraine, while use rights were ceded to Russia. The agreement has proven durable, as joint benefits have accrued to both states, even as tensions between the two countries mounted when Russia cut off gas supplies to Ukraine in January 2006.

An additional national residual rights agreement was concluded between Russia and Tajikistan in 2004 to govern what was previously a Russian neo-imperial base, hosting 5,000 Russian troops of the 201st Division. The base is now the largest Russian military facility outside Russia. Having shunned U.S. advances for a basing agreement to assist U.S. operations in Afghanistan, the Tajik government extracted a commitment from Russia to write off $240 million of Tajikistan's $300 million bilateral debt, as well as a promise to invest $2 billion in the Central Asian state's large enterprises.[111] The agreement also included a clause that granted Russia a forty-nine-year lease to use the antimissile warning station at Naruk. Although initially Tajikistan was a de facto Russian protectorate after the Soviet collapse,[112] its recent hybrid sovereignty agreements have brought more balance to the bilateral relationship and these accords now resemble those Russia concluded with Kazakhstan and Ukraine in the 1990s.

HYBRID SOVEREIGNTY ARRANGEMENTS OVER NATURAL RESOURCE–BASED ASSETS

Russia's economic ties with the NIS have more closely resembled foreign residual rights agreements, particularly in the area of natural resource exploitation. Upon the Soviet collapse, several of the NIS in the Caucasus and Central Asia found themselves with significant hydrocarbon and mineral deposits but very little technical expertise or capital available for their

[111] For details, see Kambiz Arman, "Russia and Tajikistan: Friends Again," *Eurasia Insight*, available at http://www.eurasianet.org/departments/insight/articles/eav102804.shtml.

[112] Russia's decisive intervention in the Tajik civil war firmly established its presence shortly after the Soviet dissolution. See Rubin 1994.

development.[113] Moreover, these states also found themselves constrained by the Soviet-era network of energy grids, pipelines, and infrastructure that was oriented toward and controlled by Russia.[114] Russia's control of these specific assets has allowed Russian companies to steadily reclaim foreign residual rights to many of these natural resources. Russian companies such as Gazprom (the state-controlled gas giant), Lukoil (oil company), and Transneft (which controls the oil pipeline network) now all claim large stakes of these NIS energy projects.

In the area of oil exploration and development, Russia has used its position to reclaim some foreign residual rights over lucrative oil projects and pipeline networks. In Kazakhstan, for example, Lukoil acquired a 5 percent stake in the development of the lucrative northern Caspian Tengiz oil joint venture Tengizchevroil, which is developing the world's sixth largest oil field; subsequently Transneft secured a controlling stake in the Caspian Pipeline Consortium, first established in 2001 to bring Tengiz oil to market via the Black Sea Russian port of Novorossik. Moscow's control over the export pipeline network affords it considerable residual rights and bargaining leverage over Kazakhstan.[115]

In the case of Azerbaijan, Lukoil also acquired a 10 percent stake in the famous Azerbaijan International Oil Consortium that was signed in 1994. Unlike Kazakhstan, however, Russian influence and its reacquisition of residual rights was checked by Baku's decision to construct the export pipeline Baku-Tbilisi-Ceyhan (BTC), which avoided Russian territory and Transneft altogether.[116] BTC was completed and inaugurated in 2006, thus establishing the first major new pipeline to transport oil from a post-Soviet country and avoid Russian territory and control. Until Kazakhstan is similarly able to construct an alternative export pipeline (most likely to China) that bypasses Russia, Astana will continue to be pressured into ceding foreign residual rights over its energy infrastructure to Russian companies.

Gazprom, in particular, has repeatedly used its monopoly power and pipeline grid to extract pricing concessions from NIS gas consumers and suppliers, especially those with no other alternative contracting partners. For example, Turkmenistan, which by some estimates is one of the five

---

[113] On hydrocarbons and geopolitics in the Caspian after the Soviet collapse, see Ebel and Menon 2000.

[114] Hancock (2001) catalogs a series of NIS-specific assets in her study of hierarchical governance arrangements in Russian-NIS post-Soviet relations.

[115] For details and analysis of Russia's attempts to control Kazakhstan's oil and pipelines, see Marten 2007.

[116] On the origins and politics surrounding BTC, see LeVine 2007.

richest countries in terms of natural gas reserves, has been unable to fully profit from its gas production, in part because it remains trapped by its nearly exclusive reliance on the Gazprom pipeline network and effectively has ceded residual rights to the Russian company. Since the Soviet collapse, Turkmen gas has flowed nearly exclusively into the Gazprom pipeline network and has been sold by the Russian company to European customers.[117] The Russian company has charged its European clients market prices, but has paid Turkmenistan prices significantly below these market levels, taking advantage of its monopolistic pricing power. Until Turkmenistan is able to construct a major capacity alternative export pipeline, the Central Asian country will have no choice but to accept the terms dictated by Gazprom and its foreign residual rights over the distribution of Turkmen gas. Like European firms during decolonization, Russia's natural resource companies have used their strategic position and networks to acquire significant control stakes and revenue streams from NIS natural resource development.

In sum, one can explain the emergence of these hybrid sovereignty arrangements over security and economic assets by the initial preferences of actors, the relative distribution of power, and the credibility of commitments. Both sides would prefer outright control over these fixed assets. However, with mounting costs of empire, an outright neo-imperial solution proved increasingly unattractive to Russia.[118] But the NIS were hardly in a position to push for outright and full control themselves, especially when constrained by the lack of alternative contracting partners. Even though Russia's power initially had diminished, the relative distribution with the NIS remained highly asymmetric.

Given this highly asymmetric distribution, Russia was thus less concerned than former imperial metropoles that the periphery would capitalize on their bargaining leverage and renege on these arrangements. But insofar as there were credibility concerns, these were mitigated by the similarity in regime types and institutions that emerged in the post-Soviet space. Except for the Baltics, many of the NIS opted for strong presidential, even authoritarian systems.[119] Moreover, many of the new leaders were former members of the Communist cadres of the USSR and, not

---

[117] In 1997, Turkmenistan did complete construction of a small-capacity 200-kilometer pipeline to Iran. As of 2008, other more ambitious projects have failed to develop past the planning phase. For an overview of these various proposed projects, see the U.S. Department of Energy's regional briefs at http://www.eia.doe.gov/emeu/cabs/Region_ni.html.

[118] For the economic and political costs of empires, see Bunce 1985; Spruyt 2005, 60–65, 81–86.

[119] Easter 1997.

surprisingly, the Russian government has made it a priority to strongly support NIS regimes friendly to Moscow, regardless of any of their authoritarian tendencies. In turn, many of the former Union Republics have proven to be stauncher proponents of a strong commonwealth and subsequent additional integration regimes than the Russian Republic.[120]

The Durability of Post-Soviet Agreements

Unlike the French-Algerian and Dutch-Indonesian agreements, the host countries in the post-Soviet agreements have not reneged on these agreements over time. What explains this stability?

As with other instances in which the host country holds residual rights over transaction-specific assets, one would expect bargaining leverage over time to shift to the host. Several factors, however, tempered the leverage that these countries had over Russia, and thus enabled Russia to sign such agreements without fearing hold-up or reneging by host countries. First, and quite unlike the situation during Western decolonization, reassertion of imperialism remained a distinct possibility. In French, British, and Dutch decolonization, the nationalists correctly perceived that once the metropole retreated it could only reassert its sovereign control at great cost. The imperial metropoles themselves came to the conclusion that the costs of empire had increased while the benefits of formal control had receded. By contrast, the relative imbalance of power between Russia and the NIS made imperial reassertion a distinct possibility.[121] Moreover, given the strong position of fascist and communist elements in the Russian legislature, imperial preferences could not be discounted. Thus, Russia potentially had the will and the resources to pursue a neo-imperial solution if the other states pushed too hard. Indeed, a central pillar of Russian president Putin's foreign policy was to aggressively reassert Russia's interests and influence in security and energy matters in the Near Abroad.[122]

Second, although the NIS might have preferred to gradually make these arrangements more complete, the momentum for altering the incomplete contracts generally has not favored the NIS. Given the legacy of vertical integration of production, defense, and distribution in the USSR, Russia retained key know-how as well as downstream and upstream facilities in virtually all areas of production. In other words, there were continued benefits for joint supply. Russia could hold the other states hostage should

---

[120] Of the nine participating republics, 77 percent voted in favor of the USSR during the March 1991 referendum. Admittedly, though, the questions on the referendum were vague and confusing. Lapidus, Zaslavsky, and Goldman 1992, 14.

[121] Menon and Spruyt 1997, 1999.

[122] For overviews, see Baev 2008; Krysiek 2007.

they bargain too hard. For example, Russia was criticized in the West when Gazprom shut down its gas exports to Ukraine in 2006 and did the same to Belarus in early 2007. Through these tactics and resulting intergovernmental treaties, the Russian gas giant was able to secure price increases for its gas deliveries. As gas customers, these countries have no viable alternative supplier.[123] Perhaps not coincidentally, around the same time of the Russian-Ukrainian gas dispute, the Ukrainian government declared that it would not extend the Black Sea partition and leasing agreement beyond its current deadline of 2017.[124]

Similarly, Georgia has been suspicious of Russian claims regarding technical difficulties in delivering gas, believing instead that Moscow is punishing Georgia for its pro-Western stance, including Georgia's decision after the Rose Revolution in 2003 to evict the Russian military from its remaining bases in Georgia—which since 1991 had operated under exclusive Russian sovereignty, not host residual rights arrangements.[125] Furthermore, the NIS, save the Baltic States that joined the European Union in 2004, had few alternative contracting parties when it came to the exploitation of natural resources. Russia continued to hold considerable capital and control distribution networks. And, perhaps most important, Russian pipelines were critical for bringing any resources to the world market.[126]

In sum, the governments of the NIS have not found it easy to replace Russia as a security or economic partner. The majority of significant hybrid sovereignty arrangements have endured and even expanded in scope as Russia has reasserted its power and influence in the post-Soviet space.

Conclusion

The preceding discussion shows how the nature of initial agreements exerted independent effects apart from power differentials and shared identity. No doubt realist perspectives and constructivist views are important parts in any explanation of decolonization. As already noted, power asymmetries are a key explanation for why a particular governance structure emerged. Similarly, shared identities, by making credible commitment easier, contribute to the possible emergence of hybrid sovereignty.

[123] Andrew Kramer, "Russia Cuts Off Gas to Ukraine in Cost Dispute," *New York Times*, January 2, 2006.

[124] The agreement's extension is still up in the air. Some have speculated that the Russian government will find a suitable alternative site on its Black Sea territory.

[125] See, for example, C. J. Chivers, "Georgia, Short of Gas, Is Hit with a Blackout," *New York Times*, January 27, 2006.

[126] Ruseckas and Spruyt 1999.

But the downstream consequences of postcolonial hybrid sovereignty arrangements showed dynamics that are not fully captured by descriptions of balances of power or a sense of shared community.

France was undoubtedly a much stronger power than the Netherlands. Moreover, the level of integration and its economic ties with Algeria had been very significant, while its geostrategic position put it in much better position than the Netherlands vis-à-vis Indonesia. Yet in both cases the accords broke down in short order with the host countries capitalizing on their bargaining leverage. Britain, like France, constituted a major power, even if both were declining. Yet, in contrast to the French government, Britain more readily concluded hybrid sovereignty transfers rather than pursue neo-imperial solutions, and its hybrid sovereignty arrangements proved more durable than those of the French.

Whether hybrid sovereignty arrangements survived had less to do with shared identities than with the availability of alternatives and joint benefits. Britain's choice to divest itself from Aden, and eventually Singapore, and to relocate to bases that it could hold outright (as Diego Garcia) was not driven by identity politics. Instead, Whitehall saw diminished joint gains or wished to minimize the possibility of hard bargaining by the host country. Similarly, the NIS basing and economic relations with Russia are driven less by a shared identity than by the dependence of the NIS on Russian pipelines and infrastructure.

The empirical analyses of this chapter bear out the theoretical insights developed in chapters 1 and 2. We expect hybrid governance to emerge when neo-imperial solutions are beyond the will or power of the former metropole. Yet at the same time, the previously subject territories might realize that they are still linked to the metropole in terms of trade, investment, and military resources. If pushing for full hierarchical control or complete divestment proves too costly, and if credible commitments can be made, then hybrid sovereignty agreements can emerge as intermediate solutions. Such solutions present governance arrangements than can help states in the peaceful and orderly transfer of vital aspects of their sovereignty.

With such agreements, over time, bargaining leverage will shift to the holder of residual rights, usually the host country (the former colony). The momentum in the bargaining process will usually also shift to terminating the incomplete contract or to make the contract more complete. This momentum will accelerate if joint gains diminish or if alternative contracting parties become available. Political disengagement of the two states will be the result.

However, these dynamics will be clear to the metropole. Short of empire we therefore expect the former imperial core to try to maintain residual rights of control while granting some use rights to the host country. The

Dutch, for example, brokered some of those types of agreements with the Indonesian nationalists. The former colony, by contrast, will prefer national allocation of residual rights as its second-best preference (its first preference being full sovereignty).

Both parties will face credible commitment problems. However, this is particularly the case for the holder of the residual rights of control given the future expectations about bargaining leverage and momentum. These credibility problems complicated French and Dutch decolonization and contributed to the violence in North Africa and Indonesia. Both France and the Netherlands faced rising costs of empire. They also realized that once they surrendered Algeria and Indonesia, bargaining leverage would, over time, shift to those states. Algeria and Indonesia would also likely turn to other states for support. Moreover, both Indonesia and Algeria could not credibly commit to adhering to any agreements for any long-term duration after the colonial powers had yielded sovereignty rights. The Indonesian Republic constituted at best a nascent democracy with considerable influence from the military, rather than a well-institutionalized democratic regime. Only after the crackdown on the communists and the possibility of multiparty democracy did their credibility increase. Similarly, the Algerian government emerged out of its military struggle with France, rather than out of an orderly transition to democratic institutions. Internecine battles on the Algerian side initially complicated their ability to commit the rank and file.

A shift in preferences, the realization that the balance of power favored no particular side, and increased credibility to commit propelled the respective parties to sign hybrid sovereignty arrangements rather than pursue full control. However, in both instances the accords unraveled. Alternative partners emerged for both Algeria and Indonesia. In addition, joint gains of production increasingly diminished for both the metropole and erstwhile periphery.

In the British case as well, bargaining leverage shifted over time to the Dominions and former colonies. Here, too, actors preferred to renegotiate contracts periodically with greater certitude. However, there was less momentum to unravel these agreements. For many decades, the Dominions perceived benefits from joint supply. Prior to American hegemony, there were few alternative contracting parties for Australia and New Zealand. South Africa, too, partially because of its apartheid regime, had few alternatives. Thus, joint gains and the lack of alternative contracting parties made defection from the incomplete contracts less likely in the British case. Given these dynamics, there was less fear that these incomplete contracts would soon be abrogated. Moreover, many of the Dominions and newly independent states adopted (at least initially) institutions that were quite similar to those of the mother country. This similarity in institutional arrangements between Britain and its former colonies mitigated credibility problems.

In the decades since their retreat from empire, France and Britain have followed slightly different basing strategies (see appendix 3.1): "The UK has rarely sought to establish or retain military base facilities in former colonial territories and overseas dependencies to which independence has been granted."[127] Except for deployments in Brunei (post-1984) and Belize (post-1981), London has eschewed hybrid sovereignty agreements. Its forces are instead placed in overseas territories with various legal frameworks. The United Kingdom holds rights to its overseas bases in Cyprus as "sovereign base areas (SBAs)." The Foreign and Commonwealth Office noted that Britain "has the full rights of sovereignty that we associate with the use of that word."[128] The SBA agreements that were concluded on the granting of independence to Cyprus in 1960 made no mention of the duration of the agreement or the possibility of denunciation of the agreement.[129] The bases fall under the administration of the Ministry of Defense, not the Foreign and Commonwealth Office.

Likewise, other important bases are placed in overseas territories, juridically placed under the British Crown. Diego Garcia emerged out of the separation of the Chagos island group from Mauritius in 1965. As the British Indian Ocean Territory it maintains important facilities for the United Kingdom and the United States.[130] Although the government of Mauritius has demanded that the island group be reincorporated with Mauritius, it lacks any viable means to force Britain to do so. Other important bases, such as Hong Kong (until 1997), Gibraltar, the Falklands, and Ascension Island (an important refueling area), were similarly held directly under the Crown rather than by exchange sovereignty.[131] Despite protests by Spain regarding Gibraltar and Argentina's attempted takeover of the Falklands, Britain has yielded few control rights.

France, by contrast, has pursued a different course. Although the former colonies made no concessions with regard to their overall independence, they did conclude hybrid sovereignty agreements with the metropole: "The accession to statehood in the 1960s of former French colonies in Africa was invariably accompanied by defence cooperation

[127] Woodliffe 1992, 68.

[128] Ibid., 269.

[129] Ibid., 302.

[130] Ibid., 89.

[131] Even though Britain retains considerable forces overseas, the level of its commitments has decreased dramatically. In 1966–67 overseas bases still took up about one-sixth of the naval budget. Twenty years later that figure had dropped to about 2 percent. Grove 1987, 416.

accords giving France access to bases and other facilities."[132] Madagascar, Senegal, Chad, and other states all signed such agreements. Thus, although France has yielded virtually all of its imperial acquisitions, it continues to maintain multiple hybrid sovereignty relations with many countries.

The current French overseas bases work on the principle of national allocation of residual rights, as in the earlier Algerian and Tunisian cases. The host country grants use rights to Paris for some quid pro quo. While it is well beyond the focus of this book to discuss these contemporary arrangements in detail, one example might serve to suggest the analytic value of thinking of base strategies through the lens of incomplete contracting theory.

The large semi-permanent overseas deployment in Djibouti is a case in point. Paris is of course well aware that the bargaining leverage flows to Djibouti, as the latter possesses the residual rights of control over these fixed installations. Thus, Paris has sought to diminish the incentives for Djibouti to capitalize on its leverage through issue linkages and side payments. In exchange for being allowed to station 2,800 troops, France has committed itself to come to the assistance of the Republic of Djibouti in case of external aggression (article 1). Paris has also pledged to finance joint military training, health projects, police force training, and logistical aid.[133] The agreement is also subject to periodic renegotiation. In short, the French government has pursued a strategy of creating joint gains by linking its military deployments with the provision of public goods to the small country.

The relationship between Russia and the other former Union Republics provides the starkest contrast to French and Dutch decolonization and can be explained by our theory. In this case, neo-imperialism remained (and to some extent still remains) a distinct possibility. Thus, while bargaining leverage and momentum toward complete contracting would normally shift in the host country's favor, this has not been the case in the NIS because of the stark power asymmetry. Furthermore, there are continued benefits of joint supply while few alternate contracting partners are available. Thus, strategic incentives and structural opportunities for the NIS to bargain hard with Russia remain low.

Beyond these cases of decolonization, hybrid sovereignty arrangements have also helped facilitate other notable instances of bilateral territorial disengagement. Since 1963, Finland has leased the commercially important Saimaa Canal from the Soviet Union (and subsequently Russia)

---

[132] Woodliffe 1992, 68.

[133] Report from the French Senate. Available at http://www.senat.fr/rap/r02-200/r02-2009.html.

for an annual payment. Similarly, since 1982 Bangladesh has leased the narrow Tin Bigha land accord from India, thereby enabling its territorial contiguity. In our concluding chapter, we provide further discussion of how hybrid sovereignty arrangements over water rights helped foster the Israel-Jordan peace agreement of 1993 and consider how international transitional administration can learn these theoretical and practical lessons to better govern post-conflict environments.

Having illustrated our theory's utility in explaining the dynamics of decolonization and specific assets, we now turn more specifically to how the United States military has governed its overseas basing network through incomplete contracts.

Overseas Basing Deployments of France and Britain since 1970 (Excluding Deployments in Europe, UN Operations, Iraq/Afghanistan)

Britain[a]	1971/72	1981/82	1990/91	2001/02	2007
Belize	(see Caribbean)	1 inf bn; naval and air units	1 inf bn; air det (total 1,500)	total (army) 180	army 30
Brunei	1 bn	1 inf bn	1 inf bn; air det (total 900)	1 inf bn total 1,070	army 1,120
Caribbean	1 com	(see Belize)			
Cyprus	2 inf bn, 2 air sqns (total 4,000)	2 inf bns; 2 sqns	1 inf bn; 2 inf coms; air det (total 3,800)	2 inf bn; air units (total 3,250)	army 2,110; navy 25, air force 1,140
Diego Garcia		small naval det	small naval det	small naval det	small naval det
Falkland Islands		—	1 inf com; naval and air det (total 1,600)	1 inf com; naval and air units (total 1,500)	army 450; air force 750
Gibraltar	1 inf bn; naval units	1 inf bn; naval units	1 inf bn; naval and air det (total 1,700)	army, naval, and air units (total 565)	army 235; naval and air units
Hong Kong	5 inf bns, 1 art regt	5 inf bns (total 7,100) naval and air units	1 inf bde; 3 inf bns; naval and air det (total 6,800)	withdrawn 1997	—
Malta	1 bn, 1 com, 2 sqns naval det (total 3,000)	N.I.[b]	—		
Persian Gulf	2 inf bns, naval and air det (total 6,400)	N.I.			
Sierra Leone				army and navy; (total 660)	army 100
Singapore	1 bn	—			

APPENDIX 3.1 (*continued*)

France	1971/72	1981/82	1990	2001/02	2007
Affars and Issas	2 bns, 2 sqns				
Africa					
C. Afr. Rep.	—	Para and legion (total 1,200)	inf and motor units (total 1,200)		
Chad	army and air det (total 1,300)	—	3 inf coms (total 1,100)	2 inf coms; air units (total 900)	army 1,050; navy 400; air units
Côte d'Ivoire	partial regt (total 600)	partial regt (total 450)	1 mar regt (total 500)	1 mar inf bn (total 680)	army 3,800; air units
Djibouti	—	2 inf regts; air units (total 4,000)	1 mar inf; 1 For Leg regt; air det (total 3,650)	2 inf coms; air units (total 3,200)	army 2,850; air units
Gabon	1 com (total 200)	1 com; air units (total 650)	1 mar inf regt; air det (total 800)	1 mar inf bn; air units (total 750)	army 700; navy 560; air units
Malagasy	2 regt gps, naval and air det (total 2,500)				
Niger	1 armored car gp		—		
Senegal	1 regt gp, naval and air det (total 2,000)	inf; naval and air units (total 1,300)	1 mar inf regt; air det (total 1,250)	1 mar inf bn; air units (total 1,170)	army 610; navy 230; air units
Antilles-Guyana (Cayenne)	—	3 inf regts	3 mar inf; 1 For Leg regt naval and air units (total 8,800)	Antilles: 3 mar inf regts; air and naval units Guyana: 2 mar inf air and naval (total 7,050)	army 1,300; navy 170; air units French West Indies: army 800; navy 459
Caribbean	1 inf bn			(see Antilles)	

APPENDIX 3.1 *(continued)*

France	1971/72	1981/82	1990	2001/02	2007
Mayotte, La Reunion			1 mar inf regt; 1 spt bn; air det (total 3,300)	—	army 1000 air units
Pacific Territories	2 bns and naval units				
N. Caledonia (Noumea)		1 inf regt and naval det	1 mar inf regt 1 spt bn; air det (total 3,800)	1 mar inf regt air and naval units (total 3,100)	army 1,030; navy 510; air units
Polynesia (Papeete)		2 inf regt and naval det	1 mar inf regt; 1 For Leg regt; (total 5,400)	1 mar inf regt air and naval units (total 3,100)	army 800; navy 710; air units

Sources: International Institute for Strategic Studies, *Military Balance* (London, various years); Philippe Leymarie, "Les bases en question," *Chronique Armée-Défense,* June 2, 2005.

Note: Unit size is not standardized and varies per country. Usual composition: company 100–200; battalion 500–800; brigade (regiment) 3,000–5,000; division 15,000–20,000; corps 60,000–80,000. The list is not comprehensive but serves merely to illustrate the semi-permanent deployments of France and the United Kingdom in previous colonies and dependent territories. Abbreviations used are as follows: art = artillery; bde = brigade; bn(s) = battalions; com(s) = company(ies); det = detachment; For Leg = Foreign Legion; gp(s) = group(s); inf = infantry; mar = marine; regt(s) = regiment(s); spt = support; sqn(s) = squadrons.

[a] In 1970 Britain also had basing agreements with Kenya and South Africa (Simonstown).

[b] N.I. indicates no information for that year.

Incomplete Contracting and the Politics of U.S. Overseas Basing Agreements

I believe that we should take every opportunity
to challenge the assumption that our European
allies are doing us a favor whenever they provide
us with the necessary facilities from which to
defend their own continent.
—Chester Bowles, June 4, 1962

Introduction

In the previous chapter we explored how great powers across different decades used incomplete contracts over specific assets to facilitate the process of colonial disengagement. In this chapter, we examine the political consequences of incomplete contracts in another bilateral domain of sovereignty: the evolution of post–World War II U.S. overseas military basing agreements.

The United States now stands at the center of a vast and complex global network of military bases, installations, and access arrangements.[1] Since World War II, it has secured this network through a varied set of agreements concluded with allies, nonaligned states, occupied powers, and former colonies. In some cases, the United States acquired military facilities from other great powers, such as the famous land-for-destroyers agreement (1940) with Great Britain that exchanged fifty U.S. destroyers for the right to construct bases on eight British possessions.[2] In other instances, the United States negotiated new accords to secure the use of installations in regions in which it did not have a prior presence, such as southern Europe, Africa, and the Middle East. In still others, such as in postwar Germany and Japan, it retained military facilities on the ground as it withdrew its occupation forces. Although the terms

---

[1] For broad overviews, see Calder 2007; A. Cooley 2008; Sandars 2000; Desch 1993, 1989; Blaker 1990; Duke 1989; Harkavy 1989. For more critical analyses, see Johnson 2004; Gerson and Birchard 1991.

[2] These territories were Bermuda, Jamaica, the Bahamas, Antigua, St. Lucia, Trinidad, British Guiana, and Newfoundland, Canada (Arguenta). See Sandars 2000, 42–47.

of these base bargains varied considerably across the network, all of these hosts, in accepting the U.S. military presence, agreed to cede some aspects of their sovereignty to the United States. This bundle of leases and contractual agreements governing this overseas network of American military deployments has been aptly characterized as a "leasehold empire."[3]

As former undersecretary of state Chester Bowles suggests in the opening epigraph, the status, sovereign rights, and terms of U.S. overseas military bases have routinely been politicized and contested by host countries, even U.S. allies.[4] Base-related issues frequently have dominated U.S. foreign relations with host countries. Even within the NATO community, negotiations over the terms of basing rights during the cold war were difficult, as base hosts engaged in hard bargaining and demanded quid pro quo that went well beyond standard security guarantees.

Although several excellent descriptive studies and single-country cases have been written on the U.S. overseas military presence, these works tend to focus on the overall geopolitical positioning and military functions of these facilities; they do not systematically explore the bargaining dynamics and sovereign transfers that underpin their governance arrangements.[5] Moreover, many of these studies cannot systematically explain two trends that have characterized U.S. overseas basing contracts. First, why have host countries, even ones closely allied with the United States, periodically pursued rent-seeking and demanded ever-increasing economic and military compensation packages in exchange for granting basing rights? Second, how have the terms of these incomplete contracts, especially their short-term leases and hybrid governance arrangements, endogenously contributed to these hard-bargaining dynamics during contractual renegotiations?

Our theory of incomplete contracting and mixed sovereignty arrangements offers a fresh set of conceptual tools to systematically reconsider how sovereignty is transferred in U.S. overseas basing agreements. Although the United States has some neo-imperial arrangements, most notably administering the island of Okinawa prior to its reversion to Japan in 1972, it usually relied on bilateral incomplete contracts with overseas base hosts to secure its base access.[6] In this "empire of leases," the United States ceded sovereign residual rights to the host nation. By using these

---

[3] Sandars 2000.

[4] Chester Bowles, "The Azores," *White House Memorandum to President John F. Kennedy*, Washington, DC, June 4, 1962. Accessed through the *Declassified Document Reference System (DDRS)*, 2.

[5] See especially Sandars 2000; Blaker 1990; Desch 1993; Harkavy 1989.

[6] On Okinawa, see Eldridge 2001; Johnson 1999.

residual rights of control during renegotiations, host countries extracted substantial quasi-rents from the United States while placing more restrictive limits on its sovereign rights and military functions. As long as the assets in question remained specific to the greater U.S. network, initial agreements whose terms heavily favored the United States were renegotiated and became more balanced security contracts. Over time, U.S. negotiators resigned themselves to granting compensation packages to host states that approached (but did not exceed) the relocation costs of using alternate facilities to discharge the same military functions. Thus, the greater the specificity of a host country's facilities to the overall U.S. global basing network, and therefore its "joint-use" benefit, the more leverage that country retained in the renegotiation process, regardless of the host country's relative power and/or any common identities it may have shared with the United States. Accordingly, this incomplete contracting approach to basing relations offers a more convincing explanation of the sovereign bargaining dynamics of U.S. basing accords than those potentially provided by either structural realist or constructivist theories of security studies.

In the next section we summarize and apply prevailing theories of international relations to the issue of U.S. overseas basing agreements and negotiations. In the following section, we draw on our incomplete contracting approach to present an alternate theory of basing politics and offer a set of testable hypotheses about the dynamics of specific basing assets, bargaining over quid pro quo, and contractual renegotiation. The model is then illustrated with two case studies of the evolution of U.S. overseas basing arrangements in the Philippines and the Azores, Portugal. We conclude the chapter by applying the insights of the incomplete contracting approach to current changes in U.S. basing arrangements and strategy, especially the Pentagon's Global Defense Posture Review.

Explaining the Dynamics of Overseas Basing Agreements: Prevailing Theories of International Relations

The politics and dynamics of the U.S. global basing network challenge important assumptions of both structural realist and constructivist theories of international relations. Realism and other power-based theories generally view the U.S. basing network as the product of systemic factors and pressures, such as the bipolar competition that characterized the international system during the cold war.[7] For realists, basing agreements are rarely studied as independent objects of inquiry, given that they are

---

[7] Waltz 1979. For recent modifications to neorealist theory, see Mearsheimer 2001; Schweller 1998; Walt 1987.

viewed as products of the alliances produced by state balancing and band-wagoning and the pressures generated by the systemic environment.[8] Radical analyses, similarly, focus on the asymmetries of power between the United States and its various basing hosts. From this perspective the United States imposes itself upon these weaker partners as an imperialist power, violates their rights of sovereignty, and leaves them with little option but to accept U.S. political and security demands.[9]

On the other hand, constructivist theories focus on the prevailing social norms and identities that inform relations among states and the formation of security communities. For constructivists, states relate to each other based on intersubjective social identities, not objectively defined interests.[10] Constructivists do not deny the importance of power in the international system, but they view alliances and relations between states as the results of intersubjective understandings and social processes among security allies. Consequently, constructivists argue that mutual social ties and membership in a common security community shape the terms of bilateral negotiations over basing contracts. For example, one analyst of U.S.-Italian relations has described the extensive U.S. basing network in Italy as the product of the very close pluralistic security community that has characterized their postwar relations.[11]

Certainly, both structural realist theories and constructivism offer potentially important insights into the evolution of the American basing system. Realists and radicals correctly point to the overall systemic environment and U.S. hegemonic power as a necessary condition for the establishment of these agreements, especially during their formative periods. As constructivists would expect, American policymakers also vigorously promoted a mutual security purpose with their overseas hosts when they publicly discussed the basing relationship, although such efforts were not always successful. However, a number of issues central to the basing relationship cannot be explained by either of these approaches.

First, neither realism nor constructivism can explain the extensive quid pro quo arrangements that were demanded by host countries during the renegotiation of basing agreements. Such behavior was certainly self-interested and rational, but was determined neither by external threat levels nor by the prevailing distribution of power and capabilities. In some

[8] For more nuanced assessments that combine realist insights with an independent focus on the nature of basing assets, see Desch 1993, 1989.

[9] See especially Johnson 2007, 2004, 2000; Gerson and Birchard 1991; Enloe 1989. Such commentators also focus on the social problems and tensions created by the U.S. military presence abroad.

[10] For recent representative works, see Wendt 1999; Adler and Barnett 1998; Ruggie 1998; Katzenstein 1996.

[11] See Monteleone 2007.

cases—most notably Britain and West Germany—host countries publicly recognized a shared mutuality of security interests and identities with the United States and formally demanded little in return for granting basing rights.[12] In other cases, however, host nations' behavior was driven primarily by the anticipation of extracting a quid pro quo—such as cash rental payments, military assistance, and topical political concessions—and/or improving on previous terms that were deemed unfair infringements of national sovereignty, as in the case of the renegotiation of initial basing contracts in postwar Japan, Korea, and the Philippines. At the extreme, in cases such as Portugal, Spain, Greece, Turkey, and the Philippines, host countries with formal security ties with the United States (and in the European cases, NATO membership) strategically used the threat of expulsion and the potential weakening of formal alliance structures as a bargaining tactic to extract greater concessions during renegotiations.

Second, while many of the original basing agreements reached in the 1950s asymmetrically favored the United States, the historical record indicates that over time the U.S. power differential did not guarantee favorable basing rights terms. By using their residual rights of sovereignty to renegotiate basing contracts, host countries extracted ever-increasing compensation packages and restricted American use rights over the facilities. The periodic renegotiation of these incomplete contracts and reapportioning of sovereign rights indicates a major shift in bargaining power away from the United States toward the host countries, even as the overall relative capabilities of these actors remained asymmetrical. Again, this dynamic is more consistent with the theory of incomplete contracting than it is with structural realism. And much like firms assessing market signals from competitors, host states learned to use U.S. basing agreements with other states as baselines for securing more favorable terms in their own negotiations.

Finally, neither structural realist nor constructivist theories can adequately explain the important variations in the timing of basing contract renewals and extensions over the course of the last few decades. The ebb and flow of agreements governing major American installations usually has not corresponded to major geopolitical shifts, systemic developments, or the rise and decline of international norms. Even certain high-profile base withdrawals that coincided with the end of the cold war—such as Panama and the Philippines—actually had been negotiated as "drop dead" dates of final withdrawal many years before the collapse of the Soviet Union. Even here, however, power-based theories cannot explain

---

[12] Indeed, U.S.-UK basing arrangements have always been informal. See Duke 1987.

why in the wake of the end of the cold war certain basing agreements have persisted while others have not. Although the theory of incomplete contracting cannot explain all of this observable variation, it does offer a more systematic explanation for what is otherwise a set of puzzling trends within U.S. basing agreements.

The Argument: Specific Assets, Incomplete Contracting, and Renegotiation

Incomplete contracting theory provides the basis for an alternative explanatory framework for the study of the evolution of U.S. basing contracts.[13] We argue that the overseas physical installations used by the U.S. military are made up of a global network of U.S.-governed assets. Consistent with our hypothesis (G1 in table 2.1), however, the presence of these assets on overseas sovereign host states makes it politically costly, if not impossible, for the United States to directly govern these bases as colonial outposts. Instead, U.S. officials have had to negotiate and maintain bilateral hybrid sovereignty arrangements with base hosting countries. Although many of these installations are routine and their functions are interchangeable, others remain site specific (G2). The delineation of precise use rights is governed by a bilateral agreement, usually in the form of an incomplete contract, whose terms are subject to periodic negotiation and consultation with the host country. During these periodic renegotiations, host countries use their residual rights of control over these assets to extract greater concessions from the United States and restrict its use rights.

Military Installations and Determinants of Asset Specificity

Insofar as overseas military installations perform idiosyncratic functions within the overall network of U.S. global basing functions and have no readily available alternatives, they can be considered "site-specific" assets (G2). According to James Blaker, the U.S. basing system historically has been composed of a set of distinct, relatively autonomous subnetworks, with each retaining a clear functional purpose and well-defined jurisdictional scope.[14] The exact functions and geographical organization of these networks have varied over time and have been subjected to numerous reorganizations.

[13] Hart 1995; Hart and Moore 1990; Grossman and Hart 1986.
[14] Blaker 1990, 22–23.

As within any large hierarchical organization, the challenge to U.S. military planners has been to balance the dual imperatives of attaining functional synergies and ensuring global access. Functionally, U.S. military operations consist of activities such as strategic airlift, surveillance and intelligence gathering, naval operations, tactical air forces, and ground forces (as well as related functions by other governmental bodies such as the U.S. Space Agency), with each of these functions requiring both bases of operation and bases that provide logistical support.[15] Geographically, the various functions and activities of the U.S. military are subject to the six regional commands and four functional commands that make up the unified command.[16] The geographic commands—U.S. European Command (EUCOM), U.S. Central Command (CENTCOM), U.S. Pacific Command (PACOM), U.S. Northern Command (NORTHCOM), U.S. Southern Command (SOUTHCOM), and the new U.S. African Command (AFRICOM)—control the operations, contingency planning, and force requirements of the various bases. The commands themselves are subject to occasional repositioning and jurisdictional redefinition. For example, CENTCOM's headquarters were moved from Florida to Qatar in September 2002 in anticipation of U.S.-led military action against Iraq.

Within this extensive organizational hierarchy of overseas bases, the particular "asset specificity" of each overseas U.S. military installation will depend on a number of factors, including the importance of an installation to a major theater of operation, its functional importance within a particular operational or logistics network, and/or its positional importance to a regional command. In addition, the value and specificity of a base might be subject to particular doctrinal or institutional innovations that may alter the relative strategic value of that installation.[17] Technological innovations may render certain assets and installations obsolete or increase the value of others.[18] A final factor determining the specificity of certain bases to the overall U.S. networks is the periodic consolidation and reorganization of redundant sites. For instance, in the 1940s and 1950s over thirty installations in the Pacific were terminated and their

[15] Of course, there is some variation in the number of distinct functions identified by U.S. basing analysts. Robert Harkavy distinguishes among ten different types of functional facilities: airfields, naval, ground force, missile, space, communications and control, intelligence and command, environmental monitoring, research and testing, and logistics (1989, 17–20).

[16] The functional commands are SOCOM (U.S. Special Operations Command), JFCOM (U.S. Joint Forces Command), STRATCOM (U.S. Strategic Command), and TRANSCOM (U.S. Transportation Command).

[17] Wallander 2000.

[18] See Harkavy 1993.

functions were transferred to just four sites—Guam, Hawaii, Japan, and the Philippines.[19] Thus, while the cold war or the prevailing balance of power certainly provided an important context for strategic planning and basing organization, the actual value and asset specificity of bases has depended on a host of factors that have frequently varied independently of systemic power distribution.

Incomplete Contracts, Bargaining Leverage, and Quid Pro Quo

Basing agreements between the United States and host nations usually take the form of incomplete contracts. Unable to specify every contingent detail and obligation on the part of the contracting parties, these agreements usually specify a few important sovereign rights and obligations while articulating broad statements of principle and guidelines for other issues. The exact form of these contracts has varied considerably and included bilateral treaties, executive agreements, military-to-military protocols, and diplomatic exchanges of notes.[20] Some of these agreements have been embedded within a comprehensive security treaty or a broader "defense and security cooperation agreement" (DECA), while others specifically have governed base rights. The duration of these agreements has also varied, with some contracts lasting for ninety-nine years (Philippines) or indefinitely (Treaty of Peace with Japan, 1951), whereas others have been limited to just a few years. Often, the length of the contract itself has been subject to intense bargaining and renegotiation. Historically, U.S. officials have usually preferred indefinite or long-term agreements so as to reduce uncertainty regarding the future status of the base. On the other hand, most host countries have tended to favor granting shorter contracts, given that subsequent renegotiation could provide a built-in mechanism for redressing any unanticipated problems or grievances that may arise during the course of an initial accord.

Contracting for base rights often involves granting something in exchange for guaranteeing basing rights—a quid pro quo. Sometimes granting security guarantees to the base host has sufficed for maintaining long-term basing access. The longevity of the basing arrangements that the United States enjoys with Japan, South Korea, Germany, and Great Britain is the product of ongoing joint security gains. Other times, however, hosts have demanded economic and political concessions in exchange for granting base rights. In a comprehensive report on overseas bases presented to the Eisenhower White House in 1957, Frank Nash begrudgingly

---

[19] For details, see Blaker 1990, 47–50.
[20] For an overview, see Woodliffe 1992, 29–47.

acknowledged that the mutuality of identification and security interests between the United States and its base hosts often had proven insufficient for guaranteeing base access. The report observed,

> The underlying difficulty common in varying degrees to most foreign countries and regions where the United States forces are now stationed is an insufficient identification on the part of the people of these countries with the principle or concept of collective security. In particular, the fact that the concrete implementation of the concept makes it necessary for U.S. facilities and personnel to be established on foreign territory in times like the present which, while hardly times of peace, are not times of actual hostilities, is not sufficiently understood.[21]

Increasingly, the United States added various types of side payments to basing agreements, even when negotiating with formal allies and members of NATO such as Portugal, Greece, Spain, Iceland, and Turkey, although American negotiators could not always guarantee that the U.S. Congress would approve agreed-upon levels of compensation.[22] Typically, compensation packages consisted of a mix of military hardware, military training, economic loans, import-export credits, and economic grants. Officially, U.S. negotiators refused to label such cash or military assistance payments as "rent," a policy that still remains in effect.

Furthermore, there was a direct relationship between the specificity of the assets contained in a certain country and the amount of compensation that the United States was prepared to grant to the host country. Countries that hosted assets that were specific to the U.S. network found themselves in a much better bargaining position than did countries that hosted routine or substitutable assets (B1). The Nash report addressed this relationship by calculating that compensation packages to host countries should not rise above the costs of relocating to alternate sites capable of discharging the same functions.

> Even under the best of circumstances however, we must expect to pay a direct quid pro quo for some of our facilities. Our accounting should show as clearly as possible the price which we have to pay for the privilege of maintaining such facilities. We should know, as well, what particular facilities cost us to duplicate them elsewhere. We must recognize that in these situations the price paid for facilities in one country becomes known to other countries similarly situated, and an increase in the quid pro quo granted to one is likely to create demands in other

---

[21] Nash 1957, 43.

[22] This issue became increasingly important in the mid-1980s when Congress slashed the foreign aid budget, including grants earmarked as basing agreement compensation packages. For details, see Clarke and O'Connor 1993.

countries. We should be prepared to move any facilities if the price becomes too high, since otherwise we may price ourselves out of all facilities similarly situated.[23]

The report proved especially prescient in its forecast of the reputational effects of these compensation packages. As information about quid pro quo and basing arrangements became widely disseminated across countries that hosted site-specific U.S. facilities, demands for rental payments and other forms of compensation increased significantly. For instance, U.S. base negotiators in the Mediterranean region in the 1970s and 1980s were surprised to find that host countries justified their demand for increased cash payments by citing terms reached with other host nations.[24] As a result, quid pro quo was subjected to a type of global ratcheting, as one basing-agreement "price" reached with a host country rapidly raised the expectations and levels demanded by other countries in their subsequent negotiations.[25]

The Dynamics of Negotiation and Renegotiation

The behavioral consequences of incomplete contracts became clearer as the United States began to renegotiate its initial basing contracts and leases. As outlined in our theory of incomplete contracting—specifically hypothesis B1 on bargaining leverage—countries owning the residual rights of control over U.S. assets found themselves in more powerful bargaining positions when renegotiating their contractual terms at $t + 1$ than they were initially at $t = 0$. They used the threat of expulsion or domestic political collapse to secure additional compensation and a more favorable transfer of sovereign rights. The issue of renegotiation between the United States and host countries became particularly difficult for the superpower in the late 1970s and the 1980s as countries hosting specific assets demanded dramatically increased compensation packages.[26] Furthermore, host states came to appreciate the strategic benefits of concluding short-term lease renewals, usually five years in duration, so as to be in a position within a few years to demand even greater compensation at subsequent renegotiations.

---

[23] Nash 1957, 50.

[24] Robert Kealey, "Bargaining over U.S. Bases in Europe Intensifies as Their Relative Importance Gains," *Wall Street Journal*, November 5, 1987, p. 1. Also see McDonald and Bendahmane 1990.

[25] See John W. Finney, "Kissinger Legacy: U.S. Bases around the World Are Not Cheap," *New York Times*, January 2, 1977, p. 112.

[26] See Clarke and O'Connor 1993.

Renegotiation, consistent with our hypothesis about momentum (M1), also allowed host states to more clearly specify, delineate, and restrict U.S. use rights. For the most part, the initial basing agreements reached after World War II by the United States with countries like the Philippines, Japan, Turkey, and Spain offered extremely generous terms for the U.S. military, often allocating to the U.S. military foreign residual rights or, in the case of Japan, even neo-imperial authority. Many of these initial agreements gave the United States the right to undertake almost any type of activity at its discretion and without prior consultation with the host country government. During renegotiation, however, host countries criticized these terms as "colonial" or "unequal" and renegotiated their terms to gain host residual rights and demand greater restrictions on the use of the installations. For instance, host countries insisted that the United States request formal authorization for the use of the bases for combat operations in "out of area" missions. Indeed, most European NATO base hosts denied the United States permission to use their installations in support of Israel in 1973 and the 1986 campaign against Libya.[27] Use rights tended to become increasingly restrictive with each renegotiated agreement.

Perhaps the most contentious of these use rights issues was the stationing of nuclear weapons. Throughout the cold war, the United States maintained an official policy of neither confirming nor denying the existence of nuclear weapons throughout its global network of military installations.[28] The issue caused friction in many basing renegotiations, as certain countries—most notably Denmark, Spain, and Iceland—banned them from their soil, regardless of this U.S. policy. The transit issue proved particularly thorny for U.S. naval vessels carrying nuclear weapons. For example, when in 1987 the New Zealand parliament passed a law banning the transit of vessels carrying nuclear weapons, the United States responded by dissolving its security commitment to New Zealand under the terms of the 1951 ANZUS treaty.[29]

Just as contentious as American use rights were negotiations covering the various issues of sovereignty relating to the routine operations and sovereign governance of the bases themselves. The most politically inflammatory of these was often the issue of the criminal jurisdiction procedures to govern crimes committed by U.S. military personnel, an issue that often delayed renegotiations in a number of countries.[30] Under the

---

[27] See A. Cooley 2008, 254.

[28] See Judith Miller, "U.S. Once Deployed 12,000 Atom Arms in 2 Dozen Nations," *New York Times*, October 20, 1999, p. 10. On U.S. overseas nuclear deployments, see Arkin and Fieldhouse 1985.

[29] For details of the relevant political and legal issues, see Pugh 1989.

[30] On SOFAs and criminal jurisdiction procedures, see Egan 2006; Woodliffe 1992, 169–81; Rouse 1957. On the origins of the NATO SOFA, see Delbrück 1993.

terms of the NATO Status of Forces Agreement (SOFA), the United States and the host country exercised "concurrent jurisdiction" over crimes committed by U.S. personnel according to a detailed set of legal distinctions. However, in base hosts not covered by the multilateral NATO SOFA, the apportioning of criminal jurisdiction often proved to be one of the most difficult issues of sovereignty as host countries were reluctant to cede jurisdiction to the United States.

In general, the balance of apportioned sovereign rights on bases tended to shift over time from the United States to the host country. In its initial agreements at $t = 0$ with countries such as the Philippines and Japan, the U.S. military enjoyed nearly unrestricted use rights over these facilities. Over time, however, renegotiations reapportioned and redefined this bundle of sovereign rights, bringing greater balance to the basing contract. By using their residual rights of control and bargaining leverage gained from hosting specific assets, host countries were able to extract important concessions from the United States and whittle down U.S. "use rights" to the minimum required by the United States to conduct its military operations.

Theoretical Summation and Hypotheses on Incomplete Contracts and Basing Agreements

Since World War II, a global network of overseas bases and installations has facilitated U.S. security operations. These basing contracts between the United States and the host nations have been subject to periodic renegotiation. As owners of the residual rights of control in their basing agreements, host countries in their renegotiations demanded more favorable sovereign rights, greater compensation packages, and other forms of quid pro quo from the United States; they also limited the use rights of the U.S. military. Even host nations that were members of a collective security agreement with the United States often behaved in a rent-seeking manner that took full advantage of contractual incompleteness, their residual rights of control, and bargaining leverage during renegotiation. This theoretical application of the incomplete contracting framework suggests the following specific hypotheses that derive from the general proposition laid out in chapter 2.

H1: Regardless of prevailing relative power balances, incomplete contracts allow host and foreign states to establish hybrid sovereign arrangements, short of neo-imperial control, for basing rights (G1).

H2: The greater the specificity of these military assets within the U.S. global basing network, the greater the bargaining leverage and material quid pro quo that host countries will extract from the United States during renegotiation (G2).

H3: As long as assets remain specific for the sending country, rational host states should demand compensation packages that approach, but do not exceed, the costs the United States would incur in relocating its facilities to the next best functional alternative (B1).

H4: As long as assets remain specific and benefits joint, the use rights of the United States to a military facility will become increasingly more restrictive in each round of renegotiations (M1).

H5: Rational host states will prefer short-term agreements to long-term leases so as to strategically use their residual rights of control during renegotiations.

H6: Host states will use information from other basing agreements and negotiations to demand similar sovereign arrangements and compensation packages, thereby ratcheting up the value of these agreements.

Conversely, our theoretical approach would be falsified if we found the following: basing rights agreements resembled neo-imperial complete contracting; host countries with more specific assets did not demand greater compensation than those hosting non-specific assets; the use rights of the United States to a facility became less restrictive at any given renegotiation; host countries preferred longer contracts over short-term contracts; and host states did not invoke other similar agreements when securing their compensation packages.

Illustrative Case Studies: U.S. Agreements with the Philippines and Portugal

We illustrate the usefulness of the incomplete contracting approach with the case studies of the evolution of U.S. basing agreements with the Philippines and Portugal. Despite their different histories and geographical settings, we see similar patterns of sovereign transfers under incomplete contracts. Even though initial accords afforded the U.S. military the residual rights to conduct a wide variety of military functions rent free, subsequent bargaining dynamics favored the base hosts. At later renegotiations host countries secured residual rights and then used them to extract maximum rents from the United States and to improve the terms of their sovereign arrangements. In the Portuguese case, where the Lajes installation on the mid-Atlantic Azores island of Terceira is still operating, these demands greatly decreased in the 1990s as a result of the diminished strategic value of the island's installations. And while two cases cannot offer any definitive proof for the validity of the model—they are best described as "plausibility probes" of the model's potential utility—they have been chosen based on well-established criteria for drawing scientific inference from a small group of qualitative case studies.[31]

First, in these two cases we see diachronic similarities in the type of contracting used by the United States. In the Philippines, generous base access rights were guaranteed to the United States by the Philippine independence treaty. As a result of populist domestic trends, however, the Philippines gradually revised these articles of independence and adopted sovereign residual rights. During the Marcos regime in the 1970s and 1980s it strategically bargained using a series of short-term incomplete contracts. In the Portuguese case, host authorities formally adopted short-term renewable contracts quite early, beginning in 1951, and steadily used their residual rights of control to secure political concessions on the issue of decolonization and, in the 1970s and 1980s, compensatory rent packages. In both cases, regardless of their geographical and historical differences, the adoption of short-term, incomplete contracts resulted in similar patterns of hard bargaining and rent-seeking during renegotiation periods that are consistent with the expectations of incomplete contracting theory.

Second, both cases should be relatively easy ones for structural realism, yet power-based theories are clearly inadequate for explaining the hard-bargaining dynamics that characterized basing renegotiations in both cases in the 1970s and 1980s. The Philippines was a U.S. colony until its occupation by Japan in World War II and retained very close security ties with the United States (including close military-to-military ties) following its independence in 1946. Similarly, Portugal was a founding member of the NATO alliance in 1949. Structural realist theories, whether in their balancing or bandwagoning variants, would expect a weaker military ally of a great power (or superpower) to welcome collective security arrangements and not behave in a manner that threatened expulsion and the undermining of these very alliances, especially in a bipolar systemic environment.

Similarly, these cases are not readily explainable by constructivist theories that emphasize the role of identity. In both cases, host nations and their populations shared broad security identities and political ideologies with the United States. Salazar was a vehement anti-communist, a position he proudly articulated in his foreign trips and public statements throughout the 1950s. Portugal was also a member of NATO's transatlantic security community and should have shared its collective identity.[32] Moreover, migration between the Azores and the United States,

---

[31] In this chapter we arguably process trace with variation diachronically in each case. Thus we still have variation on the independent and dependent variables. King, Keohane, and Verba 1994; A. George 1979.

[32] See Risse-Kappen 1996.

where a greater number of Azoreans live than on the mid-Atlantic islands themselves, historically has generated strong social ties and mutual identification between Azoreans and Americans. Over decades in the Philippines, governments and business communities retained bilateral ties to the United States across a broad range of spheres. President Marcos was also an unabashed anti-communist and U.S. ally, but this did not stop him from strategically using the bilateral relationship for his own political gain. In both cases, then, any initial shared identities and social understandings were undercut in the 1960s and 1970s as the process of renegotiation unfolded and host countries hardened their bilateral bargaining tactics.

U.S. Bases in the Philippines

The Nature of the Assets

The Subic Bay naval facility and the Clark Air Base constituted the two most significant U.S. military installations in the Philippines and both were to play vitally important functions for the U.S. military over the next four decades. Subic Bay was the largest naval facility west of Hawaii and, in the 1970s, was capable of accommodating two aircraft carriers as well as a dozen other ships at any time on its four dry docks. Over 60 percent of all repair work on the Seventh Fleet was carried out at Subic, with an average of ten to fifteen ships docking a day, and the facility hosted the largest naval supply in the world, eight separate U.S. commands, and a naval aircraft station capable of hosting 400 naval aircraft. Subic played a prominent role in the Vietnam War and even after a Department of Defense (DOD) report stressed its vital importance to the U.S. global basing network by concluding that "without Subic Bay, the U.S. Seventh Fleet could not be maintained at its present force level and operational effectiveness."[33]

Clark Air Base had a similar set of highly strategic functions and by the mid-1970s had become the second largest U.S. Air Force base in the world after Vandenberg in California.[34] Functionally, Clark housed a tactical fighter and tactical airlift wing, training facilities for air force units in Japan and Korea, and served as the air logistics and maintenance hub for the southwest Pacific.[35] It also functioned as a major north-south and east-west communications network hub. Taken together, Subic and Clark played critical roles in the U.S. forward defense of northeast Asia, South-

---

[33] Cotrell and Moorer 1977, 56.
[34] Sandars 2000, 119.
[35] For details, see Bowen 1988.

east Asia, the Indian Ocean, and even the Persian Gulf, and until 1988, according to William Berry, "the combination of sealift and airlift capabilities available in the Philippines would be difficult if not impossible to replicate elsewhere."[36]

Origins of the U.S. Presence and the 1947 Independence Treaty

The U.S. presence in the Philippines dates to 1898 when it acquired the islands during the Spanish-American War. The islands subsequently were governed as a colony or unincorporated territory, and U.S. authorities maintained a sizable military presence. A 1934 accord to allow independence in ten years was interrupted by the Japanese occupation, which also underscored the islands' strategic value and positioning to U.S. officials. After expelling Japanese occupying forces, the United States granted independence to the Philippines on July 4, 1946, but only after the U.S. Joint Chief of Staff secured the rights to twenty-four army facilities and fourteen navy facilities, in addition to the primary installations of Subic Bay and Clark.[37] The independence treaty—the Treaty of General Relations— explicitly excluded U.S. base facilities from this transfer of sovereignty, thereby amounting to a base rights allocation with foreign residual rights.

The precise status and terms of the bases were codified shortly afterward in the Military Bases Agreement (MBA) of 1947.[38] On the whole, the bundle of property rights apportioned in the initial treaty was very favorable to the new superpower and reflected the extreme asymmetries in power between the United States and its former colony. The United States was granted ninety-nine-year, rent-free leases to Subic and Clark along with fourteen other sites. An additional seven sites were earmarked for use "by military necessity" in exchange for the future provision of some military aid.[39] Additionally, the United States retained exclusive jurisdiction over the sovereignty of the bases, including Filipinos employed on the bases as well as the actions of American personnel anywhere in the Philippines. Strikingly, the initial agreement offered neither a collective nor a bilateral security guarantee to the hosts, emphasizing instead that the bases were almost exclusively designated for the purpose of U.S. power projection in the Pacific.

In addition, the agreement placed no effective restrictions on the use rights of the bases. The United States was permitted to govern, maintain,

---

[36] Berry 1989, 306.

[37] Ibid., 17–19.

[38] "Agreement between the Republic of the Philippines and the United States of America Concerning Military Bases," signed at Manila, March 14, 1947, *Treaties and Other International Acts Series (TIAS)* 1775.

[39] *TIAS* 1775, article I.

and construct on the facilities in any way it saw fit, as well as freely move
any equipment or weapons from one facility to another.[40] Jurisdictionally,
all facilities and personnel were exempt from any type of Philippine taxation. Finally, the agreement prohibited either government from unilaterally abrogating its terms and conditions. Understandably, soon after the
agreement was signed public resentment in the Philippines grew rapidly
against the terms of what was perceived to be an imbalanced and even
neocolonial arrangement.[41]

1948–66: The Period of Modification and Steady Revision

The security guarantees absent in the 1947 treaty were granted shortly
afterward in the early 1950s. In 1951 the countries signed a Mutual Defense Treaty as part of a broader security initiative undertaken by the
United States in Asia. The treaty laid down the principles of collective
security between the parties (article II) and stated that an armed attack
on either of the parties "would be dangerous to its peace and safety."[42] In
1953, a military assistance treaty laid the groundwork for modest
amounts of military aid and training assistance to be furnished to the
Philippines. In the following year, Secretary of State John Foster Dulles
extended the scope of the 1951 agreement by stating that "any military
attack on the Philippines could not but be an attack on the military forces
of the United States."[43] In 1954, the South East Asia Collective Defense
Treaty was signed. These agreements ignored issues specific to the U.S.
bases in the Philippines.

Growing resentment among the Philippine public over the bases
prompted calls in the mid-1950s to renegotiate certain provisions of the
1947 agreement. Media reports of crimes committed by U.S. soldiers in-
flamed nationalism and public opinion against the bases, while an overt
and thriving underground economy on the bases upset Philippine land-
owners and industrialists.[44] This growing anti-base sentiment hampered
U.S. attempts to secure the necessary agreements to allow for the expansion and modernization of Clark and Subic, even under the tenure of
the publicly pro-American president, Ramon Magsaysay.[45] The matter of
criminal jurisdiction was at the forefront of Philippine complaints, and
during unsuccessful negotiations in 1954 and 1956 U.S. negotiators re-

---

[40] *TIAS* 1775, article III, "Description of Rights."

[41] See Cullather 1992.

[42] "Mutual Defense Treaty between the Republic of the Philippines and the United States
of America," signed at Washington, DC, August 30, 1951, article IV.

[43] Sandars 2000, 110.

[44] Cullather 1994, 136–41.

[45] See the documents compiled in Cullather 1992.

fused to budge from the treaty's terms; for their part, Philippine negotiators refused to authorize new construction and the expansion of these facilities. Talks recommenced in 1958 and were concluded in October 1959 with an agreement reached by Philippine foreign minister Felixberto Serrano and U.S. ambassador Charles Bohlen.

The Bohlen-Serrano agreement was the first major amendment to the 1947 treaty and revised several sovereignty arrangements in order to redress Philippine grievances.[46] Effectively, it transferred residual rights over most issues from the United States to the Philippines. First, the agreement returned exclusive jurisdiction over the town of Olangapo and the port of Manila back to Philippine authorities and ceded over 117,000 hectares of territory back to the Philippine side. Second, the original lease period of ninety-nine years was replaced by a new period of twenty-five years, although the new period formally went into effect at a subsequent separate signing of this provision in September 1966. Third, the agreement placed a Philippine liaison officer on-site at every facility and established a joint Mutual Defense Board to hear grievances. Fourth, the 1959 agreement established certain restrictions on use rights by stating that the United States could not station any intermediate or intercontinental ballistic missiles on the bases without prior consultation with the Philippine authorities.

One area in which no progress was made in 1959 was the still contentious issue of criminal jurisdiction as Bohlen steadfastly refused to make any unilateral concessions on the matter, despite a number of highly publicized incidents involving U.S. base guards shooting Filipinos who strayed onto base territory.[47] The jurisdiction issue was repeatedly brought up by Manila, and in February 1965 new talks were held focusing exclusively on the issue. In August 1965, an agreement was reached that brought the U.S.-Philippine basing accord in line with other similar NATO accords, implementing a system of concurrent criminal jurisdiction. The United States no longer exercised jurisdiction over the criminal actions of Filipinos on the bases, while it retained its right of full jurisdiction over the actions of on-duty U.S. servicemen on the island.[48] In addition, the sides established a joint Criminal Jurisdictional Implementation Committee and agreed to waive the right to exercise exclusive jurisdiction in cases of a particular national interest.

[46] The 1959 agreement was formalized on August 10, 1965, as the "Agreement between the United States of America and the Republic of the Philippines Concerning Military Bases, Amendment of August 10, 1965."

[47] For details, see Meadows 1965.

[48] Berry 1989, 142–43.

1966–79: The Marcos Regime and the Era of Hard Bargaining

The election of Ferdinand Marcos to the presidency in 1965 marked a new era in basing relations with the United States, as the Philippine president was keen to use his country's residual rights for domestic political advantage. Even though he was publicly an ardent anti-communist and supporter of the United States, Marcos was the first Philippine leader to strategically manipulate basing renegotiations to extract substantial rental payments. During his reelection campaign of 1969, Marcos called for further renegotiations of the base agreements and demanded substantially higher levels of compensation.[49] A 1974 National Security Council (NSC) memorandum on the issue of quid pro quo for Clark and Subic facilities underscored the following:

> The Philippine government has considered grant military assistance to be a tacit quid pro quo for the strategically important U.S. military installation at Clark Field and Subic Bay. Despite the fact that the current agreement does not expire until 1991, the Philippine government has asked to renegotiate the military relationship between the two countries at the same time economic negotiations take place. The primary motivation for negotiating both at once is that the Philippines are weak in bargaining power on economic issues and would like to use the base rent–eviction threat to bolster their position. The 1976 recommendation for military assistance will be known before these negotiations are completed and could affect the Philippine position on base rights.[50]

In recommending the continued approval of allocations from the military assistance program (MAP) to the Philippines, the NSC memo commented on the specific nature of the installations and their invaluable functions within the overall U.S. basing system: "these bases are of high strategic value and are irreplaceable, and . . . the Philippine government could decide to evict the United States from Clark and Subic in the absence of a grant quid pro quo."[51]

Among the array of issues brought to the table by Philippine negotiators were the longstanding concerns over command and control jurisdiction, criminal jurisdiction, and the storage of nuclear weapons on the bases. However, the greatest Philippine demand in the 1976 negotiations was for a substantive increase in compensation. A tentative agreement

---

[49] Ibid., 131–39.

[50] Richard Kennedy, "Fiscal Year 1976 Aid Review," National Security memorandum for Brent Scowcroft, Washington, DC, December 10, 1974, #2, *DDRS*, 31.

[51] Ibid., 32.

reached in 1976 between Henry Kissinger and Foreign Minister Carlos Romulo called for a $1 billion payment over five years, but Marcos personally rejected the amount the following day and the talks collapsed.[52]

Negotiations recommenced in the fall of 1977, and an agreement on basic guidelines for a new treaty, including granting full Philippine sovereignty over the facilities and holding future renewal talks every five years, was issued in 1978 after Vice President Walter Mondale's visit to Manila.[53] In October 1978, after talks had stalled again, Senator Daniel Inouye, chairman of the Senate Appropriations Subcommittee on Foreign Operations, visited the Philippines to negotiate with Marcos a level of compensation that he claimed the U.S. Senate would accept. Inouye stressed that the Senate would not ratify any compensation package in the realm of the $1 billion previously offered and he stressed the importance of concluding an agreement in time for the fiscal year 1980 budget.[54] Convinced by the senator's arguments, Marcos ordered negotiations to recommence and an agreement was concluded on December 26, 1978, with the formal military bases agreement signed on January 7, 1979.

The completed 1979 agreement represented a major overhaul of the 1947 agreement. On almost every issue Philippine negotiators used their residual rights to extract concessions and dramatically improve the terms of the 1947 MBA and the 1959 supplement. Technically, the 1979 accords formally amended the 1947 agreement.[55] The agreement stated that the leasing period be subject to renegotiation every five years until the ultimate 1991 expiration date. Jurisdictionally, the changes in the sovereign status of the facilities were also significant. The agreement emphasized that all the territory upon which U.S. installations were built was exclusively Philippine, and a Philippine base commander was appointed to head each basing facility. In addition, for the first time the Philippines armed forces were solely responsible for maintaining the perimeter security of the facilities.

Territorially, significant modifications were made to the base areas. On Clark, the United States formally ceded 92 percent or 119,000 acres out of the original 130,000, leaving U.S. forces with about 10,550 acres.[56]

---

[52] For details and an explanation of the various components of the amount, see Bonner 1987.

[53] See "Joint Statement of President Marcos and Vice President Mondale, May 4, 1978," in Castro 1983, 139.

[54] Sandars 2000, 113–14.

[55] The formal title was "Arrangements Regarding Delineation of United States Facilities at Clark Air Base and Subic Naval Base; Powers and Responsibilities of the Philippine Base Commanders and Related Powers and Responsibilities of the United States Facility Commanders; and the Tabones Training Complex," signed January 7, 1979. *TIAS* 9224.

[56] Ibid., article I, annex I.

Similarly, annex II of the agreement delimited the territory available at Subic, reducing the U.S. facility to 14,400 acres, about 23 percent of the previously held 62,000 acres (land and water area).[57] The other facilities were also reduced and were either transferred over to Philippine jurisdiction or were consolidated and appended to the governing structures of Clark and Subic. For instance, the U.S. facilities at Wallace Air Station, the Crow Valley Weapons Range, and the John Hay Air Station were transferred to Clark, while the Zambales Amphibious Training Area and the San Miguel Naval Communications Station became extensions of Subic.[58]

In terms of compensation, the 1979 agreement also represented a huge leap forward in terms of U.S. aid guarantees. U.S. officials steadfastly refused to designate these aid payments as "rent," but the final $500 million compensation package (over five years) that U.S. negotiators agreed to make its "best efforts" to secure represented a substantial increase from the $45 million annual payment agreed in 1966. The sum of about $100 million per year established that future compensation packages would be of significant proportions.

Endgame: 1980–91

Although not as acrimonious in tone, negotiations in the 1980s until the base closings in 1991 still involved hard bargaining and the Philippines' strategic use of its residual rights of control. The 1983 agreement was concluded just a few months after negotiations commenced, a function of the Reagan regime's closer ties to Manila. In addition to the usual threat of terminating U.S. access to the facilities, the Philippine negotiating team also released to American negotiators a letter from the Soviet Union seeking closer military cooperation.[59] The U.S. side took this threat of a potential alternate contracting party seriously and concluded that negotiations should be completed expeditiously, giving in to Philippine demands for increased compensation.

For the most part, the 1983 agreement reaffirmed the major provisions of the 1979 amendments. The accord reasserted complete Philippine sovereignty over the base areas and maintained their prevailing administrative structure. American use rights to the bases were restricted even further as the agreement guaranteed that the United States would consult with the Philippine government before "the operational use of the bases for military combat operations" and that it would notify the host nation

---

[57] Ibid., article I, annex II.
[58] Berry 1989, 230–32.
[59] "Defense Memorandum of Agreement," signed June 1, 1983. *TIAS* 10699.

of any changes in force levels or weapons systems, particularly the establishment of long-range missiles on the bases.[60] The agreement also granted to Philippine base commanders increased access to U.S. facilities, except in very sensitive areas.

In terms of compensation, the U.S. aid package again ballooned from its previous level. The United States pledged "best efforts" to pay a compensation package of about $900 million over the following five years—the exact figure demanded beforehand by Philippine negotiators—a sum made up of $475 million in economic aid, $125 million in military grants, and $300 million in military sales credits.[61] Beyond the compensation payment, U.S. officials agreed to support requests for additional loans from international lending agencies, granted increased bilateral trade preferences, and agreed to back Manila on the issue of rescheduling its substantial international debt.[62]

The 1983 agreement was in effect for only a few months before major domestic political developments unfolded in the Philippines. In August 1983, opposition leader Benigno Aquino was assassinated upon his return to the country, prompting the collapse of the Marcos regime and new democratic elections that brought to power his widow, Corazon Aquino. Populist throughout her campaign and an outspoken opponent of the American presence, Aquino publicly connected the U.S. basing presence in the Philippines to the financial and military support of the Marcos regime and its dismal human rights record.[63] A new national constitution, approved by referendum in 1987, prohibited the stationing of nuclear weapons on Philippine territory and mandated that the Philippine Senate ratify all future foreign military basing accords.[64]

By the time of the 1988 renewal negotiations, the Aquino regime was driving an even tougher bargain than had the preceding regime.[65] Unable to negotiate basing access beyond the 1991 end date, U.S. officials had to settle for a supplemental three-year agreement reached by Secretary of State George Schultz in October 1988. The price for this three-year continuation yet again increased to $480 million per year, a 140 percent increase over the 1983 package.[66]

---

[60] Quoted in Berry 1989, 281–82.

[61] Berry 1989, 282.

[62] Greene 1988, 14. On the negotiations between the Philippines and International Financial Institutions during this period, see Broad 1988.

[63] A. Cooley 2008, chapter 3.

[64] Berry 1989, 286–87.

[65] For an insider's account of U.S.-Philippines base negotiations in the Aquino era, see the account of lead negotiator Alfredo Bengzon (Bengzon 1997).

[66] Sandars 2000, 118.

At the end of 1991, the U.S. presence was finally terminated as a result of the confluence of a natural disaster, domestic political intransigence, and U.S. congressional disapproval of the skyrocketing cost of compensation payments. On June 15, 1991, base rights negotiations were halted by the unexpected eruption of the Mount Pinatubo volcano, located just ten miles away from the Clark Air Base. One of the most violent of the century, the eruption effectively destroyed Clark and covered Subic in over one foot of volcanic ash. Subic reopened in July 1991. It subsequently became the exclusive focus of U.S.-Philippine negotiations. In August 1991, the negotiating sides reached an agreement to extend the U.S. presence at Subic for ten years at an annual payment of $200 million.[67] U.S. negotiators insisted that the U.S. Congress would be unwilling to approve a greater amount. However, just one month later, the Philippine Senate rejected the deal by a 12–11 vote, well short of the eighteen needed for a two-thirds majority for ratification. The last U.S. forces withdrew from Subic in November 1992.

Case Overview

The evolution of U.S. basing contracts with the Philippines illustrates many of the propositions advanced by the theory of incomplete contracting (see table 4.1). Initially, basing arrangements were an imbalanced arrangement that allocated to the United States extensive foreign residual rights over a wide range of facilities in exchange for granting the Philippines its independence. The 1947 MBA granted the U.S. military almost unchecked sovereignty over dozens of installations and imposed no substantive restrictions on American use rights. Soon after, however, renegotiations transferred sovereignty to the Philippine side and the Philippine government officials used their new residual rights of control in contractual renegotiations to curtail American use rights and reapportion subsequent sovereign rights on more favorable terms; full sovereignty was regained in 1991 when the U.S. military was forced to leave.

During the 1950s and the 1960s, Philippine negotiators focused on modifying U.S. exclusive jurisdiction on criminal procedures in accordance with NATO host countries, securing more extensive security commitments from the United States, reestablishing some symbolic Philippine sovereignty, and reasserting Philippine control over certain peripheral facilities, especially those near populated areas such as Manila. The 1959 agreement also modified the original ninety-nine-year lease into a twenty-five-year agreement.

---

[67] Ibid., 125.

TABLE 4.1
Evolution of U.S. Base Rights in the Philippines

Agreement Year (TIAS Ref. No.)	Duration	Facilities	Restrictions on U.S. Use Rights	Jurisdictional and Legal Issues	Economic Quid pro Quo Pledged ($US)
1947 (TIAS 1775)	99 years	Clark, Subic Bay, 14 other sites, access to 7 additional sites	None	Full U.S. control over bases and over Olangapo city; SOFA heavily favors U.S.	Rent-free
1958–59	Agreement to reduce 99-yr lease to 25 (effective in 1966)	Transfer of Manila Port and Olangapo city to RP	No use of bases outside of Mutual Defense pact or stationing of ICBMs w/out RP consent	Philippine Liaison at each base; Mutual Defense Board established to hear grievances, SOFA remains tilted to US	$6m; some military equipment transferred (TIAS 4019)
1966 (TIAS 6084)	25 years	Transfer of Malolos radio facilities, Camp John Hay to RP	Same as above	(1965) NATO-style SOFA adopted, 1967 natural resources development agreement	$45m per year
1979 (TIAS 9224)	25-year lease affirmed. Deals to be renewed every 5 years until 1991 end date	Reductions: 92% of Clark and 77% of Subic transferred to RP; all other sites consolidated into these 2 bases or transferred to RP	Unhampered operational use of bases in accordance with 1947 agreement; new developments and construction must be made in consultation w/RP	Exclusive Philippine sovereignty with Philippine flag; Philippine commander appointed to head each facility; RP responsible for facility perimeter security	$100m per year ($500m over 5yrs)
1983 (TIAS 10699)	5 years	Same as above	Mandatory consultation before all military combat; notification of changes in force levels/weapons systems	Allow collective bargaining for Philippine base labor force	$180m per year ($900m over 5yrs)
1988 Schultz-Manglapus Memorandum	3 years	Same as above	Storage of all nuclear weapons (but not transit) subject to RP consent	Non-removable installations revert back to RP; review labor agreement for RP workers	$480m per year
1991 (not ratified by RP Senate)	10 years	only Subic Bay, Clark closed	Same as above	Same as above	$203m per year

RP = Republic of the Philippines.
SOFA = Status of Forces Agreement.

After Ferdinand Marcos came to power, the Philippine position on bassing terms and negotiations hardened significantly. Throughout the
1970s, Philippine negotiators revisited every aspect of the 1947 and 1959
accords. They severely restricted formal U.S. use rights over the facilities
and reduced their size to the minimum of what was necessary for American operations. Also, consistent with the incomplete contracting model,
U.S. officials carefully calculated the costs and benefits of maintaining
these specific assets and/or altering their governance arrangements before
accepting these new terms. For instance, in a report to the president in
1975, one year prior to the start of renegotiations, Senate Majority Leader
Mike Mansfield reasoned,

> What would be most immediately useful is action to resolve the military
> base question. A first step in that direction on our part is an evaluation
> of both Subic and Clark in terms of a contemporary Pacific strategy for
> defending the interests and security of the United States. Until we know
> with some greater clarity and precision what the bases are worth to us
> we can hardly calculate accurately to what lengths we ought to go in
> trying to retain access to them in at least some modified form.[68]

For their part, Philippine negotiators under Marcos understood the
specificity and relative value of these basing assets to the United States
and demanded increasing compensation packages with each subsequent
renegotiation. Although U.S. officials always refused to acknowledge
these payments as pure "rent," the quid pro quo aid packages obtained
in 1979, 1983, and 1988 demonstrated just how effectively Philippine
negotiators used their residual rights to extract maximum compensation
packages that approached the relocation value of the facilities. Furthermore, by limiting basing agreements to five years, Philippine negotiators
were able to use the threat of short-term renegotiation to secure increasing
returns from the United States as well as regularly amend outstanding
legal issues. This hard bargaining occurred despite the "special relationship" between the countries and notwithstanding the fact that they were
allies and signatories to a Mutual Defense Pact. The lack of a credible
alternative site, for the United States, would have kept the momentum of
this dynamic going (per hypothesis M2) but for the intervention of the
Philippine Senate in 1991 that rejected the new agreement and effectively
evicted U.S. forces. Indeed, as will also be shown in the Azores case, common geopolitical interests merely emboldened host country negotiators

[68] Mike Mansfield, "Southeast Asia and U.S. Policies after Indochina: A Report on
Burma, Thailand and the Republic of the Philippines," *U.S. Presidential Report*, Washington, DC, September 1975, *DDRS*, 24.

to rationally drive an even harder bargain with the knowledge that the United States could neither easily nor cheaply secure viable alternatives to these specific assets.

U.S. Bases in the Azores, Portugal

U.S. military installations in Portugal have been exclusively located in the Azores, a mid-Atlantic island group located nine hundred miles west of the Portuguese mainland. Strategically positioned, the Azores since 1944 have hosted a number of important U.S. facilities including the Lajes airfield on the island of Terceira, an airfield on Santa Maria, port facilities on Praia da Vitoria and Vila do Porto, and a storage facility on Ponta Delgada on the island of São Miguel.

The most significant of these installations has been Lajes. Since 1951, it has served as a refueling station and stopping-off point for airlift and transatlantic traffic. American cargo planes used the base to support Israel during the 1973 war, and it was used as a staging area for U.S. military operations during the Gulf War, the Kosovo campaign, and Operation Enduring Freedom in Afghanistan. During the cold war Lajes also hosted the second important function of conducting anti-submarine warfare operations (ASW). The only such ASW base in the mid-Atlantic, the Azores facility enabled ASW units to track Soviet submarines within a thousand-mile radius, thereby monitoring activity from the strategic entrance to the Mediterranean to the U.S. East Coast. The Azores bases also served as a communications installation as part of DOD's Defense Communications System. In 1973, a U.S. Senate report emphasized the specificity of these assets to the global U.S. basing network, observing that the three main functions performed in the Azores bases "would not be performed as efficiently in any other location."[69]

1943–62: NATO and the Azores Agreement

The U.S. presence on the Azores can be traced to 1943, when the Portuguese government agreed to host Allied troops, including U.S. forces under British command, under an old British-Portuguese agreement.[70] Allied troops were given access to the Lajes airfield and allowed to construct a facility on the island of Santa Maria in order to protect Allied shipping

---

[69] Quoted in Duke 1989, 237–38.

[70] On the importance and functions of the Azores during World War II, as well as Churchill and Roosevelt's planning, see Herz 2004.

lanes in the Atlantic from German attacks. A November 1944 agreement effectively transferred sovereign control to the Allies and granted the United States unrestricted use rights over these installations;[71] in exchange, the United States and Allies promised to return Portuguese colonies that were occupied by Japan after the war, including reverting Timor to Portuguese sovereignty.[72] In 1946 the parties signed an agreement to guarantee U.S. access for an additional eighteen months, while the juridical sovereignty of Lajes was formally transferred back to Portugal and the facility was designed as "Portuguese Airbase 4."[73] In 1948 U.S. transit rights were extended for a further three years.[74] Within a few years Lajes became a vital Atlantic air bridge for the U.S. military, as important as U.S. facilities in Iceland and Greenland.[75] In 1949 the United States cemented the islands' strategic role by inviting Portugal to become a founding member of NATO, despite its authoritarian regime headed by Prime Minister Antonio Salazar.

The U.S. basing presence was codified by the signing of the Mutual Defense Agreement on January 5, 1951, which referred to the NATO charter, and regulated by a subsequent technical agreement that was signed on September 6, 1951.[76] The technical agreement stated that Portugal retained sovereignty over the bases, "constructions and materials," and restricted the transfer of equipment on the installations without mutual consent.[77] The agreement also allowed for the wartime use of the facilities by the United States and the United Kingdom and the agreement allowed the Portuguese government to withdraw after giving six to twelve months' evacuation notice to the United States.[78] No rental payments, monetary compensation, or overt quid pro quo was established in this initial agreement. However, in a secret addendum to the agreement provided to Salazar—who was indifferent about NATO but interested in safe-

---

[71] "Airbase on Santa Maria Island," signed in Lisbon, Portugal, November 28, 1944. *TIAS* 2338.

[72] The commitment is spelled out in the exchange of notes prior to the agreement and is included in *TIAS* 2338.

[73] "Azores, Air Transit Facilities," signed in Lisbon, Portugal, May 30, 1946. *TIAS* 2345.

[74] Calvet de Magalhães 1993, 276. "Azores, Air Transit Facilities," signed in Lisbon, Portugal, February 2, 1948. *TIAS* 2351. The text of the agreement also can be found in Vintras 1974, 178–80.

[75] National Security Council, "Base Rights in Greenland, Iceland and the Azores," Washington, DC, November 25, 1947, NSC 2/1, Digital National Security Archive, p. 1.

[76] "Mutual Defense Assistance Agreement between the United States of America and Portugal," signed in Lisbon, Portugal, January 5, 1951, *TIAS* 2187; "Military Facilities in the Azores: Agreement between Portugal and the United States," signed in Lisbon, Portugal, September 6, 1951. *TIAS* 3087.

[77] *TIAS* 3087, article III.

[78] Ibid., article VII.

guarding the territorial integrity of Portugal and its overseas possessions—the United States pledged that, if needed in a crisis, it would consent to moving NATO military equipment from metropolitan Portugal to its colonies.[79]

Initially, the 1951 agreement offered the bases in the Azores for a period of five years, an arrangement that was extended on similar terms for another year in 1956, and then for another five years on November 15, 1957. U.S. negotiators put up some argument regarding the short duration of the agreement renewal but ultimately agreed to Portuguese terms and to support Portugal's upkeep of the facilities in case they were evacuated. As with the 1951 agreement, no rental payment was charged.[80] However, the United States did commit to furnish the Portuguese military with some hardware. In 1956 it loaned two destroyer escorts to Portugal for five years.[81] A year later the United States pledged five C-64 aircraft (with a promise of four more in 1962), one squadron of F-86 fighter aircraft, and an array of modern radar and communications facilities.[82] At the time, Portuguese officials also raised the issue of U.S. decolonization policy and hinted that all U.S. "words and actions" in the next five years regarding Portugal's overseas territorial integrity might influence Portuguese attitudes toward future renewals.[83]

1962–74: Deadlock over Portugal's Colonial Policy

Throughout the 1960s Portuguese colonial policy would dominate the agenda in base negotiations and general relations between the countries. In 1962, the 1957 agreement was renewed on previous terms for an additional year, but expired on the last day of 1963 with negotiations at a complete standstill.

The Portuguese government and military held off extending the agreement as they were angry at the Kennedy administration for supporting African liberation movements in Angola and Mozambique that were fiercely clashing with the Portuguese military.[84] For their part, U.S. State

---

[79] See Antunes 1999, 151.

[80] "Portugal Defense: Use of Facilities in the Azores," signed in Lisbon, November 15, 1957. *TIAS* 3950.

[81] "Portugal Defense: Loan of Vessels," signed November 7, 1956. *TIAS* 3681.

[82] National Security Council, "Chronology on the Azores Base and Summary Survey of Selected Principal Problems and Issues Relating to the 1957 Agreement on the Azores," White House Memorandum, Reference No. NLK-78-93, Washington, DC, June 5, 1962, *DDRS*, 2–3.

[83] Ibid., 5.

[84] See Rodrigues 2004. For detailed accounts of the Kennedy administration's policy and internal debates by the same author, see Rodrigues 2002 (in Portuguese).

Department officials viewed the pro-independence Africa policy as an important counter to the tidal wave of Marxist/Leninist-inspired liberation movements flourishing in Africa, one that should not have been explicitly disavowed for the sake of appeasing Portugal. In 1961 President Kennedy reduced military aid to Portugal from $25 million to $3 million, before offering $72 million to facilitate negotiations in 1962 under pressure from a Defense Department that was not willing to sacrifice its Azores base rights for the administration's new anticolonial policy.[85] However, congressional appropriators increasingly voiced concern over Portugal's heavy-handed actions in Angola and its spotty human rights record and were reluctant to extend any type of military and economic assistance that could be misused by the Portuguese army in its African campaigns.

In response to Portuguese foot-dragging on the base renewal, the United States withheld MAP assistance in 1963 to force the Portuguese military to pressure politicians in Lisbon for a new Azores agreement. That particular policy backfired as it further fueled anti-American sentiment within the Portuguese officer corps during the 1960s.[86] Salazar was particularly incensed at the anti-Portuguese votes cast by the United States in the United Nations in debates about decolonization, actions he interpreted as "actively betraying an ally"; one observer of the base negotiations even described him as demonstrating "psychopathic" anger toward the United States on the issue.[87] As a result, Portuguese negotiators refused to grant any kind of concrete renewal or renegotiation, preferring to use the uncertain legal status of the Azores bases as negotiation leverage in getting the United States to moderate its vocal opposition to Portugal's Africa policy. The U.S. embassy in Portugal summarized the significance of the issue to Portugal as follows: "[F]or the sake of this primary consideration [Portugal's Africa policy], it has been willing thus far to forego the economic and/or military quid pro quo which it might have been in a position to exact as the price for a formal, longer-range extension of base rights."[88] As of January 1, 1964, then, the bases were operating according to an informal arrangement where the beginning of an evacuation period could be invoked with six to twelve months' notice at the discretion of the Portuguese government.

[85] Sandars 2000, 66.

[86] U.S. Embassy to Portugal, "Recommended Releases to Portugal of Military Assistance Program Arms and Equipment," Ref. A-378, Lisbon, Portugal, February 29, 1964, *DDRS*, 1–2.

[87] Central Intelligence Agency, "Portugal: Azores Base Negotiations," Ref. No. NLK-78-79, February 2, 1962, *DDRS*, 1.

[88] U.S. Embassy to Portugal, "Recommended Releases to Portugal of Military Assistance Program Arms and Equipment," Ref. No. A-378, Lisbon, Portugal, February 29, 1964, *DDRS*, 3.

With the passing of the Kennedy administration, the Portuguese government continued to wield the informal basing arrangement that constantly threatened the United States with expulsion as an important political tool. U.S. State Department officials moderated their overt public criticism of the Portuguese presence in Africa and vetoed UN proposals to hear motions on independence for Guinea-Bissau. Portuguese officials made it clear that they would evict the United States from the Azores should it participate in an economic embargo or not oppose international economic sanctions against the southern European state.[89] For their part, U.S. officials correctly observed that Portugal would not initiate expulsion unless pushed by particularly heavy-handed U.S. policy on Africa; that the bases continued to provide important economic benefits, especially to the underdeveloped island economies; and that this was Portugal's only substantive contribution to NATO. The United States considered its position precarious at the time, but it continued to observe the contractual status quo.

By 1970 both countries were back at the negotiating table under the Nixon administration and Prime Minister Marcelo Caetano, who had replaced Salazar. The Portuguese economy was in shambles, and the prosecution of the African campaigns was draining the Portuguese treasury.[90] Taking a cue from other countries' basing agreements with the United States, Caetano suggested that the agreement's renewal for the first time be tied to U.S. compensation in the form of low-interest economic loans for use exclusively within the Portuguese metropole.[91] American officials responded positively and, in 1971, the status quo was extended while the United States pledged to assist Portuguese development through a PL-480 economic loan/grant program and a credit from the EXIM bank.[92] This shift in Portuguese focus from international support on the colonial issue to economic assistance was underscored in a March 15, 1971, memo from the U.S. Embassy in Portugal to the State Department.

Bilaterally, we leave behind us a decade of differences about Africa into a period with possibilities for more constructive relations. In its relations with the U.S. Portugal will be influenced by the hope of assistance for Portugal's development needs. This new element in the USG-GOP relationship stems from the U.S. quid for quo of continued use of the

[89] Central Intelligence Agency, "Significance of Portuguese and Spanish Colonial Problems for the U.S.," July 11, 1963, DDRS, 2.

[90] See Spruyt 2005, 58.

[91] Department of State Telegram, "Initial Conversation with Prime Minister Caetano," Lisbon, Portugal, August 27, 1969, DDRS, 1.

[92] "Continued Stationing of American Forces at Lajes Base, Portugal," Signed in Brussels, December 9, 1971. TIAS 7254.

Azores bases. At the same time we should realize that part of the *de facto* price for staying in the Azores will be some international criticism for assisting unpopular Portugal.[93]

In October 1973 the strategic value of the Azores was dramatically under-scored when the U.S. Air Force used Lajes to conduct airlifts in its efforts to resupply Israel during the Yom Kippur War. Caetano was one of the few NATO leaders to grant the United States use rights for the campaign, but the decision exacted a heavy price as Arab producers afterward im-posed a devastating oil embargo against Portugal. The country was thrust into further domestic turmoil when Caetano was overthrown by a junior officer coup in April 1974, ushering in a volatile new era in Portuguese domestic politics and external relations.

1975–88: Democratization, Political Instability, and Hard Bargaining

The post-1974 period of turbulent democratization in Portugal had a pro-found effect on basing relations with the United States. Over the tenure of fourteen governments in Portugal from 1974 to 1983, the mainland Portuguese government consistently used its residual rights to demand that the United States increase its compensation for the use of the Azores and transfer more sovereign rights to the host nation.[94] U.S. policymakers were attentive to these proposals, not least because they perceived the nascent Portuguese democracy as susceptible to communist influences and a potential leftist takeover. Portuguese negotiators themselves remained suspicious that the United States was encouraging independence move-ments within the Azores, especially given the islands' extensive ties with Azoreans in the United States and their historically strong anti-communist sentiment.[95] Local leaders on the islands sought greater autonomy from Lisbon and demanded that they directly receive the economic aid pro-vided by the United States, concessions that were granted by the Portu-guese government in 1976.[96]

The political uncertainty in Lisbon and Portuguese decolonization con-vinced the U.S. Congress to open its coffers and provide base rights com-pensation. Between 1975 and 1986, it appropriated $299 million in grant

---

[93] U.S. Embassy to Portugal, "U.S. Policy Assessment," airgram memorandum to U.S. Department of State, Ref. 11 FAM 212.3-5, Lisbon, Portugal, March 18, 1971, *DDRS*, 1–2.

[94] On Portuguese foreign policy and democratization, see Maxwell 1997.

[95] See Monje 1992; Gallagher 1979.

[96] Marvine Howe, "Portuguese Act to Grant Some Autonomy to Islands," *New York Times*, May 1, 1976, p. 5.

aid, while total aid to Portugal reached over $1 billion.[97] In 1979, an agreement to extend the lease four more years was accompanied by a pledge to provide the Portuguese $80 million annually in economic aid, in addition to $60 million in defense articles and a one-off payment of an additional $140 million.[98] The total four-year package amounted to $420 million, a substantial increase over previous levels.[99] In addition to demanding greater compensation for the basing facilities, post-1974 Portuguese officials also assumed a greater role in restricting use rights and activities on the Atlantic islands. In April 1975, Portugal announced that the United States could no longer use its bases to supply Israel during a Middle East conflict and that the Portuguese government would explicitly have to approve all non-routine NATO operations.[100]

Similar demands dominated the following negotiations prior to the 1983 agreement. With knowledge of the compensation packages obtained by other NATO countries such as Spain, Greece, and Turkey, Portuguese negotiators demanded a complete overhaul of the 1951 agreement and a U.S. commitment to provide substantial aid packages as quid pro quo. Negotiations were further complicated by an American request to build additional installations on the Portuguese mainland. After the signing of the 1983 agreement, Portugal agreed to hold separate negotiations for U.S. rights to use the airfield at Beja on the mainland and to build a satellite tracking station in the southern Algarve region.[101]

The 1983 "Exchange of Notes," together with the accompanying 1984 "Technical Agreement," updated the 1951 agreement as the formal authorizing basis for the U.S. use of the Lajes airfield, the communications post in Sao Miguel, and the airports at Santa Maria and Ponta Delgada.[102] Article II recognized Portugal's "full sovereignty" over the Azores as well as Portugal's exclusive right to defend the islands with the commander of

---

[97] Sandars 2000, 67.

[98] The agreements on the base extension and aid were separate accords that were both signed on June 18, 1979, in Lisbon. See "Defense: Use of Facilities in the Azores," *TIAS* 10050; and "Economic and Military Assistance," *TIAS* 10869.

[99] Jonathan Darnton, "Portuguese Crisis Stalls Talks on U.S. Bases," *New York Times*, January 30, 1983, p. 7.

[100] "Portugal Places Curbs on American Base in the Azores But Backs NATO Commitment," *The Times*, April 9, 1975.

[101] "U.S. Renews Accord with Portugal to Use Air Base on Azores," *Wall Street Journal*, December 14, 1983, p. 34.

[102] "Exchange of Notes between U.S. Secretary of State George Schultz and the Minister of Foreign Affairs of Portugal, Jaime José Matos de Gama," signed in Lisbon, December 13, 1983, *TIAS* 10938; "Technical Agreement in Implementation of the Defense Agreement Between the United States of America and Portugal of 6 September 1951," signed in Lisbon, Portugal, May 18, 1984 (no *TIAS* number). Texts of both agreements are reproduced in Grimmett 1986.

Lajes airfield designated as a Portuguese national. In terms of use rights, the United States was guaranteed the unhindered right—only in support of NATO missions—to move freely between facilities in order to provide en route support of ships and aircrafts; maritime control; long-range air defense; command, control, and communications; search and rescue; and meteorological investigations. Furthermore, U.S. forces were granted the right to store and maintain conventional munitions and explosives at designated locations, and the U.S. commander was obliged to inform the commander of the Azores air command of the precise location and composition of these stores.[103] The annexes to the agreement specified in greater detail the use rights and property rights relating to construction of the facilities and established ceiling numbers for U.S. force levels and a schedule for their rotation. Consistent with other agreements reached with basing hosts at this time, the final treaty language committed the United States to use its "best efforts" to secure aid levels for Portugal that would increase yearly, although—as was typical for such agreements— the U.S. Congress retained the sole authority to appropriate compensation and assistance packages.

The final clause almost immediately generated renewed tensions between the signatories. Initially, the 1984 compensation package jumped as promised by U.S. authorities from $148 million to $208 million in 1985.[104] But as Congress slashed aid commitments to every country (bar Israel and Egypt), State Department requests for aid to Portugal were typically reduced by a third. Total aid packages decreased from $208 million in 1985 to $189 million in 1986.[105] For 1987 Congress approved an aid level of $147.4 million (the administration had asked for $224 million), with appropriations for 1988 totaling just $117 million ($163 million had been requested). Portuguese officials viewed these declines as U.S. reneging on the agreement and called for a full-blown renegotiation of the agreement in February 1988, the first day talks could commence in accordance with the 1983 renewal treaty.[106]

The ensuing renegotiations resulted in a temporary agreement between President Reagan and Prime Minister Cavaco Da Silva that pledged both countries would try and overcome their fiscal constraints by expanding the scope of the bilateral relationship. Secretary of Defense Frank Carlucci pledged to make up the difference in appropriated aid with

---

[103] "Technical Agreement," article IV.

[104] As in 1979, the compensation package is specified in a separate agreement. "Economic and Military Assistance," signed in Lisbon, December 13, 1983. *TIAS* 10939.

[105] Stanley Meisler, "U.S. Facing Dispute with Portugal over Pact on Bases," *Los Angeles Times*, December 25, 1987, p. 5.

[106] Ibid. See also Peter Wise, "Lisbon to Reopen U.S. Base Talks; Premier Seeks Increased Aid," *Washington Post*, September 12, 1987, A16.

equipment supplies. Nevertheless, on a visit to Washington in January 1990, Da Silva again expressed his dissatisfaction and formally requested a new agreement.

Diminishing Asset Specificity: 1991–2005

As with many nations hosting U.S. military installations, the collapse of the Soviet Union and the end of the cold war took away much of the bargaining leverage enjoyed by the Portuguese government. The new geopolitical climate diminished the importance of certain functions performed by the Azores, especially the anti-Soviet ASW activities, and President Clinton's Overseas Basing Commission targeted the two navy facilities in Lajes for termination in 1994 as part of its overall global reductions. That left the U.S. military only the Lajes airfield on the island.

The 1995 basing accord, which completely superseded the original 1951 agreement and its 1983 modification, reflected the diminished value of Lajes as a "specific asset." The United States terminated the direct financial quid pro quo that it had directly provided to the Azorean regional government over the previous decade (about $40 million annually) and replaced it with a series of mutual cooperation initiatives between the United States and the Azores. It also provided $173 million of American military equipment for the mainland Portuguese military.[107] The technical assistance measures included calls for increasing the supply of Azorean goods to the base, eradicating the Japanese beetle on the island of Terceira, and supporting cooperative research in higher education.[108] From the Azorean perspective, these were hardly substitutes for the annual $40 million payment to the regional government.[109] Although Lajes was used for logistics support during the Gulf and Kosovo wars, the strategic importance of Lajes has decreased considerably since the cold war era. As if to underscore its new diminished status, the European Command (EUCOM) took over the administration of the facility in 2002, effectively shifting it from being strategically located at the center of a special Atlantic command to the European periphery.[110]

The 1995 agreement has periodically cropped up in domestic Portuguese politics on a much smaller scale than it did in the 1980s. For in-

---

[107] "U.S., Portugal Sign Base Accord," *Washington Post*, June 2, 1995, A30.

[108] Final Minute, article IV, "Supplemental Minutes to the 1995 Agreement on Cooperation and Defense between the United States of America and Portugal," 1995. Provided to the authors by the U.S. Office of Defense Cooperation, Lisbon, Portugal.

[109] Luis Andrade, former special envoy of the president of the Azores and regional representative to the U.S.-Portugal Bilateral Commission, 1997–2004, interview by the authors, Terceira, Portugal, May 28, 2005.

[110] Authors' interviews with U.S. military and Azorean officials, Lisbon and Terceira, May 2005.

stance, in the run-up to the 2000 renegotiation, Portuguese president Jorge Sampaio stressed what he perceived to be an imbalance between the strategic value of Lajes and the quid pro quo received by Portugal. Sampaio voiced hopes that "the next negotiations of the bilateral cooperation accord between the U.S.A. and Portugal will make things more balanced, especially in terms of the training of the Portuguese, and in particular the Azoreans."[111] However, the bargaining power pendulum had swung against Portugal given that any increases in U.S. compensation payments would lead the United States to demand that Portugal play a more active role in a post–cold war NATO in terms of cost sharing.[112] After his election, Sampaio did nothing to follow up his renegotiation pledge, and the regional governments' attempts to revisit the issue were unsuccessful.[113]

The Lajes base briefly attained some renewed international prominence in March 2003 when it hosted a summit of the leaders of the United States, Britain, Spain, and Portugal on the eve of the U.S.-led military action in Iraq. Despite renewed protestations by regional representatives at bilateral commission meetings in 2004 and 2005 (most of them directed toward the mainland government in Lisbon) that the technical cooperation in the 1995 agreement had proven to be inadequate for the islands, neither the Americans nor Lisbon seemed interested in revisiting or renegotiating the agreement, especially as the United States realigned its force structure and reduced its overseas presence.[114]

Case Summary

The Portuguese case is not typically thought of as an example of hard bargaining over basing rights and is usually not placed in the same category as the Philippines or the other more contentious Mediterranean basing negotiations involving Spain, Greece, and Turkey. Upon closer examination, however, the evolution of U.S.-Portuguese basing agreements illustrates many of the patterns predicted by the theory of incomplete contracting (see table 4.2). Initially, under the leadership of President Salazar, Portugal granted the United States access to the Azores facilities with few restrictions or monetary demands. For these first agreements, it offered the United Kingdom and the United States full residual rights to build and use basing facilities in the Azores.

---

[111] Carom Rodeia, "Portugal: President Stresses Value of Lajes Air Base," Lisbon Diario de Noticias (Internet version), Foreign Broadcasting and Information Service (*FBIS*), Western Europe, July 14, 1999.

[112] Quoted in "Lisbon Losing Bargaining Power with U.S. over Lajes Base," Lisbon Diario de Noticias (Internet version), *FBIS*, Western Europe, August 6, 1999.

[113] Andrade interview.

[114] Office of Defense Cooperation—Portugal, "Minutes and Analytical Observations of the 18th Meeting of the Bilateral Commission," U.S. Embassy, Lisbon, May 2005.

TABLE 4.2
Evolution of U.S. Base Rights in the Azores, Portugal

Agreement Year (TIAS Ref. No.)	Duration	Facilities	Restrictions on U.S. Use Rights	Jurisdictional and Legal Issues	Quid pro Quo ($US)
1943 Portugal-UK accord	1 year	Lajes airfield (Terceira Island)	None subject to UK authority	Full U.K. control; U.S. under UK auspices	Rent-free
1944 (TIAS 2338)	6 months after the termination of WWII hostilities	Lajes airfield, Construction of Santa Maria airfield	None	Full U.S. control; permanent construction reverts to Portugal	Rent-free; pledge to return Timor to Portuguese rule
1946 (TIAS 2345)	18 months	Lajes and Santa Maria	Transit aviation for Germany and Japan	Facilities revert back to PORT.	Rent-free
1948 (TIAS 2351)	3 years, additional 2 upon mutual consent	Lajes	Transit aviation	US tours of duty limited to 12 months, Port. retains right to offer bases to UK	Rent-free
1951 (TIAS 3087)	5 years	Lajes, Santa Maria and new storage facilities throughout islands	For NATO purposes and missions	Portuguese sovereignty, special bilateral SOFA for Azores (tilted to US), NATO SOFA for mainland Portugal	Rent-free, some excess defense articles provided to Portugal.
1957 (TIAS 3950)	5 years	Same as above	For NATO purposes and missions	Same as above	Rent-free; loan of two destroyer escorts to PORT.
1963–1971, no formal accord	year to year	Same as above	For NATO purposes and missions	Same as above	Rent-free; US backs Portuguese claims over African territories
1971 (TIAS 72254)	5 years, retroactive to February 1969	Same as above, additional facilities classified	For NATO purposes and missions	Same as above	Rent-free; US backs Portuguese claims over African territories
1979 (TIAS 10050)	4 years, (9 years retroactive to 1974)	Same as above	Out-of-area missions subject to Portuguese consultation and approval	Same as above	$420m over 4 years: $80m annual grant, $60m defense articles, $140m additional payment (TIAS 10869)
1983 (TIAS 10938) 1984 technical implementation agreement	7 years	Lajes, Santa Maria, Ponta Delgada airfield, other airfields, Praia da Vitoria port, São Miguel communications installation	Same as above	More specified property rights, troop ceilings and deployment time limits, NATO SOFA on criminal jurisdiction	Aid package ranging from $150m to $225m annually (best efforts pledge); $40m of which goes directly to Azorean regional govt. budget (TIAS 10939)
1995-present	5 years; indefinite extension subject to 12 months notice of termination by either party	Lajes	Same as above	Same as above, exclusively designated as Portuguese airbase 4	End of $40m local payment; one-time $173m transfer of military equipment; series of local cooperative initiatives and technical assistance

However, after the signing of the first formal agreements, Portuguese attitudes toward U.S. use of its Azores facilities changed. The government of Portugal reasserted its residual rights of control after the war and then, twelve years later, used them to secure political concessions that were unrelated to the bases' actual NATO purpose. In the 1960s, Portugal used its residual rights over the Azores to prevent the U.S. government from denouncing Portuguese colonial policy within the international community. After the onset of democratization in 1974, Portuguese negotiators demanded significantly increased compensation packages, much in the same way as the Philippines did at the time. As Sandars writes, "Portugal had previously been concerned to gain international acceptance as a founder member of NATO. She now came to resemble the other, more recent, allies of the United States in the Mediterranean, Spain, Greece, and Turkey, who were concerned to maximize the financial return on the strategic assets needed by the Americans."[115] Lending additional bargaining power to the Portuguese position were the specific assets and irreplaceable functions undertaken by the U.S. military on the islands. By the mid-1970s, the Azores had become the primary transatlantic refueling or stopping point for aircraft and the primary center for the patrolling of Atlantic shipping lanes. A 1976 NSC memo noted the Pentagon's position on the specific assets–quid pro quo link: "a U.S. capability and willingness to respond to Portuguese requests for security assistance will be the *sine qua non* for their granting our continued peacetime presence in the Azores, and . . . there is no suitable geographic alternative for the vital ASW and other functions performed by these facilities."[116] Although Portugal became frustrated with the diminishing levels of aid provided by a thrifty U.S. Congress in the mid- and late 1980s, its call for a formal renegotiation did not translate into more compensation after the collapse of the Soviet Union. As the strategic significance and asset specificity of the Azores declined in the 1990s, a new basing accord was signed in 1995 that reflected this diminished Portuguese bargaining leverage and provided much lower levels of compensation.

The Global Defense Posture Review: The End of Specific Assets?

The logic of incomplete contracting also offers important insights into the most recent attempts by the Pentagon to fundamentally revamp its basing posture. The Global Defense Posture Review (GDPR), first introduced in 2003, calls for the most fundamental reorganization of the U.S. overseas

---

[115] Sandars 2000, 70.

[116] National Security Council, "Memorandum to the White House," [1976; exact issue date unknown], declassified January 23, 1997, *DDRS*, 15.

military basing network since World War II. The GDPR aims to establish a global network of smaller, bare-bones bases and installations, while drawing down troops from larger military bases of the cold war era in Germany, Japan, and South Korea.[117] These new bases will be termed either Forward Operating Sites (FOSs), small installations that can be rapidly expanded, or Cooperative Security Locations (CSLs), host-nation facilities with prepositioned equipment, access agreements, and logistical capabilities. Should a crisis or military need arise, U.S. planners would be able to expand these sites and rotate troops and materials through them. These FOSs and CSLs will be positioned throughout the world, including in areas where the United States has not traditionally maintained an on-shore basing presence, such as Africa, the Black Sea region, and Central Asia.[118] Washington, in other words, has sought to decrease the bargaining leverage of its basing partners by giving itself alternatives.

Strategically, the GDPR reflects the passing of the cold war era in which the basing posture was designed to fight large-scale land wars. Consistent with the U.S. National Security Strategy of 2002 and 2006, the more skeletal nature of the new facilities and their global positioning are rooted in defense planners' perceptions that force postures should be located on-shore in regional security hotspots and remain flexible and adaptable so as to cope with the new security threats of the post–September 11 era, such as terrorist networks, warlords, and criminal gangs. Accordingly, U.S. base negotiators have been demanding broad "use rights" over these facilities—what they term "strategic flexibility—while insisting that quid pro quo be kept to a minimum. In addition, a small onshore presence in different hotspots and areas where governance is poor is also deemed to be an effective way to prevent the rise of incubator states for terrorist groups, the way Afghanistan developed after the Taliban.[119]

Assessing the GDPR with Incomplete Contracting Theory

Incomplete contracting theory can illuminate some of the political logic behind the GDPR as well as flag some of its potential pitfalls. Politically, the overall logic of creating a network of smaller sites is very much consistent with the bargaining logic outlined by incomplete contracting theory. Theoretically, if new sites are of a minimal size and just one component of a substitutable chain of installations, no one particular country that hosts a site will be of vital importance or "specific" enough to potentially

---

[117] For an overview, see A. Cooley 2008, chapter 7; Overseas Basing Commission 2005; Campbell and Ward 2003.

[118] See A. Cooley 2008.

[119] See Barnett 2004. This flies in the face of the U.S. traditional role as an "offshore balancer"; see Mearsheimer 2001.

hold up U.S. operations and/or disrupt planning. Politically, U.S. planners hope to avoid a replay of the hold-up that took place in Turkey in February 2003. The Turkish government bargained hard and negotiated a $15 billion aid package in return for allowing the United States to establish a northern front for its military campaign in Iraq. However, the Turkish parliament failed to approve the measure and U.S. forces were prevented from landing.[120] Under the GDPR posture, if one particular host of an FOS or CSL demands excessive quid pro quo or unduly curtails U.S. use rights, then the United States would have the possibility of moving elsewhere, thereby undercutting such bargaining attempts *ex ante*.

But incomplete contracting also offers some cautions regarding the political feasibility of the GDPR. For one, while the GDPR aims to depoliticize each base within a broader network, this logic only holds if the nature of the military threat and operational theater remains at a global scale. However, threats and military operations, even those that are part of the "Global War on Terror," actually remain very much regionalized and localized, thus rendering certain bases and installations that may be small by absolute standards still relatively specific to that particular campaign or mission. Moreover, the ill-defined, ambiguous, and non-transparent nature of many of these FOS and CSL contracts actually renders them more incomplete and potentially subject to unilateral revision by overseas hosts than were the standard five-year renewable contracts the United States signed with its base hosts during the cold war.

Consider, for example, the recent cases of the U.S. bases in Kyrgyzstan (Ganci airbase in Manas airport) and Uzbekistan (Karshi-Khanabad airbase or "K2"). Both installations were rapidly established after September 11 to support combat, surveillance, and humanitarian missions in neighboring Afghanistan.[121] With each facility retaining the capacity to house 1,000–2,000 U.S. military personnel, both were considered representative of the type of FOSs that the United States wanted to establish globally.[122] Yet in July 2005, the Uzbek government actually evicted the United States in response to U.S. criticisms of its heavy-handed crackdown on anti-government demonstrators in the eastern city of Andijon.[123] Soon after the expulsion, Uzbekistan signed a security cooperation agreement with Russia, a country that had staunchly backed the heavy-

[120] See Richard Boudreaux, "The Reasons Turkey Rejected U.S.," *Los Angeles Times*, March 3, 2003.

[121] See A. Cooley 2008, 2005b.

[122] See, for example, Cornell 2004, 6; Ann Scott Tyson, "New U.S. Strategy: 'Lily Pad' Bases: U.S. Forces Are Repositioning Overseas Forces, Opting for Smaller, Transitory Bases in Places Like Kyrgyzstan," *Christian Science Monitor*, August 10, 2004, p. 6.

[123] A. Cooley 2005b.

handed tactics of the Karimov government. In Russia, Uzbekistan found an alternative contracting partner to the United States, one that would not criticize or threaten its regime authority, and did not hesitate to break the relationship.

As a result of the Uzbek eviction, certain base functions and operations were transferred to neighboring Kyrgyzstan and Ganci airbase. However, for about a year after the K2 eviction, the new Kyrgyz government led by Kurmanbek Bakiyev—successor to former president Akayev, who was swept out of office by pro-democracy protestors in March 2005—demanded a renegotiation of the terms of the initial Akayev-era accord and a substantial increase in economic benefits, including a hundred-fold increase in the $2 million annual rent paid by the United States.[124] After a prolonged negotiation, the two sides concluded a renegotiated five-year deal in July 2006, one that increased rental payments of the base to $20 million annually and promised a total of $150 million in annual fees and government assistance to be paid by the U.S. government to the Kyrgyz Republic.[125] Kyrgyz officials expect any extension of the agreement beyond 2010 to also be subject to hard bargaining and a possible increase in quid pro quo.[126] Despite K2's relatively small size, its loss and the resulting increased value of Ganci for the ongoing campaign in Afghanistan afforded Kyrgyz negotiators significant residual rights and bargaining leverage that they exploited in their subsequent renegotiation. This behavior is consistent with the expectations of our incomplete contracting model.

Conclusion

This chapter has applied concepts from the theory of incomplete contracting to offer an explanation of the politics of U.S. overseas basing arrangements that differs from those offered by prevailing theories of international relations. The United States was able to establish a global network of military installations by entering into a series of incomplete

---

[124] See Vladimir Socor, "Kyrgyzstan Asks for Manifold Increase in U.S. Payments for Manas," *Jamestown Foundation Eurasian Daily Monitor*, January 26, 2006. Available at http://jamestown.org/edm/article.php?article_id=2370703.

[125] Officially, and consistent with past practice, the United States does not regard the $150 million as a base rights quid pro quo. By contrast, Kyrgyz officials do interpret the agreement and the figure as a base rights package. Authors' interviews with U.S. and Kyrgyz officials, Bishkek, Kyrgyzstan, January 2008. The public announcement of the July 2006 diplomatic exchange of notes can be found on the U.S. Embassy to Kyrgyzstan's Web site: http://bishkek.usembassy.gov/july_14_joint_statement_on_coalition_airbase.html.

[126] Authors' interviews with Kyrgyz officials, Bishkek, Kyrgyzstan, January 2008.

contracts with allies and partners. As these contracts came up for renegotiation, host countries used their residual rights of control to extract quasi-
rents in the form of monetary and/or political concessions from the United
States. Even longstanding allies and partners of the United States engaged
in hard bargaining over the use of these military assets.

As the detailed case studies of the Philippines and Portugal demonstrate, such behavior is dramatically at odds with both structural realist
and constructivist theories of international relations. In both case studies,
host countries engaged in calculated hard bargaining and threatened the
United States with expulsion. Similarly, common perceptions of identity
or security communities did not inhibit these countries from behaving in
a predatory and rent-seeking fashion vis-à-vis the United States. More
detailed case studies are needed to validate this approach, and there may
be some cases that do not conform to the rent-seeking pattern (most notably, cases like Britain and Germany where joint security gains have persisted absent quid pro quo). Nevertheless, we hope to have shown that
the incomplete contracting framework has important insights to offer the
study of U.S. overseas basing and, more broadly, the study of security
contracts in international relations.

Nor should the approach be limited to cold war cases. Although the
end of the cold war has altered the overall security priorities for the United
States, the current GDPR will offer important organizational and political
challenges that are consistent with the incomplete contracting model, as
shown by recent developments in U.S. base relations with Uzbekistan
and Kyrgyzstan. Similar types of hard bargaining over quid pro quo have
also characterized U.S. relations with Djibouti, which since 2002 has
hosted a strategically important U.S. FOS on the Horn of Africa.[127] Beyond the GDPR, the United States is also likely to confront similar dilemmas regarding bases and bargaining in the future in Afghanistan and
Iraq, especially as it withdraws troops and consolidates and legalizes its
presence on a more contractual basis. Finally, new global defense initiatives may still necessitate negotiations over specific assets and their
positioning. For example, the Bush administration's development of a
National Missile Defense (NMD) will necessitate establishing an overseas
network of sites to position NMD installations. As such, we would expect
countries that will host future NMD facilities eventually to replicate the
bargaining tactics and demands discussed in this chapter.[128] Indeed, by
late 2007, both Poland and the Czech Republic, as potential future hosts
of NMD interceptors and radars, had adopted new demands for quid

---

[127] The terms of the U.S.-Djibouti basing deal, including compensation arrangements,
remain classified.

[128] ON NMD negotiations and Greenland, see Archer 2003; Dragsdahl 2001.

pro quo from the United States for accepting missile defense installations, including requests for bilateral security guarantees, substantial military assistance, and the upgrading of their air defenses.[129] As with other cases of transferred sovereignty, negotiations for overseas U.S. military installations have followed the logic of incomplete contracting, even as military technologies, strategy, and the international system have fundamentally changed.

[129] See Judy Dempsey, "Poland and Czech Republic Will Coordinate Negotiations on Defense Shield," *International Herald Tribune*, January 10, 2008.

Incomplete Contracting and Modalities of Regional Integration

Introduction

In the preceding chapters we explored how states negotiated transfers of sovereignty over territory and installations in bilateral settings. How did France negotiate a decolonization agreement with Algeria that allowed it to maintain military bases and to exploit hydrocarbons in its former colony? How did the Philippines and the United States apportion the sovereignty of U.S. military installations on Philippine territory? How did Russia sign agreements with some of the Union Republics that left the Baikonur cosmodrome and military installations in Russian hands? All of these agreements transformed previously hierarchical relations into hybrid sovereignty relations among independent states.

In this chapter we inquire whether incomplete contracting theory can shed light on the converse. What kinds of institutions do states design when they transfer sovereignty toward a more hierarchical relationship, as occurs in regional integration? Regional integration agreements differ in various respects from the incomplete contracts we discussed in earlier chapters. In those cases, the parties tried to reach a bilateral agreement regarding the particular division of control and use rights following territorial separation. Each was particularly concerned with the bargaining leverage that would flow to the holder of the residual rights of control. By contrast, in the case of regional integration, particularly when it incorporates some elements of supranational decision making, states have to decide whether and to what degree a new actor, the regional organization, will acquire rights held previously by the member states. We thus investigate whether the theory has explanatory power in a different set of issue areas and cases from those we have discussed so far. In this sense we investigate the scope of the deductive propositions that we developed in chapters 1 and 2.[1]

Aside from the potential introduction of a supranational entity, this chapter also extends the discussions in the previous chapters by demonstrating the relevance of incomplete contracting theory in understanding

---

[1] For a discussion of probing the extension of one's theory to other cases, see Laitin 1999.

multilateral agreements rather than bilateral accords (although NAFTA started out as a bilateral agreement between Canada and the United States) and by examining the transfer of sovereignty in areas that do not primarily involve transaction-specific assets.

The number of sovereign functions ceded by states to regional organizations and the depth of this integration vary considerably across regional institutions. When regional organizations pool sovereign functions such as monetary policy, trade policy, and legal jurisdiction, they provide particularly salient examples of modes of governance that constitute neither anarchical nor purely hierarchical relations.[2] In other instances regional integration resembles standard intergovernmental contracting, with sovereignty residing with the independent states.

Among the many regional organizations, the European Union (EU) has been the most far-reaching. Today its twenty-seven members make up the largest economic community in the world. But NAFTA, the Latin American Mercosur, and Asian regional organizations such as the Association of South East Asian Nations (ASEAN) and the Asian Pacific Economic Community (APEC) have all affected state autonomy to various degrees.

The EU's evolution, institutions, and governance have been extensively analyzed by scholars. For our purposes, we will concentrate on the formation of the European Coal and Steel Community (ECSC) in 1951 and particularly on the creation of the European Economic Community (EEC) in 1957. The institutional choices made at that time laid the basis for the extensive sovereign transfers found in the current EU. We will contrast regional integration in Europe with NAFTA by focusing on the formative phases of both, and clarify why they continue to look so different today.

No institution has blurred the distinction of anarchy and hierarchy more than the EU.[3] Indeed, even when the EEC still stood in its infancy, Jean Monnet proclaimed that already 80 percent of state policies resided at the European Community level. Perhaps Monnet had reasons of his own to claim the supremacy of Community institutions, but it cannot be gainsaid that today, trade policy, labor directives, and fiscal and monetary policies have increasingly come under Community discretion. Fifty years after its formation, the EU shows considerable vertical integration and a high level of supranational decision making over an increased number of issue areas and functions. Yet the foundational agreement that

---

[2] Sbragia (1992) sees in this pooling of sovereignty in the EU a hybrid form between the anarchy of sovereign states and the creation of hierarchy and a new (federal) state.

[3] The European Union has been the name of the organization since the Treaty of Maastricht (1992). Depending on the time frame to which the particular segment of our narrative refers, we will focus on the European Economic Community (EEC) or the European Community (EC).

formed the EEC in the Treaty of Rome in 1957 was remarkably sparse and functioned as a classic incomplete contract. Andrew Moravcsik thus rightly labels the treaty a "framework agreement."[4] Giandomenico Majone notes that "A relational contract settles for a general agreement that frames the entire relationship, recognizing that it is impossible to concentrate all the relevant bargaining action at the *ex ante* contracting stage. The Rome Treaty, for example, may be conceived of as a relational contract."[5] Consequently, we classify the European integration process as a case of incomplete contracting with creation of supranational or third-party institutions.

We compare and contrast the European foundational agreement with NAFTA. Although arguably the most institutionalized regional organization after the EU, it demonstrates a low degree of transfers of sovereignty to supranational decision making and a much higher degree of *ex ante* precision in legislation. Frederick Abbott thus observes, "NAFTA embodies a high degree of precision and obligation and a moderate degree of delegation of decision making authority. The European Union, in contrast, embodies a high degree of obligation and delegation and a moderate level of precision."[6]

Indeed, European integration from the outset looked markedly different. The brevity of original treaties, wide in scope but short on details, contrasts with the length of the North American agreement (that originated between Canada and the United States in 1987 followed by Mexican accession in 1994), which was far more limited in its aims but highly detailed. The European states embarked on their course with many of the details still to be worked out. Important elements of European integration, such as the Common Agricultural Policy (1962), the relation of European laws to national laws, and regulations on fiscal policy, only emerged years after the 1957 Treaty of Rome.

The level of supranational decision making in the European case was also higher from the outset. The ECSC institutionalized supranationality through the High Commission and was intended to regulate the key coal and steel sectors of the Western European economy.[7] Similarly, supranational decision making expanded in the years after the beginning of the Community—even if the organization had to deal with periodic setbacks

---

[4] Moravcsik 1998, 152, 157.

[5] Majone 2005, 73. He observes, furthermore, that in relational contracting parties do not agree on detailed plans but on general principles, on the criteria to be used to decide unforeseen contingencies, on who has the power to act, and on dispute settlement mechanisms (72, 73).

[6] See Abbott 2000, 519.

[7] The locus classicus is Haas 2004 [1958]. Also see Mikesell 1958; R. Gordon 1962.

such as the Luxembourg compromise in 1965 that seemingly gave individual states veto rights. Similarly, the European Commission was created to promote European objectives rather than narrow state interests (the latter were to be represented by the Council of Ministers), and with multiple directorates and a large bureaucracy, it lacks any equivalent in NAFTA.

Their respective judicial milieus also differ markedly. The European Court of Justice (ECJ) has taken a key role in codifying these transfers of sovereignty by asserting the supremacy of EU law over national legislation to the extent that some observers suggest "governments do not control legal integration in any determinative sense and therefore cannot control European integration more broadly."[8] Arbitration in NAFTA, by contrast, remains an intergovernmental, not supranational, ad hoc settlement mechanism. Indeed, any claim to the contrary would meet an American constitutional challenge. NAFTA thus constitutes a case of intergovernmental agreements with complete contracting.

This chapter thus focuses on two key questions. First, what explains the institutional variation between NAFTA and the EU? Simply put, why does the creation of NAFTA look like a set of intergovernmental complete contracts while the creation of the European Community looks like a set of incomplete contracts with transfers to supranational entities? Second, what consequences do these different modes of contracting have on the subsequent institutional development of these organizations?

This chapter starts with a discussion of some of the literature that, following Oliver Williamson's work, suggests the level of integration might be partially explained by the degree of exchange of transaction-specific assets. This is a useful starting point. However, we will argue that although both NAFTA and the EU have led to frequent state interactions and the subsequent exchange of transaction-specific assets, both modes of organization, from their origin to the present, have differed markedly.

We subsequently suggest that incomplete contracting theory can more accurately shed light on the various modalities of regional integration. Governments, and the constituencies they represent, have to balance a variety of competing objectives. On the one hand regional integration aims at economic gains by pooling some aspects of state sovereignty. Yet simultaneously, states fear hard bargaining by stronger members in future specification and delineation of the agreement if elements of the contract are left underspecified.

---

[8] Stone Sweet and Brunell 1998, 73. They submit that intergovernmentalists, who argue that the EU institutions cater to and are the epiphenomenal result of negotiations aimed to foster state interests, are wrong. See also the discussions in Burley and Mattli 1993; Alter 1998, 2000.

More specifically, following the logic of our incomplete contracting perspective, contracting parties will be concerned with the bargaining leverage accruing to the holder of residual rights of control. If member states are the holders of the residual rights (the ability to specify the terms of the incomplete contract at $t + 1$), then contracting parties will be particularly concerned with asymmetric bargaining advantages for the more powerful states. If residual rights are held by international organizations or third parties (such as the supranational institutions in the EU), governments will be concerned with the bargaining leverage that flows to such institutions as time progresses. And, following our logic, once supranational institutions acquire residual rights, they will use them to delineate and institutionalize the new scope of their authority.

We discuss three issues. First, we clarify the divergent motives for political elites that led to the formation of the ECSC in 1951, the EEC in 1957, the Free Trade Agreement (FTA) in 1987, and NAFTA in 1994. Admittedly, these factors are exogenous to contracting theory proper. For example, some of these variables, such as the German reunification question, are clearly idiosyncratic to the case at hand. We do not claim to provide new insights into the European or North American states' motivations to contract with each other. We leave in the middle whether one can prove that geopolitical concerns mattered less than commercial concerns as Moravcsik avers, which runs counter to Mahant's account, or whether Moravcsik's explanation of motives differs greatly from Alan Milward's account.[9] We instead build on the insights from various authors to show how motives influenced rational elites to choose particular allocations of residual rights of control. We then attempt to show that the choices for such allocation had downstream consequences.

Second, we turn to the question of institutional design, especially regarding elite concerns about the allocation of residual rights. Here we capitalize on the insights of an incomplete contracting perspective. Given that residual rights were allocated differently in the two cases we discuss, we would expect the institutional designs to address the concerns of the parties ceding such rights.

Third, we argue that due to the divergent allocation of such rights at their foundation, the subsequent trajectories of these organizations show marked divergence rather than convergence. We thus argue that expectations following from an incomplete contracting approach suggest that NAFTA will continue to resemble clear-in and clear-out specific contracting, little vertical integration, a high degree of *ex ante* legislation, and only ad hoc arbitration. The European integrative process, by contrast,

---

[9] Mahant 2004; Milward 1992; Moravcsik 1998. On the importance of European elites and the ideational construction of the European project, see Parsons 2003.

will continue to exemplify incomplete contracting, *ex post* legislation, and supranational adjudication over sovereign issues and functions.

In our final segment we will clarify how our views differ from realist and ideational accounts. Moreover, we submit that an incomplete contracting approach provides an alternative perspective of the role of courts in this process, particularly of the European Court of Justice. More specifically, such an approach differs from principal-agent perspectives that see the Court as merely an agent acting at the behest of national governments.[10] Accordingly, this chapter not only illustrates the theoretical expectations of incomplete contracting theory but also makes a contribution in its own right to understanding the underlying organizational dynamics of European integration.

Regional Integration and Williamsonian Contracting Theory

As discussed in our earlier theory chapters, Oliver Williamson explains governance structure among firms as a function of uncertainty, the frequency of transactions, and asset specificity. Firms will tend to integrate vertically when they interact frequently, when their interactions involve a high degree of uncertainty, and when their contracts cover transaction-specific assets.[11] Similarly, governments will create formal governance structures, with rules, norms and procedures, to regulate interstate relations that are frequent and that involve transaction-specific assets.[12]

A similar logic might be used to explain regional integration. Following Williamson's contracting model, transaction specificity and the frequency of interaction will determine the depth of integration and the degree to which formal hierarchy is exercised by a supranational institution. The various agreements that created and subsequently expanded the EEC to its current form have increased investments of transaction-specific assets, and public and private actors have expended considerable costs adjusting to EEC legislation and harmonization. The frequency of transactions between the contracting parties has also risen, as evinced by increased intraregional trade and cross-border mergers and investments. Katja Weber, for example, fruitfully uses a transaction cost approach to explain why firms in the EU would prefer integration and vertical control. She extrapolates then from firm preferences to explain state policies in favor of further integration.[13]

[10] For arguments that see the Court as relatively constrained, see Garrett 1995; Garrett, Keleman, and Schulz 1998.

[11] O. Williamson 1985, 1986.

[12] Yarbrough and Yarbrough 1992; Frieden 1994.

[13] Weber 2000. See also Weber and Hallerberg 2001.

At first glance then the Williamson model adequately explains the increasing levels of supranational decision making (in the expanded powers of the Commission, the increase in majority decision making), and the expansion of European Court of Justice prerogatives. However, although powerful in many respects, the Williamsonian perspective leaves several key questions unanswered.

First, it does not clarify whether hierarchy precedes or follows from greater cross-border transaction specificity.[14] Transaction-specific arguments demonstrate correlation between hierarchy and the nature of assets but do not clarify the causal chain. This is particularly relevant in regional integration. No doubt the development of the EU has shown an increase in transaction-specific investments across European borders, but did this cause the trend toward greater supranationality or did the development of EU institutions entice private actors to make such investments?

We argue that the mode of contracting and the degree of delegation to new institutional sites determine the subsequent integration process. In signing an incomplete contract, the contracting parties required credible commitments from their partners to minimize reneging or hold-up. In finding a supranational solution to the problems of incomplete contracting and the need for credible commitments, the European arrangements *logically* propelled subsequent cross-border investment.

Second, unlike the executives of firms, political elites do not merely seek to maximize the economic benefits for their states. Strategic politicians fear a loss of office and diminishing autonomy. Even if regional integration might yield significant economic gains,[15] governments will fear other more powerful states when it comes to future distributions of such gains, or fear a supranational authority that might contradict national political objectives. Moreover, information difficulties and uncertainty will diminish the possibility of complete contracting, particularly as the time horizon lengthens. Governments will likely refrain from engaging in potentially costly vertical integration if the future is uncertain and gains may be distributed asymmetrically. Politicians will fear hold-up by the other partners. Consequently, political elites will concentrate on how rights are allocated in regional contracts. Who holds the residual rights, and who will have bargaining leverage in subsequent rounds of negotiations? Our contracting model thus takes into account how politi-

---

[14] This problem arises, for example, in Frieden 1994. As Frieden recognizes, transaction specificity and hierarchy no doubt correlate but the causality of which influences which is difficult to disentangle. Process tracing might provide a partial answer to such quandaries.

[15] The Cecchini report, for example, predicted an overall 4.5–7 percent GDP growth in the EC (Emerson et al. 1988). Likewise, Mexico anticipated significant economic gains from NAFTA (Cameron and Tomlin 2000).

cal elites engage in a broader calculus regarding economic gains and the possibility of hold-up.

Third, Williamsonian theory suggests that regional governance forms differ simply because of the nature of the assets exchanged and the frequency of transactions. Thus, we would expect regional organizations only to diverge in the degree of vertical integration, not in their institutional logic. If NAFTA shows less supranational integration than the EU this must be the result of lower transaction-specific investments. Over time with increasing cross-border investments one would expect it to resemble the EU.

That expectation is incorrect. The logic of European integration differed from the beginning. The ECSC was devised from the outset as a supranational institution. The EEC in 1957 already contained elements that required more supranational decision making in the near future—even if some states were hesitant to embrace such aspects. Moreover, within just a few years after the creation of the EEC, the European Court proclaimed the supremacy of EEC legislation over national legislation in landmark cases such as Costa Enel and Van Gend and Loos. In NAFTA no such supremacy is in sight two decades after the FTA emerged in 1987. The scope of the agreement remains unchanged. Nor has NAFTA created the supranational bureaucracy and legislative institutions that emerged immediately with the birth of the EEC, Euratom, and ECSC.

In short, NAFTA was, and remains, an intergovernmental agreement with residual rights remaining with national governments. In the EEC, by contrast, states from the outset devised plans to grant some residual rights to supranational entities with subsequent agreements yet to be negotiated. The key distinction between NAFTA and European integration lies in how rights were allocated from the start and in the degree to which the former is a complete contract and the latter an incomplete one. The remainder of this chapter thus aims to clarify the motives behind the original institutional designs and the subsequent consequences of those institutional choices.

An Incomplete Contracting Approach to Regional Integration

We argue that incomplete contracting theory addresses some of the weaknesses in Williamsonian theory. Regional integration exemplifies various features of incomplete contracting. The duration of the contract extends over time, the environment of the negotiating parties is susceptible to change, and the contract contains no "clear-in and clear-out." Indeed, the very notion of contract performance remains open to interpretation.

Furthermore, while political elites may claim credit for the increased provision of public goods and economic growth that has resulted from regionalization,[16] the size and distribution of such benefits in the future is opaque. Actors might, therefore, constantly try to renegotiate the terms of the contract to deal with new and exogenous changes in their environment. Other scholars have similarly noted the incomplete character of European integration and how EU institutions have used new broad directives to expand and then consolidate their power.[17] Moravcsik submits that the pooling and delegation of sovereignty "can be viewed as solutions to the problem of 'incomplete contracting.'" He also notes that without such delegation and pooling, it becomes "more difficult to structure intertemporal trade-offs. Issues must be negotiated in large unwieldy bundles."[18] The latter situation, we suggest, typifies the NAFTA agreement. While negotiating the contours for the North American agreement, the contracting parties found it difficult to engage in intertemporal trade-offs. Thus the agreement required the actors to specify terms in great detail even if the agreement covered far fewer areas of integration than the European accord. We build on these insights to show how an incomplete contracting perspective can shed light on the institutional variation and the consequences of assigning (or not assigning) residual rights to regional organizations.

A Priori Expectations and Varieties of Regional Integration

The nature of the contract and the degree of delegation to a new institutional site will first of all depend on the relative power of the contracting parties. Governments of weak states will be concerned with the exercise of asymmetric power by the more powerful members.[19] Even intermediate range powers, such as Britain, have been reluctant to surrender sovereign prerogatives out of concerns that France and Germany would dictate EU policy. What holds true for Britain holds a fortiori for smaller states.

But all states will also be concerned that regional institutions might acquire more residual rights as the integration process proceeds. Thus,

---

[16] Mattli (1999) demonstrates this well for the EU. Winham (1988) clarifies the Canadian logic for concluding the Canadian-U.S. Free Trade Agreement (CUSFTA, also simply FTA), while Cameron and Tomlin (2000) provide a detailed account of Mexican motives.

[17] Pollack 1997, 104. Hix (2002) suggests that an incomplete contracting view can shed light on the expansion of the powers of the European Parliament in the last decade.

[18] Moravcsik 1998, 74.

[19] This can largely be determined simply by the relative size of the respective economies. The larger state will have more means of leverage over the smaller state. Note that Moravcsik (1998, 7) speaks alternately of relative power and asymmetric interdependence. That is, countries that stand to gain the most from regional integration, usually smaller countries, will be more likely to make concessions in order to finalize an agreement.

member states such as Britain are now also concerned with the supranational institutions within the EU decision-making process that have residual rights of control and retain the potential for a subsequent unsanctioned expansion in jurisdictional authority.

Power asymmetries, and concerns about expansionist international institutions, thus influence actors' calculations in deciding whether regional arrangements should take on a supranational or intergovernmental character and whether the agreement should take the form of a complete or an incomplete contract. In bilateral settings, this is relatively clear. The holder of residual rights of control, usually the host country, will have bargaining leverage over the home (or investing) country. With regional agreements, sovereign states initially are the holders of residual rights. They have to decide whether to relinquish residual rights of control over various functions or issue areas (i.e., create a supranational entity) or whether to retain their residual rights (as in an intergovernmental agreement). They also have to decide whether they wish to leave the contract relatively open-ended, and thus subject to *ex post* contracting, or write—as close as possible—a complete contract *ex ante*, that is, a fully specified contract at the time of signing.

We thus have four sets of possible outcomes for states that pursue regional economic integration. With intergovernmental complete contracts, states retain residual rights, and the contract is fully specified *ex ante*. This process describes regional agreements such as NAFTA or the more recent Central American Free Trade Agreement (CAFTA). An intergovernmental incomplete contract confers bargaining leverage in bilateral cases to the holder of residual rights—in our previous cases this entailed the holder of residual rights to transaction-specific assets. In cases of regional integration incomplete contracting would confer bargaining leverage to the more powerful economies. Postcolonial economic blocs that are established and dominated by the former metropole power would fit this cell. For instance, this would describe France's role in the CFA Franc Zone in West Africa or Russia's economic dominance of the Commonwealth of Independent States (CIS) and its successor European Economic Community (EURASEC) customs union.[20] In supranational complete contracting, the states confer residual rights to a new institutional site or international organization, but fully specify the terms of the contract *ex ante* with little further development beyond the original terms. The World Trade Organization (WTO), with its bounded authority over trade issues and regularly used dispute settlement mechanism, does not amount to a full transfer to a third party but goes further than the ad hoc arbitration

---

[20] For a comparative discussion of post-imperial economic integration and disengagement, see Abdelal 2001.

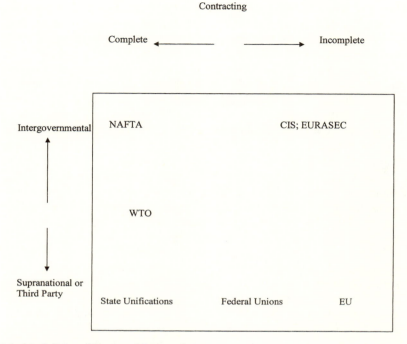

5.1. Modalities of Regional Integration.

that typifies the NAFTA agreement.[21] Although the WTO dispute settlement mechanism is partially based on the earlier NAFTA procedures, it differs in that the WTO has a standing permanent organ—the Appellate Body—whereas NAFTA arbitration panels remain ad hoc.[22]

Extending even beyond that point, parties may relinquish their independent status and agree to form a new unit with a distinct authority structure as occurs, for example, when previously independent units merge to form a new state or strong federal union. They may sign a complete contract, fully allocating authority to the new entity, especially if they seek to lock in commitments of other states.[23]

---

[21] As Drezner (2007) notes, even realists concede that the dispute settlement body of the WTO constitutes a significant case of supranational authority when enforcing decisions that go against powerful states.

[22] Thus the WTO system establishes a permanent international judicial body, whereas NAFTA establishes a quasi-judicial body or arbitral panels. See the classification in the Project on International Courts and Tribunals, available at http://www.pict-pcti.org/publi cations/synoptic_chart/synoptic_chart1.htm. Also see http://www.wto.org/english/tratop _e/dispu_e/dispu_e.htm#dsb.

[23] Rector 2003.

Finally, with incomplete contracting and the creation of supranational institutions, the contract develops dynamically over time with institutional reconfiguration at the supranational level. Which of these is likely to develop in practice?

Explaining Institutional Choice: Preferences, Relative Power, and Demand Symmetry

The institutional design of regional organizations will depend on the actors' initial preferences, their relative power and symmetry in demand. Accounting for preferences alone does not provide a sufficient explanation. Even if states are similarly predisposed towards integration, power asymmetries and variation in economic interdependence (asymmetry in demand) will lead to different institutional choices across regions.

If states were to pursue regional integration through incomplete contracts that leave considerable residual rights with the individual members, then the more powerful states will likely seek to reinterpret and redraft the initial terms of the agreement. Less powerful actors that agree to the incomplete contract at time t must fear subsequent defection and the bargaining leverage of the more powerful state at time $t + 1$. Weak states will thus prefer a complete contract, making subsequent negotiations less important. We expect them only to consent to an incomplete contract if the larger and more powerful economic actors credibly bind themselves through supranational institutions.

By contrast, a powerful state will be less inclined to favor an incomplete contract with considerable powers vested in supranational institutions. Such an arrangement would diminish the position of the stronger state and subject it to external, third-party legislation and adjudication. That is, if residual rights flowed to a supranational entity, the bargaining leverage of the stronger power would diminish. Ceteris paribus, such a state would prefer incomplete contracts without supranational authority, as Russia has pursued in the CIS. Concerns over bargaining leverage and power asymmetries thus inevitably raise the issue of credible commitment. If the more powerful states want smaller states to contract with them they must credibly bind their authority. Even though the weaker powers might gain from an incomplete contract they will be reluctant to surrender some sovereign rights without mechanisms to constrain the more powerful actors. Supranational delegation is one way of signaling future compliance by stronger states, but if power asymmetries are stark, as in a hegemonic environment, the stronger power will not consent to such constraints of its autonomy. This generates the following corollary to our earlier propositions regarding credible commitment (table 2.1).

C3: In regional integration agreements the larger economies face credibility of commitment problems.

The powerful economic actor must thus weigh the benefits it gains from regional integration against the costs of surrendering some sovereign rights. If the demand for regional integration largely originates from the weaker economies, then the stronger state(s) will not consent to the creation of new institutional sites but will retain residual rights of control. The stronger state will thus be willing to sign an intergovernmental agreement given the gains from trade liberalization but will not surrender sovereign prerogatives. Weaker states without such supranational binding mechanisms will in such situations push for complete contracts, with intergovernmental complete contracting as the result.[24] In lieu of an agreement on supranational institutions, stark power asymmetries will thus yield complete contracting without supranationality. We expect *ex ante* legislation (full specification and high formalization), little third-party arbitration and adjudication, and weak institutionalization beyond the intergovernmental level. This yields a final corollary.

C4: Given credibility problems in regional integration, small states will opt for complete contracting unless the powerful states agree to transfer residual rights to a third party.

Conversely, regional organizations with modest power asymmetries will more likely yield *ex post* legislation (low specificity and formalization in the founding document), more third-party arbitration and adjudication, and a higher degree of supranational decision making. The stronger states will be more inclined to acquiesce to binding, supranational institutions through which they can credibly commit, partially because balancing coalitions are possible. Modest power asymmetries will make such commitments more credible and thus small states will be more willing to leave negotiation to future, *ex post* decision making.

Besides initial preferences and concerns with relative power, demand symmetry will influence the nature of the contract and the degree of supranational institutionalization. The state in which the demand for integration is lower than in other states will have bargaining leverage over the actors whose demand for integration is high. Thus, if the weaker states have more to gain from integration, given that they stand to gain the

---

[24] In addition the number of contracting actors might mitigate the relative salience of power asymmetries by facilitating countervailing alliances. This in turn will make it easier to create institutional binding mechanisms. Our conclusion would correspond with the hypothesis of Koremenos, Lipson, and Snidal (2001, 794) that larger numbers tend to correlate with more centralized institutional mechanisms or quasi-legislative institutions that are empowered to adjust the agreement. However, they attribute this to renegotiation costs.

most from access to larger economies, then the latter will be in a stronger bargaining position and reluctant to surrender residual rights of decision making. Conversely, if both weak and powerful states stand to gain in roughly equivalent fashion, the stronger economies will be more pliable. They will be more willing to surrender rights as the costs of contracting with lesser states that fear defection.[25]

Bargaining over Sovereignty in European Integration

Throughout its history European integration has had to deal with many unforeseen issues. Indeed, writing in 1958 one observer even doubted whether the Treaty of Rome would stand the test of new challenges and that "a general crisis, arising for example from a major recession, might cause the Treaty almost to become a dead letter."[26] But, to the contrary, the European Economic Community of the late 1950s transformed itself into a much larger organization, covering much more than just trade liberalization and acquiring many more members.

As neo-functionalist theory recognized early on, regional integration inevitably brought issue linkage and the extension of decision making to many new areas. For example, the EEC treaty of 1957 outlined the desire to reduce internal tariffs, create a common external tariff, and reduce unfair competition; further trade liberalization required the creation of the Common Agricultural Policy by 1962 and attempts to regulate exchange rate stability. The subsequent moves to free trade in all factors of production has propelled the EU to tackle numerous other issues such as pension payments, gender equality, mutual recognition of standards, monetary union, and the movement of peoples and refugees. While expressing their interest in "ever closer union," the contracting parties of 1957 could hardly foresee the many dimensions that EU integration would have.[27]

Exogenous shocks and crises have also played a role. For example, the various enlargements have been driven by external events, such as the fall of the Mediterranean authoritarian regimes in the mid-1970s and the breakup of the Eastern Bloc in the late 1980s. Particularly the latter, and the "big bang" extension of the EU to ten Eastern European states, could

---

[25] Moravcsik (1998) uses different terminology but argues similarly that asymmetric interdependence determines concessions. Those who stood to gain the most made the most concessions.

[26] Hurtig 1958, 381.

[27] Overviews of the early stages of European integration and its various institutions are too numerous to count, but see, for example, Archer 1990; Dinan 1999; S. George 1985; Harrop 1989.

hardly be anticipated by the original contracting parties of 1957, or even by the drafters of the Single European Act of 1986.[28] In the midst of all this, states had to face oil crises and economic downturns.

Despite early pessimism, the six-member state organization of 1957 has blossomed into a vibrant continent-wide organization, with substantial powers delegated to supranational institutions. The institutional design of the European "Founding Fathers" has played a significant role in producing these outcomes. The initial constitutive treaty remained relatively brief. Contrary to the NAFTA agreement (thousands of pages in its original form), the EEC agreement reflected statements of principle. Subsequent details were filled in by national and supranational lawmaking bodies. The development of the *acquis communautaire*—the body of rules that comprised treaty laws and a host of subsequent secondary legislation—would be a key element in settling the details for the future.

Given the uncertainties of final objectives and ultimate ends of the nascent regional organization, member states opted for little *ex ante* legislation. Indeed, the open-endedness of the treaty conveniently allowed member states to sidestep difficult decisions that would likely precipitate opposition from domestic constituents. For example, as long as the exact degree of supranational decision making, or the level of social harmonization, remained vague French decision makers could get around opposition in the Assemblée.

This level of *ex ante* legislation, however, required members to rely on *ex post* arbitration and supranational decision making, particularly through the Commission. At first, the European Court of Justice was expected to only play a relatively minor part in the process.[29] Nevertheless, the Court has taken on roles heretofore unforeseen. Key principles and Community legislative supremacy emerged without clear stipulation by the national governments that Community law would be supranational and have direct effect. In other words, not dissimilar in impact to such American landmark cases as *Marbury v. Madison* or *Martin v. Hunter's Lessee*, the ECJ appropriated an entirely new realm of authority for itself, with the ECJ at the judicial pinnacle.[30]

European integration thus started from the outset as an incomplete contract that delegated some residual rights to supranational authorities. Why did the European states agree to do so? What were the procedural elements of this constitutive agreement that gave the states confidence in

---

[28] On the determinants of EU expansion into Eastern Europe, see Vachudova 2005.

[29] Moravcsik 1998, 155.

[30] One could see the U.S. Constitution as an example of incomplete contracting as well. Because of the brevity and vagueness of the founding document, the Supreme Court *had to* step in as a supreme arbitrator and settle many issues *ex post*.

assigning certain residual rights to supranational institutions? And what have been the consequences of these institutional designs in the long run?

To answer such questions we must start with the foundation of the ECSC and subsequently the EEC in the 1950s. The choices made at that juncture influenced the European trajectory over the next five decades.

The Motives of the Contracting Parties

European political elites, commercial interests, and the general public had been profoundly affected by the experiences of World War II. To prevent another conflict, federalists favored a lofty goal of full integration. Others, by contrast, were reluctant to surrender national prerogatives. Still others were motivated more by concerns about European economic decline and American ambitions than security issues. In the midst of such discussions the French-German axis emerged as a critical force in propelling European integration. What enticed these states to surrender some of their sovereign rights to these nascent European institutions?

Recognizing the particular historical circumstances that affected the initial preferences of Western European elites, we submit that two key factors influenced the institutional design: relative symmetry of power and relative symmetry in demand. Both conditions were necessary with neither one being sufficient to account for the subsequent mode of integration. Symmetry of power made credible commitments possible and unilateral hegemony impossible. Mutual interdependence made such integration desirable, as all stood to gain considerably from integration.

Realists are correct that security greatly concerned Paris and Bonn. Initially France pursued policies aimed at diminishing German power and any chance at revival. It sought control over the Ruhr and Saarland, giving it access to critical industrial resources. But with deteriorating relations with the Soviet Union, the United Kingdom and the United States opposed such a strategy. Instead France together with the United Kingdom, the Benelux, Germany, and the United States formed the International Ruhr Authority in 1949, which aimed to control coke, coal, and steel in the area. With the recognition of the sovereign Federal Republic of Germany that same year, Germany soon opposed such control over its resources and wanted alternative arrangements. Given its wartime past it had to temper its desire to gain full sovereign control by consenting to institutional mechanisms that checked such a revival of German power. Britain and the Americans simultaneously pushed for a revived and more integrated Europe. They soon fixed their gaze on the coal and steel sector where economic and security interests combined.

This sector was a critical component of reindustrialization and a key component of any war effort. With the war only a few years past, there was general unease about a rebuilt and unhampered Germany. Economically the French steel industry was also dependent on German coke. French mines and steel mills also feared a lack of competitiveness in the face of rebuilt German heavy industry. All Western European countries also feared that their governments lacked adequate control given the high degree of cartelization in the private sector.[31]

A strong proponent of federalism, Jean Monnet, drafted the treaty for the European Coal and Steel Community. While Monnet's idea of a supranational planning body—no doubt influenced by French dirigiste ideas—ultimately failed, the treaty did establish important institutional components that would later inform the EEC. The High Authority was thus constructed as a supranational institution over and above the Council of Ministers of the Member States (the Benelux countries, France, Germany, and Italy). It also established the European Court of Justice to arbitrate disputes between states, firms, and European institutions. The common market in this sector prohibited import and export duties, quantitative restrictions, and discriminatory practices.[32] It also sought to eliminate an important source of price distortions by equalizing transport rates—which represented 20–25 percent of the price of steel.[33]

The common market in coal and steel was thus from the outset about much more than lowering barriers to trade. Indeed, as Haas notes, "there had been no tariffs applicable to these commodities previously."[34] It involved pricing agreements, control over investments, cartel policy, the elimination of subsidies, transparency in labor practices, and so forth.[35]

Alter and Steinberg argue convincingly that the High Authority never took on the management of coal and steel as the drafters of the treaty envisioned. However, it did establish an important precedent by introducing supranational institutionality and by moving far beyond the narrow realm of overt tariff barriers. The broad scope of this form of integration would make any attempt at complete contracting very difficult. Commenting in 1958 on what the experience of the ECSC forebode for the EEC, Raymond Mikesell concluded, "The experience of the High Authority in this field—which has been confined to the problems of regulating competition in only a few related industries—is not reassuring. The task for formulating policies and regulations . . . of perhaps hundred of industries . . . seems almost overwhelming. Experience in dealing with discrimination and competitive practices indicates a need for an adminis-

---

[31] R. Gordon 1962; Mikesell 1958.
[32] Archer 1990, 55.
[33] Mikesell 1958, 436.
[34] Haas 2004 [1958], 60.
[35] Alter and Steinberg 2007, 91.

trative and quasi-judicial authority with supranational powers over a rather broad area."[36]

These experiences entered into the discussions for a more comprehensive community beyond coal and steel. By the mid-1950s, the cold war had reached its zenith with tensions surrounding Berlin, the Hungarian uprising, and suspected communist meddling in the European colonies. As NATO allies, all six contracting parties shared the threat posed by the USSR.

Despite this common threat, France and increasingly Germany saw a revived, unified Europe as a potential Third Force. French disagreements with the United States were longstanding, going back to France's position in the wartime alliance and disagreements about French handling of Indochina and the Algerian War. German chancellor Adenauer increasingly distrusted American motives. The Suez Crisis of 1956 had not only exposed European weakness. It had also showed Washington's willingness to exercise heavy-handed leadership.[37]

It had furthermore become increasingly clear that Germany would regain its preeminent position on the continent. By 1954 it had joined NATO as a critical ally in the effort to deter the Warsaw Pact, thus becoming once again a "normal" state rather than the postwar pariah. German economic growth was obvious as well. Consequently, France sought an institutional means to bind Germany to international agreements that would constrain German options.[38] French foreign minister Pineau thus assured the Soviet Union that European integration was not directed against it but "to insert Germany into a European community."[39]

Recognizing the importance of such concerns, Edelgard Mahant suggests that geopolitical considerations provided a necessary but not a sufficient condition for integration. Common economic interests emerged as well. German industrialists realized that they would bear the costs of protectionist measures, as in agriculture, but they were willing to do so given the expected benefits of integration.[40] Moreover, German agriculture too had protectionist measures that would benefit from EEC policies in this regard.

Areas of potential contention could be settled. For example, although French elites and interest groups were concerned that the high level of

[36] Alter and Steinberg 2007; Mikesell 1958, 437.

[37] Mahant 2004, 102, 128, 131.

[38] Even as economists debated the benefits of integration, they recognized that a key objective was to embed a rearmed and economically strong Germany in a European Community. See, for example, Gehrels and Johnston 1955.

[39] As cited in Mahant 2004, 132.

[40] Ibid., 45, 47, 62.

French standards with regard to the work week and benefits would be diluted by a European agreement, in practice this proved not to be the case. Indeed, by one calculation social policies had already converged to a great degree. And even the overseas territories did not derail the agreement. While Germany had no material stake in giving the French overseas areas preferential access, Paris had made clear that an EEC agreement would have to make provisions, if there was to be any deal. Bonn, realizing the importance of these areas for France (the Algerian war was by then in full swing), conceded the issue. Indeed, if seen within the broad view of keeping the colonies outside communist embrace, the expenditures could also be fit into geopolitical strategy.[41]

Moravcsik puts even less weight on geopolitical concerns. He argues for the primacy of commercial interests in the deliberations, although he admits that such motives could only surface after key geopolitical concerns were settled.[42] More generally, Moravcsik argues that changes in capital movements and intra-industry trade altered social actors' preferences in favor of greater integration. Political elites, in turn, catering to their respective constituencies, then negotiated the specific institutional configurations to coincide, as best as possible, with the national preferences.

Regardless of the relative primacy of geopolitical factors versus commercial interests, we follow the logic that political elites pursued their national objectives by strategic calculation. French and German elites in particular negotiated the institutional contours through which to pursue their aims.[43] For both supranational institutions loomed large in French and German minds. Germany sought a means to reintegrate itself within Western Europe, while France sought institutional means to curtail a rising Germany. Both pursued their respective security and economic interests. For German elites this meant a desire to promote industrial exports; for France this entailed a greater emphasis on agricultural markets.[44] Germany thus stood to gain considerably from access to the other European states. The smaller states similarly would benefit greatly given that Belgium and the Netherlands were heavily dependent on international trade.

[41] Ibid., 112, 119, 127, 146–47.

[42] Moravcsik 1998, 6. Interestingly, he adds that without such geopolitical concerns the Community might have resembled something more along the lines of NAFTA or the WTO. He also notes that geopolitical considerations by Adenauer greatly influenced the German position (94).

[43] Britain also had interests in a unified Europe, but because of Commonwealth and imperial considerations, as well as French reluctance, it opted for a Free Trade Area rather than the EEC. See particularly Schenk 1996; Butt 1966.

[44] Moravcsik 1998, 87, 94–97, 103, 111.

Interdependence, in other words, was symmetric. Capital movements and increasing intraregional trade gave German industry an incentive to support a supranational bargain as it stood to gain considerably from further integration. And indeed, during 1952–55 intracommunity trade in steel and coal increased by 170 percent, trade in other goods by 42 percent, and trade in capital goods (excluding iron and steel) by 59 percent.[45]

Matching Preferences with Institutional Forms

The European geopolitical and economic environment thus propelled a disposition among political and social elites to tolerate a significant degree of supranational decision making with relatively low levels of precision *ex ante* in legislation. Nevertheless, they still required institutional safeguards before they actually yielded sovereign prerogatives.

Even if states are generally concerned with absolute gains rather than relative gains, as neoliberals contend, the contracting states will want some assurance that subsequent gains will not flow disproportionately to the stronger states. The Benelux states worried that the more powerful states (France and Germany) would gradually usurp more power in such institutions. Given their lack of relative power and dependence on access to the market of their larger counterparts, those concerns were warranted. Consequently, the larger states needed to make credible commitments, without which weaker contracting parties would refrain from any initial agreement.

All contracting parties also had to be apprehensive of a loss of control to supranational institutions. Bargaining leverage after all would gradually shift to those institutions if they gained residual rights of control. Institutions thus had to be designed to alleviate such concerns. How were the six member states able to create institutions that could at once credibly commit the larger states and assuage fears of runaway supranationalism?

First, the six negotiating parties faced modest power asymmetries—measured in terms of relative comparability in overall economic strength. The moderate power asymmetries within Europe provided the smaller states (the Netherlands, Belgium, and Luxembourg) some measure of comfort in signing on to the founding treaty. Although the German economic miracle "Wirtschaftswunder") was making Germany the preeminent economic power by the late 1950s, it still had to contend with a substantial French economy (going through its own economic miracle), as well as with Italy.

[45] Mikesell 1958, 438.

TABLE 5.1
Economic Performance among the EEC Member
States, 1957 (GDP in billions of US dollars)

Belgium	9.8
France	53.7
Italy	21.8
Luxembourg	0.4
Netherlands	8.4
West Germany	43.1
United Kingdom	53.0 (nonmember)

Sources: United Nations, *Statistical Yearbook 1958*
(New York: United Nations, 1958). Data for France
are from International Monetary Fund, *International
Financial Statistics* 11 (1958): 1–6. Data on Britain from
International Institute for Strategic Studies (London:
IISS, 1971).

Note: Data are GDP figures for 1957, except data for
France (figures for 1956 and report GNP). We provide
figures on the United Kingdom as Britain loomed at one
point as one of the potential contracting members.

Moreover, the three smallest states, which stood to gain the most from
trade liberalization, operated jointly on several issues. Indeed it was the
joint action of the Benelux at the ministers' conference in Messina in
June 1955 that initiated the subsequent negotiations that led to the EEC.
The Benelux also entered negotiations on the common external tariff as
a coherent unit, countering the French preference for a common external
tariff that would be higher than the tariff of any member state, given that
the Benelux already had negotiated a low common external tariff at an
earlier date.[46] The small states showed they could band together for bargaining leverage.

Although the contracting parties only foresaw a gradual shift toward
majoritarian decision making rather than consensus, they also realized
that guarantees had to be built in to assuage the fears of the smaller actors.
Thus, the weighted voting system then envisioned guaranteed that the 3
smaller states could not be outvoted by the three larger ones.[47]

Thus, although it was evident that West Germany would soon be the
preeminent European power, it could be checked by other relatively powerful actors such as France and Italy or the Benelux when it acted as a
coherent unit. Germany could not have accomplished its objectives without binding itself. With moderate power asymmetries Germany could

[46] Hurtig 1958, 348. The result was a common external tariff based on the arithmetical
average of the duties in the four customs territories.
[47] Mahant 2004, 94; Moravcsik 1998, 153.

not have unilaterally dictated the terms of agreement.[48] Moreover, Germany needed to reinsert itself within the European Community in order to allay fears of a resurgent German power. France clearly wanted to bind Germany, and Adenauer understood that self-binding by Germany was a *sine qua non* for his nation to be accepted as a "normal" state. Consequently, given its motives to acquiesce in institutions that would limit its room for maneuver, and given the ability of others to check any German ambitions, Bonn had both the will to commit to supranationality while the configuration of forces also allowed it to do so in a credible manner.[49]

This does not mean that the states fully envisioned the depth of contemporary European integration from the outset. Nor did they consciously delegate these functions to European-level institutions. How could they? Even though the agreement left considerable room for interpretation by supranational institutions such as the European Commission and the European Court of Justice, the contracting parties curtailed their ability to stray too far from elite preferences. Although some states supported a strong more supranationally oriented Commission, Germany and France favored more authority for the intergovernmental Council of Ministers. Thus, although the Commission could initiate legislative proposals, the Council of Ministers had the ability to block proposals.[50] The European Parliament at this stage had feeble powers at best, and a direct election of the parliament was not to occur until two decades had passed. The ECJ, too, was not envisaged with broad powers.[51] While the Court soon took on vastly expanded powers in broad interpretations of its jurisdictional competency, it has also realized that in substantive matters, legislation from the member states could nullify the aims of the Court. Thus it selectively expanded its prerogatives.

We need not retell the story of how the EEC came into being as the result of various efforts at integration. Some of these efforts failed, as the attempt to form a European Defense Community and a European Political Community. Despite such setbacks many economic and political groups wanted to forge ahead with integration in such areas as transportation, oil, and atomic energy. The Benelux countries led the way in trying to forestall stagnation and found allies in Jean Monnet and French prime minister Faure. The Benelux memorandum of 1955 and the subsequent

---

[48] The German war record of course would make such a unilateralist effort even more problematic.

[49] Even Joseph Grieco (1995), who sets out to defend a realist perspective of integration, ends up pointing to the modest power asymmetries and the willingness and ability of Germany to credibly commit—blending neoliberal institutionalist arguments with realist views.

[50] Mahant 2004, 95.

[51] Moravcsik 1998, 155.

Messina negotiations from the outset envisioned a deep integration in multiple economic areas.

The eventual signing by the six of the Treaty of Rome in 1957 encapsulated the breadth of the European ambition, far beyond simply lowering barriers to trade or equal treatment as demanded by the principles of the General Agreement on Tariffs and Trade. Instead the treaty enumerated eleven activities including an end to customs duties; quantitative restrictions; a common external tariff and common external policies; freedom of movement of persons, services, and capital; a common agricultural policy; undistorted competition; and coordination of economic policies.[52]

Institutionally, the treaty established an assembly, a Council of Ministers, a European Court, and the European Commission. It copied from the ECSC the notion of a supranational court. And the Commission would take a somewhat similar position as the High Authority in its supranational orientation but without the expansive powers that had been granted to the latter.

In sum, the EEC started from the outset with supranational institutions in its makeup—even if their subsequent powers were still unrecognized. Furthermore, given the vast scope of the intended integration, the treaty could not hope to resolve all related issues *ex ante*. Indeed the agreements that truly opened up the movement of persons and capital, the Schengen agreements and the European Monetary Union, would take decades to achieve. In other words, the treaty was an incomplete agreement with virtually all issues to be held over for future legislation and adjudication. The formative treaty of European union is thus an exemplar of incomplete contracting with supranational institutionalization.

The Consequences of Assigning Residual Rights to Supranational Institutions

MEANINGFUL SUPRANATIONALISM

As a consequence of incomplete contracting and the low level of specificity, the contracting states have had to allow the ECJ to develop meaningful review of national decision making and test government policies against EEC legislation. The ECJ has gradually expanded its powers to become a truly supranational force. Already in 1963 the ECJ proclaimed in the Van Gend and Loos case that European Community legislation had direct effect. The Court, not national governments, would test the applicability of EEC law in the particular case. Individuals, moreover, had standing in proceedings against their own government. As the Court stated, "the

---

[52] For a quick overview, see Archer 1990, chapter 5.

Community constitutes a new legal order of international law for the benefit of which the states have limited their sovereign rights."[53]

The *Costa v. Enel* case, decided one year later, reinforced the Van Gend and Loos decision.[54] Contrary to the Italian dualist view that international law needed national transformation in order to be effective (and thus that later national law superseded earlier international agreements), the Court decided that EEC law was directly applicable and thus supreme to national law.[55] In later decisions the ECJ also passed judgment on the effect of directives beyond regulations and decisions. Subsequent Court decisions over the past decades have expanded the prerogatives and the judicial scope of the Court's holdings.[56]

Such decisions from the ECJ came at the very time that political elites, particularly the French government, balked at any further inroads to supranationality.[57] Thus despite the Luxembourg compromise (1965), which limited progress toward supranational decision making, the Court managed to forge ahead with supranational implications.[58] Why did governments abide by such rulings?

The ability of the ECJ to proceed while political elites, particularly in France, sought to limit the powers of the Commission and curtail supranational legislation suggests that the particular status of the Court was instrumental to the entire EU process. That is, elites were willing to go along with the expansion of juridical powers because integration required procedural solutions to the problems associated with incomplete contracting and little *ex ante* legislation. The Court had to be given great leeway because elites could not know where long-term contracting would lead and could not engage in highly specific *ex ante* legislation.[59]

Germany and France have, by and large, followed ECJ decisions that have gone against them. That is, without the ability to unilaterally dictate

---

[53] *Van Gend and Loos v. Nederlandse Administratie Belastingen*, ECJ 26/62 1963.

[54] *Costa v. Ente Nazionale per L'Energia Elettrica (Enel)*, 6/64 1964. The Simmenthal decision (1978) further expanded on this. National courts were instructed to see to it that community law was implemented and "to set aside any provisions of national law which conflict with it." See Dinan 1999, 34.

[55] See Alter 1998.

[56] See the numerous examples in Alter 1998, 2000.

[57] For the argument that the ECJ had an important independent role in moving supranational decision making forward, see Burley and Mattli 1993.

[58] Qualified majority became possible but the compromise entailed that consensus would be required on all "important matters." The individual states would determine when they wished to invoke the "important matters" clause.

[59] Moravcsik (1998, 75) notes that delegation occurs when joint gains are available, distribution conflicts are moderate, and the environment is highly uncertain. These expectations are very similar to the expectations we deductively derive with regard to the motives to sign incomplete contracts and our expectations regarding the durability of incomplete contracts. See chapters 1 and 2.

the terms of subsequent *ex post* legislation and decision making, the larger states have consciously sought to tie their own hands.[60] Even France, although the most ardent proponent of state sovereignty, holding back the move to majority decision making in the Luxembourg compromise of 1965, has nevertheless gradually given way to more cases of majority decision making enshrined in the Single European Act, the Maastricht, and Amsterdam treaties. France has even given way on the ECJ's monist position of EU law with the Conseil d'État changing its view.

In another example, in the Cassis de Dijon case (1979), the Court disallowed the use of German national standards to operate as non-tariff barriers. The decision that national standards deserved mutual recognition had vast implications for the ability of national governments to shield their economies from unwanted competition. The losing party, the German government, in abiding by the decision, simultaneously enhanced its own reputation to credibly commit and sanctioned an important judicial decision that would affect the liberalization of trade throughout the EU.

Thus the Court did not simply interpret regulations and directives but took an active stance in actually propelling integration forward. The ECJ has handled such diverse cases as those involving tariffs and non-tariff barriers, equal pay (the Defrenne case), and abortion rights (the Irish abortion cases). The expanded powers of the Court are not simply derivative of governments' delegated power, nor should they be construed as tacit state consent before the ECJ rulings, as Geoffrey Garrett's intergovernmental perspective would assert.[61] Indeed, even powerful states have consented to adverse judgments in order to establish reputation and credible commitment. If the Court were merely epiphenomenal to immediate state interests, it could not perform the necessary function of impartial adjudication. And if it were closely connected to state interests, it could not serve as a mechanism for the stronger states to tie their own hands.

At the same time our argument differs from, but does not contradict, Burley and Mattli's argument. They suggest that the ECJ worked as a "technocratic" institution outside the purview of political oversight.[62] We argue instead that the ECJ gained considerable independent powers exactly because it provides a logical function in the incomplete contracting process of the EU. It was not because of a lack of oversight but because credible commitment in such incomplete contracts requires that

---

[60] For a realist argument that large states have strategic incentives to restrict their own latitude for maneuver, see Grieco 1995.

[61] Garrett 1995; Garrett, Keleman, and Schulz 1998. For a discussion of the intergovernmental perspective and neo-functionalists, see Grieco 1995; Mattli 1999.

[62] Burley and Mattli 1993.

such supranational institutions must be given latitude outside of immediate state oversight.

Similarly, the Commission capitalized on the residual rights granted to it by the initial treaty to expand and institutionalize its authority. Consequently, it has often been at the forefront of devising a vast body of directives and regulations to implement the original treaties in practice. As Mark Pollack notes, although various oversight mechanisms are in place to curtail the power of the Commission, these oversight mechanisms are costly, thereby giving the Commission considerable latitude in certain areas.[63]

The EU members have thus largely used *ex post* legislation and supranational adjudication as a strategically motivated solution to regional contracting under high degrees of uncertainty. For this solution to work effectively, the European Commission, and perhaps even more so the ECJ, have been given considerable independent latitude.

RUNAWAY SUPRANATIONALISM? THE BARRIERS TO REVERSAL

But even if *ex post* legislation and supranational arbitration are functional responses to credible commitment problems and incomplete contracting, why have governments been willing to live with the expanded powers of the ECJ and Commission? Why, given that residual rights of control have given supranational institutions increased bargaining leverage over time, has not this led to a clash between national governments and EU institutions?

Some of this might be attributable to the continued relative symmetry of power within the European Union, even after German unification. Even though the German economy is paramount, other states, such as France, Italy, the United Kingdom, and Spain, are sizable in their own right. Moreover, the French-German axis, rather than German hegemony, continues to form an important basis for European cooperation. Furthermore, the increased number of actors since the inception of the EEC has diminished relative power considerations. As other states have joined the Community, the ability of any one state, such as Germany, to unilaterally dominate decision making has declined. The increasing number of member states combined with the move toward qualified majority rule in many areas requires even the largest states to create supportive coalitions. At the same time, any move to block legislation cannot simply be based on unilateralist obstructionism. Germany thus has had to appeal to Dutch and French sentiments to form a veto coalition. Similarly, the

[63] Pollack 1997.

Mediterranean countries have had to find common ground to pursue their preferences.

Nevertheless, it is true that contracting parties have tried to control supranational authority by limiting ECJ activism and by maintaining a substantial degree of intergovernmental input during the drafting of EU legislation. The Court, consequently, has had to balance judicial activism with the possibility of unilateral defection should a state fail to adhere to an adverse judgment. The ECJ has been careful not to expand its judicial activism to areas that would impose very high costs on individual states. For example, in delineating that pension schemes could not differentiate between male workers and female workers it has not required the states to implement its decision retroactively.[64] The costs of doing so would be prohibitive and increase the likelihood of state defection. At the same time any potential defection by a contracting state will lead to a loss of credibility and reputation on its side. Court and contracting parties are thus constantly gauging the probability that ECJ decisions will indeed be implemented.

The costs of defection, however, are not static. If states can mobilize some of their fellow contracting parties to reverse the effects of ECJ activism, then the diminishing reputation costs increase the likelihood of defection. Given sufficient resistance the contracting parties can either renegotiate particular terms of the Community treaties or they can push for regulations and directives that in effect nullify the Court's decisions.[65] In this sense, the contracting parties have built-in reversibility in the procedural mechanisms of integration. This occurs when subsequent phases of the incomplete contract threaten to yield results that are unacceptable to powerful states, but at the same time requires those states to mobilize a quorum sufficient to challenge the implications of the ECJ decisions.

Given the number of actors involved in the EU legislative process, mobilizing a substantial number to oppose the ECJ is extremely difficult. Karen Alter, following Fritz Scharpf, refers to this as the "joint decision trap."[66] This explains why the Court has been able to expand its powers, while national governments have often been unable to mount serious challenges. Mark Pollack also notes how the ECJ, even more so than the Commission, has been able to maneuver with limited oversight by national elites because ECJ decisions are difficult to challenge in the second instance.[67]

---

[64] The Defrenne case (1971) had struck down wage discrimination, and the ECJ ruled that the treaty's provision had direct effect. See Dinan 1999, 309.

[65] Garrett, Keleman, and Schulz 1998.

[66] Alter 1998, 2000.

[67] Pollack 1997.

We might also note how the presence of multiple veto opportunities diminishes the likelihood of policy change, a move from an achieved equilibrium position.[68] For example, the contracting parties in 1957 came to an agreement regarding equality of pay among men and women (article 119 of the Treaty of Rome). This constitutes the policy equilibrium position and falls within the win set of all the member states. Suppose that the ECJ in reaction to an individual appeal interprets this legislation to mean that pension plans must be uniformly applied to male and female employees (the Defrenne case). Assume that this was unforeseen by the contracting parties. Yet this ECJ decision now threatens to become policy even though it fell outside the scope of the original win set. The ECJ decision in essence has become the status quo. The onus of shifting from the status quo would now fall to the individual state that opposes the ruling, and if consensus decision making were in place the multiple allies required to draft new legislation would raise considerable hurdles to design a new policy equilibrium.

THE ADOPTION OF QUALIFIED MAJORITY VOTING

But while the costs of reversing ECJ decisions are high, this does not mean that states cannot resist ECJ rulings. Turning the conventional argument around—that the shift to qualified majority voting (QMV) has expanded supranationality—one might argue that QMV might actually allow for easier oversight of the ECJ in the second instance. The conventional argument notes how since 1965 the Luxembourg compromise governed decision making. All important matters had to be decided by consensus, with the individual states deciding which issues they deemed "important," thus establishing a veto. However, the adoption of the Single European Act (SEA) in 1986 and the Maastricht Agreement (1992) limited the ability of states to veto legislation by moving toward qualified majority voting. The Amsterdam Agreement (1997) further expanded the areas in which qualified majority voting is applied.

On one dimension this indeed limits the ability of individual states to forestall legislation approved by the majority of members in the Council and Commission in a subsequent stage. Conversely, however, one could argue that qualified majority voting allows a recalcitrant state to challenge supranational decisions—should a government feel that EU decisions go against its key interests—by passing offsetting legislation with a majority coalition in the Council of Ministers. Integration thus proceeds as a two-stage process. Initially, progress in integration (as a process of incomplete contracting) necessitates that states relinquish some aspects of national

[68] Tsebelis 1995, 1999; Immergut 1992.

sovereignty. As argued earlier, states have to make credible commitments to future agreements and do so by surrendering some of their authority to supranational institutions.[69] This is even true for powerful states. Nevertheless, states also fear loss of control over these supranational institutions and threats to sovereign prerogatives. Consequently, they will seek to find remedies to check such behavior. In this sense, the move to qualified majority voting has made it easier to mount a challenge to the Commission or ECJ decisions in the second instance.

That decisions in the Commission and the Council are de facto often made by consensus rather than qualified majority voting, as Lynn Dobson has noted (except when strong domestic preferences are present), does not vitiate this argument.[70] Indeed, the very fact that QMV is rarely used indicates that the Court has seldom ventured into areas where it believes its rulings will not find broad support. That is, the Council and the Commission have not had to pass much legislation in the second instance to reverse earlier Court decisions. Moreover, the argument that only cases with strong domestic constituent interests give rise to QMV might suggest that the "fire alarm" mechanism functions quite well. When actors with strong preferences see those preferences jeopardized by European-level institutions, QMV allows them to more readily amend earlier decisions by passing legislation in the second instance. QMV thus allows for more expedient fire alarm oversight by the contracting states than does consensus decision making.

States can resist runaway supranationality in other ways as well.[71] Thus, while the Commission, the ECJ, and the Parliament have gradually taken on new responsibilities, conforming to the expectations of incomplete contracting, the member states have also created mechanisms to renegotiate the original contract periodically and to monitor the level of delegation to the supranational institutions. The Council of Ministers thus acts as the second reader of Commission legislation, and even with qualified majority voting, voting blocs can forestall legislation that goes against key state preferences.

This argument—that the EU process has largely been a process of incomplete contracting and continuous negotiation—squares to a considerable extent with explanations that see the EU process as driven by agreements between elites, as the intergovernmentalists suggest. As Moravcsik has pointed out, a fundamental change in the EU structure requires a shared

[69] See Moravcsik 1998.
[70] Dobson observes that only in cases in which particularistic, strongly entrenched domestic constituents are involved is QMV used (remarks made at the International Studies Association conference, 2003, Portland).
[71] See Pollack 1997.

understanding about the ultimate aims of the EU.[72] The Single European Act (1986) could only come into being after Mitterrand's conversion from dirigisme, and by assuaging Thatcher's fear that British sovereignty would be tarnished. Integration revolved around agreement on broad principles, with the specific details to be worked out over the long run. Moreover, Nicolas Jabko recently has shown how, starting with the SEA, the Commission itself strategically deployed the "logic of the market," with its calculated ambiguity and flexibility over what that the term actually meant, to forge cross-cutting coalitions within states that would support the completion and institutionalization of the single market's institutions at the supranational level.[73]

But we disagree with those who suggest that the EU today should simply be seen as an intergovernmental agreement from which states can extract themselves at any juncture. While the initial choices in the creation of the European Community no doubt reflected state interests, that Community subsequently has entered a realm of supranational decision making. While its forays into new issue areas and governance functions, detailed by each new agreement, individually have the potential to be reversed or checked during their initial introduction (as we saw with the collapse of the constitution in 2005), once institutionalized these supranational bodies have rarely transferred back actual sovereign authority or jurisdiction to member states. The logic of incomplete contracting and the need for credible commitment have rendered the original intergovernmental agreement an obsolescing bargain.

Regional Integration in North America

In contrast to incomplete contracting in European integration, the North American Free Trade Agreement, since its adoption, has manifested complete contracting. The integrative process remains also decidedly intergovernmental with more modest objectives than the supranational decision-making process of the EU. In contrast to the EU, NAFTA evinces a much higher degree of *ex ante* contract stipulation and less *ex post* judicial and legal activism.[74]

NAFTA remains limited to a free trade agreement, whereas the EEC set out to form a customs union and an economic community virtually from the outset. Even if explicit references to supranationality in the EEC treaty in 1957 were muted (partially because of the debacle sur-

---

[72] Moravcsik 1991, 1998.
[73] Jabko 2006.
[74] Abbott 2000.

rounding the European Defense Community),[75] many of the supranational aspects of the EEC evolved quickly in the subsequent years. Moreover, the EEC members did not insist on *ex ante* clarity to the same extent
as did the NAFTA parties even though the intent and scope of the EEC
in 1957 was much broader than the intent and scope of the Canadian-
U.S. Free Trade Agreement (CUSFTA or FTA) of 1987 and the NAFTA
agreement in 1994.

As with our analysis of regional integration in Europe we ask three
questions. First, what were the underlying motives of the contracting parties to the agreements? Second, what kinds of institutions did the actors
design to deal with their specific concerns in the contracting process?
More specifically, how did the states manage to mitigate the dangers of
reneging and hold-up in later stages of the agreement? Third, how did the
particular allocation of residual rights influence the subsequent development of regional integration?

Motives and Objectives of the Contracting Parties

Similar to the European states, the North American contracting parties
were motivated by a mix of geopolitical considerations and economic
concerns. To a considerable extent, movement toward regional integration in North America was driven by the developments in European integration. In all three states domestic political and economic elites also
started to converge in their preferred policies for trade liberalization.

NAFTA finds its roots in, and indeed is a direct extension of, the 1987
Canadian-U.S. FTA. It built on the Canadian-American automobile accord of two decades earlier.[76] Despite the automobile accord, the United
States and Canada had not pursued further integration. Canada still opted
for a more interventionist government policy than did the United States.
It also retained ties to the United Kingdom and the Commonwealth preference system. The United States, on its side, still pursued a global liberal
agenda, even if by 1972 it had to retreat from fixed exchange rates. The
Tokyo Round of negotiations in the context of the General Agreement on
Tariffs and Trade (GATT) had been quite successful, even if some issues
as trade in services and agriculture continued to bedevil agreement.

By the 1980s, the situation had changed dramatically.[77] Canadian Conservative prime minister Mulroney was far less inclined to interventionism
than his predecessor, Pierre Trudeau. The United Kingdom had also
clearly moved toward European integration, rather than pursue economic

---

[75] Dinan 1999, 32.
[76] See the discussion in Winham 1988; Hufbauer and Schott 1992, chapters 1 and 2.
[77] Winham 1988, 44–46.

agreements with the remnants of the former empire. With 80 percent of Canadian exports going to the United States, Ottawa became increasingly interested in opening up the cross-border trade with its powerful southern neighbor, particularly in view of its weak domestic market in the 1980s.

However, despite economic setbacks in the 1970s, the United States, with its multilateral rather than regional focus, still proved a reluctant partner. Only fears of relative U.S. decline, the threat of a "fortress Europe" following the SEA, and the difficulties of getting the Uruguay Round started made the United States think of a regional alternative.[78] The "NAFTA" track would serve as an incentive for Europeans and the Japanese to be more amenable to American demands. The carrot of an agreement on GATT was balanced by the stick of a regional alternative.

A similar set of calculations informed U.S.-Mexico negotiations in the late 1980s. Mexico had initially pursued protectionist policies and had frowned on foreign influences on its economy. Indeed, foreign ownership of Mexican oil deposits was constitutionally prohibited. Lopez Portillo's government had walked away from a very favorable GATT protocol in 1979, which would have given Mexico fifteen years to adjust.[79]

But the fall in oil prices in 1980 and the debt crisis put an end to that strategy.[80] The Mexican governments of de la Madrid and Salinas did a dramatic about-face, pursuing export-led growth and foreign investors. Salinas, a product of the de la Madrid *camarilla*, expanded on de la Madrid's turn to trade liberalization.[81] Staffing their administrations with technocrats, de la Madrid and Salinas forged a coalition between state elites favoring liberalization and large business enterprises.[82] In particular, the lure of American investments in Mexico proved enticing to these corporations. The way forward lay in pursuing access to the North American market, while at the same time seeking GATT membership.[83]

Once again, the United States proved reluctant. The American agenda remained focused on progress in the Uruguay Round. The continued dif-

---

[78] As Bhagwati (1993) interestingly points out, as early as the 1960s some voices in the United States saw regional free trade agreements as an alternative to the EEC and multilateralism. By the 1980s, with the Europeans reluctant to start the Uruguay Round and with European integration picking up steam, the regional alternative reemerged in the minds of politicians.

[79] Cameron and Tomlin 2000, 57–58.

[80] Even explanations that focus on the impact of ideas and ideological conversion suggest that the impetus for change came from the international economic shock of the early 1980s. See, for example, Golob 2003.

[81] Camp (1990) describes the importance of this *camarilla* (clique) in Mexican politics.

[82] Thacker 1999. The losers in the process were farmers, the urban poor, and the middle class, who were kept out of the ruling coalition and the deliberations on NAFTA.

[83] Mexico gained GATT membership in 1986 on much less favorable terms than were offered in 1979. See Dufey and Ryan 1994.

ficulties in concluding a final agreement, however, made the United States more amenable to Mexican overtures. A GATT agreement by the late 1980s seemed more remote than ever with disagreements on agriculture, services, and the protection of property rights. Even worse, a possible trade war loomed with Europe in view of the Spanish and Portuguese accession that raised tariffs for American soy exporters.[84] A broader regional fall-back option, beyond the bilateral deal with the Canadians, gained gradual momentum in Washington.[85]

Canada, too, was initially uninterested in a trilateral agreement, though it had started bilateral discussions with Mexico. It had few economic connections with Mexico and Mulroney did not see a broad North American deal emerge in the 1980s.[86] Canada, nevertheless, also changed its position. The Canadian government feared that the United States and Mexico would sign a bilateral deal, thereby allowing Washington to create a hub-and-spoke pattern through its treaties with its neighbor to the north and south. Moreover, a Mexican-American bilateral deal would likely siphon American investments from Canada. Thus Ottawa thought it wiser to maintain its seat around the bargaining table.

In short, like the Western European states, intraregional openness would provide considerable economic gains.[87] However, for most of the postwar decades the North American states had different geopolitical considerations, variant economic strategies, and divergent domestic interests. And the United States had no need to embed itself in a regional community as Germany had had to do (because of its wartime past).

By the 1980s, however, first Canada and then Mexico sought to pursue greater liberalization in North America. The United States, however, was less interested. Only greater domestic convergence of Canadian, Mexican, and American economic policies and the threat of a unified Europe brought the U.S. negotiators to the table. Mexico and Canada sorely needed access to the American market, whereas the United States had

[84] Odell and Matzinger-Tchakerian 1988.

[85] Domestic rifts in the United States were significant, with many labor and environmental groups opposing and larger businesses favoring the deal. Erstwhile presidential candidate Ross Perot became one of the most vocal critics of NAFTA. In the end the agreement passed its biggest hurdle, the House of Representatives, with a thirty-four-vote margin. Keith Bradsher, "After Vote, Labor Is Bitter but Big Business Is Elated," *New York Times*, November 18, 1993, A21. See also David Rosenbaum, "House Backs Free Trade Pact in Major Victory for Clinton after a Long Hunt for Votes," *New York Times*, November 18, 1993, A1.

[86] Hufbauer and Schott 1992, 24. The Canadian public also seemed less than enthusiastic about what the CUSFTA had yielded. See, for example, Clyde Farnsworth, "Canada's U.S. Trade Experience Fuels Opposition to the New Pact," *New York Times*, October 3, 1993, p. 1.

[87] For an assessment of the benefits of NAFTA, see Hufbauer and Schott 1993.

multiple options. Its trading relations across North America, East Asia, and Europe made a North American agreement less imperative for the United States than for the smaller economies. Not only was the U.S. economy considerably larger, but because the demand in the other states for integration was stronger than on the American side, the United States was in the driver's seat. The preponderance of the American economy in the NAFTA region allowed the United States to get what it wanted by bargaining and bilateral or trilateral deals. U.S. officials could thus clearly set the terms of the agreement. For example, from the outset, Washington stipulated to the Mexican government that any mention of free movement of labor would terminate the discussion.[88] Other issues that were likely to arouse controversy were bracketed and addressed in side deals.[89] Yet other items required last-minute concessions by Mexico, such as on sugar and citrus.

While all states opted for North American liberalization, the asymmetric demand worked wholly in favor of the United States.[90] Washington, therefore, had little incentive or need to submit to supranational organizations or to third-party binding arbitration that might hinder the pursuit of American objectives.

Intergovernmentality and Complete Contracting

Even if there had been greater enthusiasm in the United States for a far-reaching agreement, the asymmetry of power would have made it difficult to create binding institutional mechanisms. The asymmetry of power between the North American contracting parties is far more pronounced than between most of the European member states. The 1987 FTA coupled two advanced capitalist states of highly disparate power. In 1984 American GNP came to $3,947 billion dollars, dwarfing that of Canada ($346 billion).[91] The inclusion of Mexico in the accord in 1994 similarly highlighted power disparities between Mexico and its counterparts. The American GDP in 1991 was still nine times that of Canada and more than twenty times larger than the Mexican GDP.[92] The Mexican GDP per capita was one-seventh of that in Canada and the United States.

---

[88] Cameron and Tomlin 2000, 71.

[89] The environment thus required a side agreement to allay some opposition. See Baker-Fox 1995.

[90] To give a recent example, when the Mexican government asked for a renegotiation of the opening of its corn and beans market in 2008, Washington flatly refused. The Mexican government responded in turn that it would dutifully abide by the earlier terms, even though roughly 3 million small and less efficient Mexican farmers fear the adverse effects of U.S. competition. http://www.Bloomberg.com, June 6, 2006.

[91] Bueno 1988, 107. Figures from World Bank, World Development Report 1987.

[92] Hufbauer and Schott 1992, 5.

In the European case, as we discussed, even though the German economy led the others, its power could be checked by other major powers. In other words, although the German economy was strong, it did not occupy the hegemonic position the Americans enjoyed. Germany accounted for roughly one-fifth of EC output, whereas the U.S. economy accounted for almost 85 percent of the NAFTA region.[93] With only a few contracting negotiating states, there was no hope of an offsetting coalition.

Consequently, Canada and Mexico had to distrust American hegemony. Indeed, at one point during the negotiations, Washington—to the dismay of the Canadians—threatened to restrict binding binational dispute settlement procedures only to the FTA and not extend such procedures to the NAFTA dispute settlement. Ultimately, NAFTA did incorporate the FTA procedures, but Washington signaled strict limits as to how far it would allow its sovereignty to be curtailed.[94]

Mexico, in particular, had to fear "being too far from God and too close to the United States," as dictator Porfirio Díaz once lamented. Even Salinas, while staunchly advocating multilateral liberalization, feared as late as 1988 that "there is such a different economic level between the United States and Mexico that I do not believe such a common market would provide an advantage to either country."[95]

Counterfactually, even if the United States had consented to greater delegation to supranational institutions, its commitment to abide by any such legislation or adjudication would be less than credible. Canadian and Mexican dependence on access to the American market, as well as the ability of the United States to pursue multilateral options, gave Washington the ability to renege unilaterally if it so chose. That is, the very preponderance of the United States made it difficult to design institutions that could credibly constrain the hegemon.

Consequently, without agreements that would constrain American preeminence, the weaker parties had little incentive to put their fate in a relatively open-ended agreement. The contracting parties preferred to negotiate complete contracts and exchange specific quid pro quos up front rather than relegate points to further negotiations. Given the level of formalization *ex ante*, and the level of complete contracting, ad hoc arbitration, not *ex post* legislation and supranational adjudication, became the norm.

[93] Grieco 1994.

[94] Cameron and Tomlin 2000, 48, 49. As one observer rightly noted, "it was Mr. Salinas who staked his Presidency on the trade agreement, often dragging a reluctant nation into partnership with a powerful neighbor it has always feared." Tim Golden, "Mexican Leader a Big Winner as the Trade Pact Advances," *New York Times*, November 19, 1993, A1.

[95] Quoted in Cameron and Tomlin 2000, 59.

The Consequences of Complete Contracting and Intergovernmentalism

As a consequence of leaving the residual rights of control with the contracting parties, NAFTA has not progressed much beyond the terms of the initial agreement. Unlike European integration, which quickly expanded into various areas of economic and political cooperation, and accepted many more members, NAFTA has expanded little. Canada, despite its gains from liberalization with the United States, remains wary of domination by its more powerful neighbor and has excluded certain areas from the regional agreements, such as sectors deemed important to its cultural heritage. Canada has also been reluctant to accept a customs union and has explicitly sought to capitalize on foreign investment in Canada (particularly by Japan), using Canada as a convenient back door entry into the U.S. market. Voluntary Export Restraints (VER) in steel and automobiles imposed by the United States on Japan and European states only accentuated the attraction of Canada in the 1980s.[96]

With the extension of the FTA to Mexico, both the United States and Canada have excluded full factor mobility, specifically of labor. Environmental concerns with a rush to the bottom and lower standards have weighed in as well. The agreement has remained limited to diminishing trade barriers between these states rather than creating a customs union, let alone full economic integration. In lieu of common external tariffs, the parties have instead devised more stringent local content laws and "transformation tests."

In NAFTA ad hoc arbitration has sufficed because *ex ante* stipulations were far more extensive. Arbitration has also been rare. By one count the number of cases brought under chapters 18 and 19 of the FTA and chapters 19 and 20 of NAFTA numbered no more than eighty-one by 1999.[97] Actors know what the terms of the agreement are and their preferences were incorporated into the agreement's original terms.

Not only have few challenges emerged, but most cases have been relatively straightforward, with the norm being consensus decisions.[98] NAFTA dispute settlement panels allow each state to choose two individuals from a roster of specialists with the fifth to be agreed upon by both. Although one might expect that such panels would fragment along national origins, this has not happened.

---

[96] See, for example, Dufey and Ryan 1994.

[97] Stevenson 2000.

[98] Goldstein 1996; Stevenson 2000. For a discussion of the general settlement mechanism, see Hufbauer and Schott 1993, 102–4.

In short, NAFTA has differed in two key aspects from the European agreements for integration. These differences have had profound effects on the subsequent process. First, NAFTA institutions lack the supranational equivalent of the Commission, Parliament, or Court. Instead, political leaders brokered the terms of the agreement *ex ante* and in great detail, whereas the intergovernmental bargain in the EU only set the broad contours of agreement.

Second, arbitration panels in NAFTA are ad hoc and their composition needs the approval of the contracting parties. Panels decide single complaints rather than expand the domain of regional legislation. With no standing court, there is not an institutionalized mechanism through which the arbitration procedure can establish precedent and expand the supranational aspects of integration. Consequently, fears of a loss of sovereignty and usurpation by the regional organization remain moot.

Incomplete contracting with supranational institutions builds into the agreement, and indeed virtually demands, further development along supranational principles and creates dynamic incentives for further integration. Intergovernmental complete contracting, by contrast, virtually precludes such developments.

Rival Explanations

This comparison of the European and North American integration through the lens of incomplete contracting theory provides a rival explanation to realist and ideational accounts.[99] Moreover, our argument, while sympathetic to principal-agent arguments and neo-functionalism, provides a different perspective from these two views.

Realists see regional integration as derivative of shared security concerns. In the face of common threats, states cooperate in the political and economic sphere. Regional integration is thus driven by shared external security concerns combined with internally diminished security dilemmas. But if so, realism is then poorly equipped to explain the emergence of the early phases of European integration, as the ECSC. Indeed, if anything the internal security dilemma of how to deal with a rebuilding Germany would lead one to predict less integration in Europe in the 1950s. Instead, European integration was consciously pursued in order to reduce the in-

---

[99] A methodologically sound comparison between East Asian regional integration and NAFTA or the EU, by contrast, would be far less rigorous because of the variation in many causal variables. East Asia demonstrates a much lower level of intraregional trade, multiple security dilemmas, and considerable variation in regime type.

ternal security dilemma.[100] Integration was not epiphenomenal to the solution of underlying fears, but instead was a means to prevent those fears from translating into reality.

It is also too simplistic to derive motives for integration solely from the external security environment. Realist arguments fail to recognize that in the early years of integration, European countries could pursue different strategies even if the external threat of the cold war became clear. With strong left-wing sentiments in many Western European countries in the immediate postwar years, the potential contracting parties could not be sure about each state's ultimate commitment to free trade and noninterventionist economic policies. Indeed, while French conservatives agreed on capitalism as the model to emulate, the Gaullists disagreed about the extent and depth of integration, and the Socialists only converted to free market principles by 1983–84. Britain opted out of the Community altogether and created alternative sets of agreements with the Commonwealth and the countries in the European Free Trade Association (EFTA) zone. Even in Germany preferences were divided. Adenauer was challenged by his own economics minister, Ludwig Erhard, who favored association with the much looser structure of the EFTA rather than the EEC.[101]

Moreover, the security environment alone does not give us leverage on why the institutions look so different, or why the EU remains so robust more than a decade and a half after the end of the cold war. While it is true that the move toward a European constitution momentarily stalled because of the Dutch and French votes in 2005, most provisions were in fact adopted in the Lisbon Agreement of 2007.[102] Prior to Lisbon, the landmark Maastricht, Amsterdam, and Nice agreements and the move toward monetary union all dated from after the fall of the USSR.

In addition, after early concerns regarding West Germany diminished by the mid-1950s, the European Community looked much like its later North American counterpart. Both regional organizations consisted of states that were allies, or at least had no reason to fear an existential threat from their trading partners. The EEC thus grouped together Western European NATO members. Similarly, the United States, Canada, and Mexico have had benign security relations for many decades. One might even expand the notion of an external threat to also constitute an eco-

---

[100] Grieco (1995) tries to reconcile realism with an institutional logic, arguing that European institutions led to the binding of great power ambitions. But this contradicts key tenets of realism, which claim that international institutions only have a marginal causal effect. See Mearsheimer 1994–95.

[101] Mahant 2004, 122; Moravcsik 1998, 100.

[102] The French Assemblée and the Sénat agreed in February 2008 on a constitutional amendment that opened the door to ratification of the EU constitutional treaty.

nomic challenge. One might thus aver that the EEC emerged in response to European decline and the competition of the United States and Japan. The FTA and NAFTA arose in response to challenges posed by the expected imminent failure of the Uruguay Round and the SEA.

Thus, if realist arguments are correct then NAFTA and the EEC should be motivated by a similar logic and show similar institutional traits.[103] Both, in reacting to external economic or security threats, would be expected to show similar institutional designs. Both regional organizations should show similarities or, given the head start of the EEC, a trend toward convergence as NAFTA matures. However, here too the evidence contradicts such expectations. They differed from the start in their institutional configuration and continue to do so.[104]

Our argument also differs from ideational accounts such as those of Craig Parsons, who suggests that key political actors managed to drive the process, acting on their own deeply held views.[105] We do not gainsay that individual perspectives and views are key features of political life. Preferences cannot simply be deduced from attributed material interests. We also know that Europeans held widely different opinions on the level of integration and the degree to which sovereignty should be transferred to international institutions.[106]

However, we claim that given that political leaders have relatively short time horizons, given uncertainty about the future, and given the huge complexities of integration, the elites of that time could do no better than design an agreement based on general principles with many details to be worked out down the line. The very nature of incomplete contracting subsequently, and logically, precipitated that supranational authorities would pick up the slack. No doubt leaders such as Robert Schuman and Monnet were driven by deeply held beliefs. But the reason why the agreements ended up looking the way they did had as much, if not more, to do with the relative power symmetry between actors and their equivalent demand for deep integration. The complexities of such an agreement combined with necessary institutional guarantees led to the structure of ECSC and the EEC. Counterfactually, if power and demand symmetry

---

[103] Grieco 1995.

[104] Even the sophisticated discussion of the relative merits of neo-functionalist and intergovernmentalist arguments in Mattli (1999) goes too far in focusing on the efficiency gains of public goods provision. Arguably, both organizations would show gains by further integration, yet they remain markedly distinct in logic.

[105] Parsons 2003.

[106] Survey analysis in the 1950s revealed, for example, that German leaders and supporters of the governing Christian Democrats were far more in favor of integration than was the opposition Socialist Party. Kriesberg 1959.

did not exist, no level of supranational entrepreneurship could have carried the day.

Moreover, while realist and ideational explanations both add to explanations of why these organizations emerged, they provide little purchase on explaining the important institutional differences between the two. They give insights into the diverse motives of the political actors involved, but they do not explain the variation in institutional design or the consequences of such variation.

This last observation thus also signals the difference between our view and extant neo-functionalist and principal-agent arguments. Our discussion agrees with Mattli and Slaughter's argument that debates over whether governmental elites or neo-functionalist dynamics ultimately drive European integration are not fruitful.[107] European laws and directives and ECJ rulings are not merely epiphenomenal to state interests. European legislation is not, and—based on our incomplete contracting argument—cannot be, beholden to intergovernmental compromises at every juncture of the decision-making process. Given the incomplete nature of the contract—the lack of information about the future, uncertainty about the future distribution of benefits—contracting parties must surrender some of their control, even if political elites initially exercise a great deal of influence on setting the framework for subsequent cooperation. The long-term horizon (i.e., frequency of interaction), the limited reversibility of investments (economic and political), and the need to establish reputation to credibly commit require that elites tie their own hands as well as those of fellow signatories. Debates between those who emphasize the role of governmental elites versus those who put primacy on neo-functionalist explanations remain unfruitful because both processes result from the same logic of organization. Incomplete contracting between elites provided the institutional space for European-level institutions to pick up the slack. Indeed, incomplete contracting required it.

Our perspective thus differs from neo-functionalists who argue that supranationality is the result of spillover, or supranational institutions usurping power with national elites only marginally involved in the integration process. We argue instead that elites rationally designed such institutions and allowed them a measure of autonomy, without which European cooperation would be impossible.

It should also be evident that our perspective differs from the view that regional organizations are simply extensions of the state interests. That argument holds for NAFTA, as it is an intergovernmental complete contract. But it is not correct that the institutions created by the EEC, and

---

[107] Mattli and Slaughter 1998.

which are now still at the basis of the EU, are simply agents acting at the behest of their governments.[108] Thus one might argue that what starts out as delegation by governments (principals) to the agent (the EU institutions) ends up increasingly within the realm of agent autonomy. We argue that EU activism is not the consequence of a loss of principal control over the agent, but that some of the EU institutions, such as the ECJ, were not—and indeed, given the logic of the incomplete contract, could not be—mere agents.

We thus support Giandomenico Majone's claim that principal-agency theory misunderstands the nature of European Community structures. Simple delegation on an intergovernmental basis would not greatly enhance credibility. Instead, Majone argues for an alternative understanding of the relationship of national governments to European-level institutions, which he calls fiduciary delegation. Discussing the role of the ECJ in this mode, he observes that "in policy areas where the Community is *exclusively* competent, the power to exercise public authority has been irrevocably transferred. . . . Since the treaties did not contain an explicit list of areas of exclusive Community competence, it has been up to the Court to build up such a list."[109]

As a result of the incomplete contracting nature of the EEC treaty, and because of the need to credibly commit, European Community institutions required the states to give up meaningful authority. This is not simply a question of principal-agency "slippage" but a logical response to how state elites can solve contracting problems. National elites and supranational institutions are involved in a delicate balancing act of meaningful autonomy and runaway activism. In the European case, if European institutions were simply designed to carry out the interests of the more powerful states, the contracting parties could not have agreed to such an open-ended and wide-ranging agreement.

Conclusion

In previous chapters we argued that incomplete contracting theory can shed light on questions of territorial partition and the reallocation of rights over site-specific assets. Similarly, we argued that such an approach can illuminate bargaining dynamics regarding overseas bases. When site-specific assets are involved, the bargaining situation over time uniquely favors the host country, even if the host country is manifestly weaker in

---

[108] For discussions of agency theory, see Eisenhardt 1989. Doleys (2000) has sketched some of these concerns for the EU.

[109] Majone 2005, 77.

terms of power resources. Once the home country has sunk investments, the host country will seek to renegotiate the terms of the agreement. One solution to the contracting problem is the full allocation of sovereign rights, that is, hierarchy. Short of hierarchy, the holder of residual rights of control will have the bargaining advantage as time progresses.

In this chapter we relaxed the condition of transaction-specific assets and asked whether incomplete contracting theory could illuminate the reverse of territorial disintegration, that is, regional integration. Although transaction-specific assets may be involved, for example, by facilitating cross-border foreign direct investments, we examined the specific allocation of residual rights of control. States may choose to retain those rights themselves or grant some of those rights over decision making to regional institutions.

As we have seen in the preceding analysis of European integration, the contracting parties had objectives different than those of their North American counterparts. From the outset, the six founding members of the ECSC and the EEC favored comprehensive agreements regarding internal and external tariffs, competition policies, agriculture, and the overseas territories. But the very extensiveness of their ambitions diminished hopes that such agreements could be concluded without relegating matters to future discussions and renegotiations. It required political elites to hold over the details of such agreements for future discussions.

Pending institutional solutions to their contracting problems, however, such a leap of faith would have been foolhardy. Without specific institutional designs, the contracting environment would normally favor the more powerful states. Although small states would have much to gain from trade liberalization given their own limited domestic markets, they would have to fear that the more powerful states would capitalize on their position in the future. In order to circumvent such problems associated with a regional agreement that left many elements underspecified, the stronger states consented to mechanisms that would curtail their room for maneuver. Consequently, important residual rights of control were assigned to regional institutions.

Over time this led to increasing supranational judicial review and increased ECJ activism. At the same time the European Commission was granted considerable powers in drafting additional legislation. Greater supranational legislation (by qualified majority voting) and judicial review raised prospects of a fundamental disjuncture between states' objectives and European-wide institutions. To prevent such a disjuncture, states developed means of fire alarm oversight in the second instance, for example, by passing supranational legislation that could counter runaway ECJ activism.

NAFTA shows a different process. The United States, unlike Germany, had little incentive to tie its hands by supranational institutions. Even if it had wished to do so, power imbalances are so pronounced that the U.S. commitment would lack credibility. Power asymmetries combined with asymmetric preferences. Canada and Mexico were in greater need of an agreement than the United States. Given U.S. reluctance to tie its own hands and Canada and Mexico's concerns about American leverage, the parties have been reluctant to engage in an open-ended incomplete contract. NAFTA is thus a less comprehensive agreement in terms of the range of issues covered, but with full specification on the issues that it does cover. NAFTA exemplifies classical contracting with clear specification of the terms of the agreement and ad hoc arbitration. Without supranational decision making, oversight issues have not arisen.

This analysis challenges realist expectations that European regionalization will stall. Realists aver that the cooperation among the European countries, particularly in its supranational aspects, will decline with the end of the cold war and the declining American presence. Concerns about relative gains will become more pronounced with fears of German dominance.[110]

Instead, the logic of incomplete contracting can explain why EU institutions have become catalysts, driving the integration process forward. Given the incomplete nature of the European foundational treaties, these institutions inevitably acquired broad mandates to expand on the earlier agreements. The very incompleteness of the contract thus required further action if states wanted to capture the full benefits of their earlier agreement.

Finally, the iterative nature of European contracting, the decades of progress to ever closer union, and the expanded powers of supranational adjudication have institutionalized the incomplete contracting process in the EU. Subsequent Court decisions and supranational directives from EU organizations have produced a ratcheting up effect as a result of the dedication of assets following such decisions. Reversal of policies will be more costly than moving forward. That dynamic in turn has also facilitated the credibility of commitment of even the largest powers in the EU.[111]

We also argue that regional differences will persist, contrary to expectations that the EU and NAFTA will converge as time progresses. Their

---

[110] Grieco 1995; Mearsheimer 1994–95.

[111] The economic gains of joining the EU have also become clearer to nonmembers. Following the logic of Richard Baldwin's gravity model of trade, the costs of nonmembership have gradually increased as the membership of the group has expanded. Baldwin, Haaparanta, and Kiander 1995.

variant institutional designs impel different behaviors on the part of national elites and regional institutions. Incomplete contracting will spur further negotiations and specifications by supranational institutions. NAFTA as a complete contract will not.

Thus, the EU and NAFTA will continue to manifest diverse institutional practices through which they pursue the benefits of regional integration. Their institutional configurations have launched the signatories on diverse trajectories. At this point the EU proceeds with a built-in dynamism, while NAFTA is an example of a complete contract agreement with limited objectives to expand vertically into other areas. Accordingly, the likelihood that other regional organizations such as ASEAN and Mercosur will come to resemble either the EU or NAFTA will greatly depend on whether their member states choose to adopt incomplete contracting or a complete contract as a governance mechanism.

Chapter 6

Further Applications and Conclusions

Introduction

We have argued that the nature of contracting in international relations affects how sovereignty is transferred among states and other international actors. In our historical case chapters we have offered new theoretical explanations for the timing and nature of post-imperial extrication, the evolution of U.S. overseas military basing agreements, and the varied institutional forms of regional economic integration. Our case studies included areas encompassing security issues, as well as the study of regional economic integration and contracting over specific economic assets.

The cases examined sovereign transfers in bilateral settings, such as decolonization and U.S. basing arrangements, as well as contracts in which third parties, such as the supranational bodies of the EU, shared sovereignty with states. Throughout all of these topics, we explored the conditions under which incomplete contracting and hybrid sovereignty arrangements emerged, looking at relative power imbalances and the importance of credibility of commitment. We also assessed the consequences of incomplete contracts once they were adopted, especially as they influenced the bargaining dynamics between the actors, contractual renegotiation, and the durability of these contracts.

The cases in the preceding chapters, however, hardly constitute the entire universe of cases of sovereign transfers that incomplete contracting theory might illuminate. Rather than recapitulate our findings in detail, in this final chapter we seek to extend the insights of the incomplete contracting approach to a number of additional theoretical debates and policy questions that relate to sovereign transfers. We believe that incomplete contracting theory can fruitfully illuminate issues that traverse the fields of both international relations and comparative politics. The theory also suggests important lessons for how we can improve the design of sovereign transfers and the institutions that govern them.

We sketch out these additional applications in three concluding mini-cases. In the first we apply incomplete contracting to the study of the durability of ethnofederal states and examine the circumstances under which federal bargains are likely to promote, rather than ameliorate, separatist ethnic antagonism in a constituent unit or even secession from the broader federal polity. In our second case, we show how the institutional design explored in the decolonization chapter applies to other cases of bilateral territorial extrication. Here we examine how institutions that promote joint sovereignty—especially over site-specific assets such as water resources—might help facilitate a resolution in the Arab-Israeli conflict and underscore the potential political problems that such governance arrangements might entail. Finally, we explore how incomplete contracting may apply to a new area of third-party sovereign transfers increasingly used in post-conflict settings—the international administration and governance of a post-conflict territory. We conclude the book by assessing the implications of our study for scholars and policymakers as they consider the institution of sovereignty in the contemporary world of international politics.

Case 1: Federalism as an Institutional Solution to Managing Nationalism

The insights of incomplete contracting theory may be just as relevant to studies of how governance rights shift within larger federal polities as they are to understanding sovereign transfers between states. A central concern among a broad range of comparative scholars is the capacity of federal arrangements to promote the peaceful and stable coexistence of different ethnic groups through selected decentralization and autonomy. Successful federal contracts foster interethnic stability by allowing for autonomy and local governance over issues deemed especially important for preserving group identity.

While for the most part the track record of federalism as an institutional solution is good,[1] some exceptions have led scholars to explore why certain ethnofederal states might become unstable or even disintegrate. Henry Hale has observed that ethnofederations with a strong core ethnic region make instability and collapse much more frequent than those without a core.[2] Dawn Brancati has argued that the prevalence of ethnicity-based regional parties within a political party system can make decentralization politically destabilizing.[3] Others have pointed to democratization and the propensity of new elites to make appeals to nationalism as the key destabilizing force in the collapse of federations.[4]

---

[1] Amoretti and Bermeo 2003; Stepan 1999; Lijphart 1977.
[2] Hale 2004.
[3] Brancati 2006.
[4] See Snyder 2000; Leff 1999.

The striking exceptions to the more general successful cases of federalism are those of the communist multinational states, especially Yugoslavia, the Soviet Union, and Czechoslovakia. In their comprehensive study on federalism and political stability, Ugo Amoretti and Nancy Bermeo hypothesize that the communist cases were exceptional because outside actors imposed these institutions and did so coercively. Other scholars of post-communism have explained the remarkably rapid unraveling of the communist federations as a function of their institutional characteristics such as the structure of the Communist Party, their constitutions, or contradictory nationalities policies.[5] These institutions established a number of parallel identities for federal units that over the long run could not be managed and, in fact, eventually generated incentives for republican elites to push for secession. Thus, over the long term, communist ethnofederations as political organizations were predisposed toward their own demise. However, the main problem with such institutional accounts is that they do not explain why these same federations remained stable for a number of decades before they unraveled so quickly. Nor is the "inevitability" of communist institutional collapse supported by the case of China, where devolution has been more adaptive and stable, or even the post-Soviet institutional persistence of the Russian federation itself (with the notable exception of Chechnya).[6]

An Incomplete Contracting Explanation

From our perspective, a critical institutional feature that helps account for the stability displayed by certain federalist systems over others is the type of contract that underpins the federal bargain. Complete contracts that clearly delineate the rights and obligations of each party do, indeed, offer an important institutional mechanism for managing nationalism; they decentralize control over a number of issues to national federal groups. Clearly specified rights, duties, and obligations can successfully empower regional or ethnic subunits and satisfy demands for autonomy, but retain an overall federal structure in political equilibrium. On the other hand, when federal contracts are incomplete or changed, new holders of residual rights face severe credibility problems as they have the potential to act opportunistically, appropriate greater rents and jurisdictional powers, and demand ever-greater concessions during renegotiation. As with relations among states, holders of the residual rights of control in federalist arrangements—either the center or the federal unit depending

---

[5] See especially Cornell 2002; Bunce 1998; Brubaker 1996; Roeder 1991.

[6] On Chinese economic devolution as a special type of federalism, see Montinola, Qian, and Weingast 1995.

on the issue area—will face credible commitment problems that may well encourage preemptive rebellions or mobilizations along ethnic lines.

We argue that institutional accounts of the collapse of the communist federations miss a critical analytical step: prior to the unraveling of these federations, longstanding complete federal contracts had been renegotiated, for political reasons, into new incomplete contracts that reapportioned the residual rights of control over key issues and functions. In the cases of the Soviet Union and Yugoslavia, well-institutionalized federal systems only collapsed *after* the terms of these federal contracts were altered by the center. Prior to these renegotiations the center and republics had maintained well-institutionalized and highly specified federal contracts that dictated the scope and terms of center-republican interactions, property rights arrangements, and decentralization. Rather than create a renewed federal framework to manage ethnic relations that gave more flexibility and power to the republics, these contractual changes generated deep uncertainty and raised doubts over the credibility of the republics' commitments to honor the territorial integrity of these federations. The political dynamics generated by these new incomplete contracts were different in Yugoslavia, in which the center tried to recentralize, and the Soviet Union, in which Moscow experimentally decentralized. But in both cases contractual abrogation fatally escalated tensions between the center and constituent republics over future institutional design, bargaining power, and the allocation of political rights.

In the Yugoslav case, important sectors in both the economy and security—decentralized since the adoption of the 1974 constitution—were recentralized during the 1980s.[7] In the economy, under external pressure from the IMF, the Yugoslav center reasserted centralized control over monetary policy, taxation, and international financial transactions, thereby undermining the monetary authority of republican-level banks and economic institutions.[8]

Similarly, in the realm of security, the center's organizational reshuffling of the Yugoslav military (JNA) and the disbanding of the Territorial Defense forces in 1990 breached the 1974 constitutional guarantee of a standing defense force to each of the republics.[9] In both the economic sphere and in security affairs, as well as in other key social sectors, recentralization attempts by the Serb-dominated central state to strengthen federal institutions not only fundamentally violated previous constitutional bargains and property rights distributions but, without a formal new legal framework, created severe commitment problems regarding the

---

[7] For more on this interpretation, see A. Cooley 2005a, 127–36.

[8] See Woodward 1995.

[9] See especially Gow 1992.

Serb-dominated center's political aspirations. Ultimately, the countermo-
bilizations by Slovenian and Croatian republican elites were not targeted
toward the terms of the 1974 constitution but were reactions to the seemingly unilateral reassertion of central power by the Serb-dominated center
without an accompanying set of credible guarantees about the necessity,
duration, or exact scope of these new arrangements. After this new incomplete contract that shifted residual control rights back to the center, republican elites faced overwhelming pressure to secede from the federalist project altogether.

In the Soviet case, prevailing complete contracts were renegotiated in
the opposite fashion to that of the recentralization observed in Yugoslavia. After ascending to power as general secretary, Mikhail Gorbachev
initiated ambitious new constitutional and institutional reforms in the
political and economic spheres. Perestroika—the devolution of decision-
making authority to local economic units and administrators for the purposes of economic experimentation—was the greatest alteration of the
central Communist Party contract with its constituent republics since the
formation of the Soviet Union.[10]

Although Gorbachev's reforms at the time were hailed in the West as a
bold step toward modernizing and increasing the Soviet system's flexibility, the incomplete nature of the reforms actually accelerated the superpower's collapse. Rather than encourage innovation as a means toward
saving the viability of the union, this contractual redefinition of the precise obligations and balance of power between the central and republican
parties generated deep uncertainty regarding new property rights arrangements and the planning process, with very poor mechanisms for central
oversight. As Steven Solnick has argued, this type of new contractual
environment effectively initiated a "bank run" on the assets of the Soviet
state, as republican and local officials appropriated the center's property
and authority out of fear that this devolution might be reigned in at some
later point.[11] Unable to adequately monitor or enforce its ill-defined new
rules over these new residual rights holders, the center had no choice but
to acquiesce to its own collapse as nationalist movements in the Baltic
States, Caucasus, and even Russia demanded outright independence.[12]
The program of experimentation that sought to provide a new institutional basis for the modernization of the Soviet system ended up creating
a new incomplete contract that triggered the centrifugal forces that
quickly destroyed it.

---

[10] See the institutional account provided in Roeder 1993, 210–45.
[11] Solnick 1998.
[12] On the dynamics of these national movements, see Beissinger 2002.

Implications for the Study of Federalism and Devolution

We share the general optimism about the efficacy of federal systems and their institutional capacity to manage democratization and minority rights for territorially bound ethnic groups. However, we caution that the type of contracting involved in institutionalizing these decentralizing solutions should be as complete as possible—the degree and scope of devolution should be delineated in full *ex ante*. Although we are unlikely to see the type of deep institutional uncertainty in other cases that was generated by the renegotiation of the federal contract in the communist cases, we do believe that rapid decentralization without adequate specification of residual rights of control over territorially specific assets and key functions may do more harm than good, even if it does not promote outright secession. For example, Spanish president José Luis Rodriguez Zapatero's plan to devolve a number of central government functions—including justice, immigration, labor regulation, and technology policy—has created the most important reorganization of current center-periphery relations in Spain since the 1975 transition from Franco's rule.[13] Yet it is still unclear whether these plans will necessarily quell the demands for separatism in the Basque region, Catalonia, and Galicia or fuel them; this new incomplete contract may empower local nationalist elites to demand further concessions, such as demands for referenda on independence, and create new baselines of autonomy for other regions. Much will depend on the structure of the contract, the designation of residual rights, and what is left for future renegotiation.

Finally, from this perspective, we view the emerging design of Iraq's federalism with great concern. Many have pointed to a federalist solution as the best possible institutional framework for accommodating the political interests and concerns of the country's three main identity groups, the Kurds, Sunnis, and Shi'a. We believe that trends toward incompleteness in the design of the Iraqi constitution may bode ill for the future integrity of the country. As the International Crisis Group commented about the draft constitution during the lead-up to its fall 2005 ratification vote, "Key passages, such as those dealing with decentralisation and with the responsibility for the power of taxation, are both vague and ambiguous and so carry the seeds of future discord. Many vital areas are left for future legislation that will have less standing than the constitution, be more vulnerable to amendment and bear the sectarian imprint of the Shiite community given its likely dominance of future legislatures."[14] Indeed,

---

[13] On the politics of devolution and constitutional revision in Spain, see Losada and Maiz 2005; Encarnacion 2004.

[14] International Crisis Group 2005.

the only way an eleventh hour agreement prior to the October 2005 ratification vote was secured was by guaranteeing to Sunni representatives that the agreement itself would be renegotiated.[15]

Further, without clear governance arrangements to manage the country's oil wealth, Iraq's three sectarian groups may use their existing residual rights of control to appropriate these specific assets for their own in-group purposes and not for the development of the country's central institutions.[16] By institutionalizing incompleteness within the document, future renegotiations will be subject to hard bargaining, intransigent sectarian demands, and acute credibility problems. At the extreme, the long-term viability of Iraq's future territorial integrity may actually have been undermined by the adoption of the incomplete contract embedded in the 2005 constitution.

Case 2: Contracting over Water Rights in the Arab-Israeli Conflict

Similar to our discussion of decolonization in chapter 3, the Arab-Israeli conflict involves rival property claims to transaction-specific assets, specifically water resources. In the wake of the Oslo Accords, Israel and the Palestinian Authority (PA) tried to establish hybrid sovereignty arrangements to allocate sovereign rights over these resources. An incomplete contracting approach sheds additional light on why these have been relatively unsuccessful.

The Evolution of the Contest over Water Resources

Control over water resources has historically been one of the many contested issues in the Arab-Israeli conflict. Indeed, disputes about water supplies were among the causes of the 1967 Six-Day War and the 1982 Israeli incursion into Lebanon.[17] As a consequence of Israel's territorial control over the West Bank, and until recently over Gaza, such control inevitably intertwines with property rights disputes over the subterranean water supply as well as over the surface waters of the Jordan River. As with other disputed site-specific assets, the contesting parties are thus faced with the

---

[15] See *Washington Post*, October 13, 2005, A16; *Los Angeles Times*, October 12, 2005, A1.

[16] We note, for example, the regional oil deals announced by the Kurdish government in the fall of 2007. See Mark Gregory, "Iraqi Kurds Sign Four Oil Deals," *BBC News*, October 4, 2007.

[17] Lowi 1999; J. Cooley 1984.

question of how to divide such assets. With varying degrees of success, Israel and the PA have tried to implement a form of divided sovereignty to address the question of control over this critically important resource.

Israel and the occupied territories draw their water from three main sources. The coastal aquifer runs from northern Israel and terminates in the Gaza Strip. Inland, the mountain aquifer stretches across northeastern Israel into the West Bank.[18] Finally, the Jordan River and the Jarmuk River service Lebanon, Syria, Israel, Jordan, and the Palestinian territories. The upper Jordan flows into the Sea of Galilee and from there on the lower Jordan flows to the Dead Sea. It provides a third of Israel's consumption.[19]

Disputes over the region's water supplies have increasingly taken center stage in the overall Israeli-Palestinian conflict and the occupied areas. First, the coastal aquifer is being seriously depleted. With 1.5 million Palestinians crammed into the Gaza Strip and booming urban centers on Israel's coast, water is being used at such a rate that the saltwater of the Mediterranean is penetrating the underground aquifer.[20] The large discrepancy between Palestinian per capita use and the use by the Israeli settlements in Gaza—prior to their retrenchment, settlers received more than four times the amount that Palestinians received—further reinforced the conflict between locals and Israeli settlers.[21]

The Jordan River basin, too, has been contested territory. The bordering Arab states have accused Israel of using a disproportionate amount of water from the river. Israel has in turn argued that some of the headwaters of the Jordan are being siphoned off before flowing into Israeli-controlled territory.[22]

Finally, the mountain aquifer has been a key source for the West Bank settlements, Israel proper, and the Palestinian towns and refugee camps, and has thus also been a major source of contention. Loehman and Becke observe that "the Mountain Aquifer lies for the most part under the West Bank. It is the source of about 30% of the fresh water supply in Israel and is the most important source of fresh water for Palestinians in the West Bank."[23] Here, too, Israeli per capita use for home, agriculture, and

---

[18] The water resources are classified in various ways. Some analysts thus distinguish among a Western Aquifer, an Eastern Aquifer, a North Eastern Aquifer, and the Coastal Aquifer, of which the Gaza region is one part (Nassar 2006, 49). The groundwater resources that service the West Bank may be further distinguished in three aquifers as well (Isaac 1999).

[19] Luft 2002; Inter Press Service News, April 23, 2003.

[20] Gat 2006, 93.

[21] Isaac 1999.

[22] Lowi 1999.

[23] Loehman and Becke 2006, 265.

industrial purposes greatly surpasses the Palestinian use. Pollution and salinization further diminish this scarce resource.[24] The Palestinian Authority has also accused Israel of deliberately damaging wells and transportation pipes in this area. Availability is so low that many Palestinian families do not obtain the minimum level required to sustain themselves (per UN standards).[25] After Israel seized the West Bank in 1967, its Water Commission Administration granted the Palestinians no more than 20 percent of the groundwater. The rest went to Israel proper and the emerging settlements.[26]

For all these reasons, control over water supplies has been a hotly contested issue. The Oslo II agreement (1995) explicitly aimed to redress this source of the conflict. At the signing of the agreement at Taba in September 1995, Israel committed itself to withdrawing from more than 450 Palestinian towns in exchange for Palestinian recognition of Israel's right to exist and an end to the violence. More specifically regarding water resources, under article 40 Israel formally recognized Palestinian water rights in the West Bank.[27] Israel would also transfer control over water resources in the Gaza Strip, except for the resources that were used by the settlers (roughly 7,000) and military installations. It further mandates that Israel transfer 70–80 million cubic meters of water to the Palestinian Authority.[28]

Some progress has indeed been made in allocating water resources. Thus Israel submits that it has continued to try to implement the terms of Oslo II, although the outbreak of the Second Intifada made it more difficult to deliver the requisite quantities of water. Even after the Intifada erupted, some joint management continued, with the Palestinians authorizing some new supply lines to Israeli settlements in 2002.[29]

The Palestinian perspective is quite different. Seen from their side, Israel has carefully guarded its control over water. Even after Oslo, and certainly after the outbreak of the Second Intifada in September 2000, Israel had used its control rights over the water supplies to deny Palestinian use rights. The Israeli Defense Forces (IDF) have controlled the territory and have largely denied the Palestinians the opportunity to dig new wells.

[24] Gat 2006, 92.

[25] For the Palestinian perspective on how Israel uses water as a means of control, see the Water and Sanitation Hygiene Monitoring Project (WaSH MP), http://www.phg.org /wash-mp/.

[26] Lowi 1999, 385.

[27] Stephan 2006; Rouyer 1999. See also http://www.transboundarywaters.orst.edu /publications/.

[28] Inter Press Service News, April 23, 2003.

[29] Selby 2006, 333.

Foreign Residual Rights and Israel's Bargaining Leverage

These conflicts over water rights and the difficulties of creating stable agreements on this issue conform to our expectations. Prior to Oslo II, Israel had full control and use rights over the water resources in the occupied territories. As we would expect, Israel's first preference would be to maintain full control over this transaction-specific asset. However, with international pressure mounting after the first Gulf War, and with increasing resistance in the occupied territories, as evinced in the First Intifada, it became more difficult to unilaterally exert full control. Moreover, following the Oslo Accords of 1993 and the 1994 Israeli-Jordanian peace treaty, Jordan relinquished its claims to the West Bank. With the door opening to a possible Palestinian state, Israel came to recognize that in such an event full control over the resources in the occupied territories would gradually have to be ceded. Yet, at the same time, Israel looked askance at a fully independent Palestinian state over which it would have little control. Thus, although Israel remained unquestionably the more powerful actor, the costs of pursuing full hierarchy (analytically the same solution as empire in the cases of decolonization) rose significantly.

Given the need to rearrange existing governance structures and in order to deal with these trans-boundary resource issues, Israel and the Palestinian Authority have tried to develop hybrid governance arrangements.[30] The Oslo agreement thus created a Palestinian Water Authority (PWA). The PWA would take on the management and control of all Palestinian water resources. Palestinian citizens of the future state would be granted use rights but not ownership of water resources, which would remain with the state. The agreement also established a joint umbrella organization, the Joint Water Committee (JWC), for the shared management of water resources. Procedurally, the JWC required consensus decision making. One critical observer noted that "through this mechanism Israel maintains a veto power . . . over all decisions (licensing, drilling, increased extraction . . .) in water resources management in the West Bank, including over proper Palestinian resources as the Eastern basin of the Mountain Aquifer."[31]

The process subsequent to Oslo II has been anything but smooth. Israel relinquished some use rights in taking on obligations to provide the PA with a given quantity of water. But while it committed itself in Oslo II to a complete transfer of resources in Gaza (except water used by the settlers and the IDF), it only committed to ceding partial control to the PWA in

---

[30] Rouyer 1999.
[31] Stephan 2006, 69.

the West Bank. The issue of ownership was to be negotiated in the context of the permanent status talks.

As we would expect, the holder of residual rights (Israel) has used its control to put pressure on the actor holding only use rights. With the breakdown of negotiations following the failure of the Camp David negotiations (2000) and the outbreak of the Second Intifada, Israel has firmly insisted on maintaining residual rights over the water supply for the West Bank. And indeed it has used its control over the supply to engage in hard bargaining, as evidenced by its decision to withhold water that it is supposed to supply the Palestinians according to Oslo II. More recently, Israel has used the security barrier and the geographical dispersion of the various Palestinian enclaves to maintain control over the distribution network. Indeed, the water supply has been largely handled by Mekorot, Israel's national water authority.[32] The Palestinian population has complained that it should be given use rights to the water within the territorial boundaries controlled by the PA. De facto, however, Israel has limited the drilling of new wells for Palestinian use as well as control over the infrastructure for transportation of the water.

In our taxonomy this situation thus resembles allocation with a foreign power holding the residual rights (see figure 3.1). As the holder of the residual rights it can severely restrict the Palestinian latitude of actions. Israel's current desalinization project demonstrates this logic succinctly. As said, despite a breakdown of the larger peace process, under Oslo II Israel is bound to deliver a fixed quantity of water to the Palestinian Authority. Given demographic growth, and given that Israel does not provide water from the Jordan to the Palestinians on the West Bank, this means that Israel would have to increasingly tap into the mountain aquifer or allow the Palestinian Authority greater access to the subterranean water resources of the West Bank.[33] Instead, Jerusalem explored an alternative plan. It aimed to supply the Palestinian areas with water produced by a desalinization plant in Caesaria, located on Israel's coast. Thus Israel would still maintain control over the fixed asset (the aquifer) and over the water supply since the desalinization plant and the pipelines to transport the water would all be located in Israel.

The project was not driven by economic efficiency. According to Israeli water expert Arie Issar, "it would be foolish to desalinate water on the coast and push it up the mountains when there are underground water resources up there, which cost only a third as much."[34] Jerusalem aimed

---

[32] For a discussion of Mekorot's general role in water management, see Selby 2003.

[33] Israel submits that the water from the Jordan River is already shared by Syria, Lebanon, and Israel. Jerusalem argues, moreover, that it already supplies water to Jordan. Inter Press Service News, April 23, 2003.

[34] Quoted in *New Scientist*, May 27, 2004, http://www.newscientist.com/article/dn5037-israel-lays-claim-to-palestines-water.html.

to get U.S. financial aid to develop this system, which was vastly more expensive than the alternative. The proposal was driven by a desire to retain control rights over the aquifers rather than by economic motives.

Not surprisingly, the Palestinian Authority had serious concerns about this plan. Although Israel would technically be fulfilling the terms of Oslo II, bargaining leverage would continue to reside with Israel. The Palestinian Authority had reason to fear that Jerusalem would engage in hard bargaining and use its leverage to put pressure on overall Palestinian policy.

The Gaza Strip provides another example. Here, Israel turned full control rights over to the Palestinians following the withdrawal of the settler population in 2005. But the coastal aquifer is already being depleted at an alarming rate. While the aquifer could supply 60–65 million cubic meters a year on an ongoing basis, it is currently being tapped at 150 million cubic meters. Seawater is consequently infiltrating, with the remainder seriously polluted. Thus, while Israel's transfer of authority over Gaza gives the Palestinian Authority political control, Israel still retains bargaining leverage in that the Palestinian demand for water exceeds long-term supply. The authorities in Gaza will thus have to rely on supplies from Israel, giving the latter continued influence.[35]

With residual rights shifting to the PA, the burden of credible commitment shifted from Israel to the Palestinians. Continued infighting in the Palestinian camp and questions about the legitimacy of the corrupt PA leadership have raised doubts about the PA's ability to credibly commit.[36] The conflicts between the Palestinian Authority and Hamas only further complicated this inability to make credible commitments.

To conclude, Israel continues to assess water issues in the framework of its overall security, as it did in the past. As early as 1977 Prime Minister Begin asked for an evaluation of possible zones of withdrawal from some of the occupied territories that would not jeopardize Israel's water supply. The Cator Commission subsequently drew a red line delineating which territories would meet that criterion.[37] A 1991 study by the Jaffee Center similarly drafted a map that delineated areas that could be returned but would still give Israel control over key water supplies.[38] Israel's retention of foreign residual rights "has left Palestinians in a situation where they are increasingly dependant [sic]on Israeli water infrastructure . . . Israel

[35] Amira Hass, "The Settlers Are Gone, the Polluted Water Remains," ZNET Mideast, August 26, 2005, http://www.zmag.org. An externally funded project is currently under way to build a desalinization plant in Gaza.

[36] The Palestinian intellectual Edward Said decried the PA as "at bottom a kind of Mafia" (2000, 22).

[37] Arsenault 2006, 195.

[38] The report was subsequently censored because the Israeli position at the time was to maintain control over the entire West Bank. See Wolf 1995.

has been responsible for its maintenance, where deemed necessary, and regulation."[39] Indeed, some observers have likened the existing relationship to creeping colonization. It is thus analytically closer to a neo-imperial situation than to allocation with national residual rights of control.[40]

Israel's position as well as the breakdown of the Oslo provisions on joint sovereignty over the relevant water resources fully comport with our expectations. The incomplete nature of the Oslo agreement made it inevitable that both parties would seek to obtain future bargaining leverage. Israel realized that it could maintain hegemonic control over the Palestinians as long as it retained residual rights of control. Conversely, the PA sought to gain more residual rights to diminish this leverage.

Consequently, both sides needed to demonstrate credibility in commitment. However, decades of conflict made it difficult to establish credibility by reputation. Moreover, the open-ended nature of the criteria for gradual transfer of sovereignty rights made it easy for Israeli and Palestinian opponents of the Oslo Accords to claim that the other side had not fulfilled the preconditions stipulated in Oslo. What exactly constituted a full cessation of hostilities as Oslo required? If extremists on either side engaged in violence, did this mean that the governments in question had violated the terms?

Both sides also lacked the institutions to commit credibly. The internal divisions among the Palestinian elites and the stalemate between Hamas and the PA raised doubts about the ability of their leadership to control the various factions. Similarly, the fragmented nature of Israel's cabinets raised doubts its ability to commit as well.[41]

With poorly specified hybrid sovereignty arrangements and weak credibility to commit, the incomplete contract was in trouble from the start. Combined with a lack of perceived joint gains, the breakdown of the Oslo water accords should come as no surprise.

Case 3: International Transitional Administration: The Case of Kosovo

Finally, our theory of incomplete contracting and sovereign transfers can contribute to understanding the dilemmas and governance problems that confront international administrators in post-conflict states.

---

[39] Arsenault 2006, 198–99; see also Selby 2003.

[40] For this critical assessment of the water arrangements in Oslo II, see Selby 2006, 326.

[41] See Spruyt 2005 on the consequences of weak coalitional governments in Israel. Shikaki (2002) notes how Arafat's support and the legitimacy of the PA had shrunk precipitously even before the Second Intifada.

Transitional Administration: Third-Party Incomplete Contracting

Since the end of the cold war, the international community has governed a number of post-conflict territories and regions under a UN mandate.[42] In cases such as Bosnia, Slavonia, East Timor, and Kosovo, the UN established bodies staffed with international administrators who were granted formal governing powers. In general, this "transitional" authority was designed to facilitate the eventual complete transfer of sovereignty to a target government or to a nascent government of an emergent independent state. UN bodies such as the UN Transitional Administration in East Timor (UNTAET) or the UN Transitional Administration for Eastern Slavonia, Baranja, and Western Sirmmium (UNTAES), unlike earlier international peacekeeping missions, actually governed a wide variety of state-building functions within these post-conflict states including election administration, internal policing, revenue collection, legal reform, and education.[43] Scholars have noted the similarities between these new UN bodies and previous historical colonial missions and/or the mandate system of international trusteeship authorized by the League of Nations.[44] This revival of international administration in post-conflict situations has been accompanied by a renewed academic interest in the broader merits of creating new institutions to "share sovereignty" between weak states and the international community.[45]

Our theory of sovereign transfers and incomplete contracting can illuminate some of the political and institutional challenges faced by the administrators of these post-conflict international bodies. Like our discussion of European decolonization, international transitional administration has helped facilitate territorial disengagement by creating hybrid sovereignty arrangements in post-conflict environments or disputed territories. In areas such as the Balkans and East Timor, international administration helped facilitate the emergence of new sovereign states in the international system.

But unlike decolonization, which usually was characterized by bilateral contracting between the former imperial core and periphery, the introduction of transitional administration involves the transfer of sovereignty to a third party—the international community. In turn, this international body of administrators will gradually cede power to the new institutions of the governed territory, but in so doing will ensure that the host govern-

[42] For overviews, see Chesterman 2004; Caplan 2002.

[43] See Marten 2004; Paris 2004.

[44] On colonial analogies, see Marten 2004. On trusteeship and its similarities to today's international missions, see Bain 2003; Chesterman 2004, 11–47.

[45] See Krasner 2005, 2004; Fearon and Laitin 2004.

ment abides by the commitments it has made to the international community regarding its state-building goals. Thus, analytically, international transitional administrators must sequence and design the sovereign transfer so as to ensure both political stability in the emerging state and its adherence to international standards of democratic governance. Our theory of incomplete contracting can help clarify these challenges.

An Example: The Evolution of the Kosovo Case

The evolution of the case of Kosovo, the former province of Yugoslavia and then Serbia, illustrates some potential contributions of incomplete contracting theory to the study of international transitional administration. Kosovo has undergone a number of different complete and incomplete contractual arrangements. Under the Yugoslavian constitution, from 1974 to 1989 Kosovo was an autonomous province, after which Serbia reasserted direct governance over it. Throughout the 1990s, Kosovo retained this diminished status even as constituent republics seceded from Yugoslavia, while ethnic tensions spiraled into interethnic violence between Serbs and Kosovars. By 1998 the United States and the EU had imposed sanctions on Yugoslavia and threatened military action in the region to protect the Kosovars. In March 1999, after Yugoslav president Slobodan Milosevic rejected the Rambouillet conference proposal for the province's increased autonomy, NATO launched a bombing campaign to compel the Serbian military to abandon Kosovo.[46]

Although the UN Security Council did not authorize the military action, the end of the war was marked by the adoption of UN Resolution 1244. The resolution placed Kosovo under the mandate of the United Nations Interim Mission in Kosovo (UNMIK) and authorized the deployment of the Kosovo Force (KFOR). SCR 1244 gave no guarantee of Kosovo's eventual independence; rather, it mandated that UNMIK grant the province "substantial autonomy within the Federal Republic of Yugoslavia" for an interim period.[47] UNMIK assumed almost complete governing authority, essentially designating the Balkan province a UN protectorate, and was charged with developing Kosovo's "democratic self-governing institutions." Thus, in the immediate postwar phase, UNMIK exercised neocolonial powers as a third-party sovereign authority.[48] As Simon Chesterman points out, in a rather curious reversal of usual patterns, UNMIK during this initial phase often found itself on the defensive when answering to human rights organizations for not

---

[46] For an account, see Bellamy 2002.
[47] Quoted in Chesterman 2004, 132.
[48] See the detailed account in King and Mason 2006, 49–92.

imposing stricter martial law to protect human rights and maintain social order.[49]

In 2001, this neocolonial phase gave way to a period equivalent to the foreign residual rights outcome. In this phase, which lasted until the summer of 2002, the territory adopted a constitution, held its first elections, and established a working dialogue with Belgrade.[50] Under a constitutional framework adopted in May 2001, UNMIK was to gradually transfer specific domestic sovereign responsibilities and functions to the new Kosovar-controlled body called Provisional Institutions of Self-Government (PISG). The PISG would be made up of an assembly to elect a government (including a president), a legislature (including a prime minister), and a judiciary. However, UNMIK would retain control over all other sovereign decisions and the conduct of foreign affairs, as well as actively monitor the newly constituted Kosovo Police Service. Once these local institutions were established, UNMIK began to transfer its foreign residual rights over local governance to the new local government. Over the course of the summer and fall of 2002, Kosovar Albanians assumed control over ten governance portfolios previously administered by UNMIK, all of which were converted into newly formed ministries.[51]

But after the Kosovar Albanians appropriated increased sovereign power and the institutions of basic statehood, Serbia and Serbian minorities within Kosovo bitterly protested the competence and democratic commitment of the Kosovar Albanian authorities. Kosovar Albanians were criticized for failing to protect Serbian minorities, discriminating against them in legal decisions, and inadequately guarding Serbian cultural sites and churches from communal violence.[52] Consistent with our theory, authorities in Pristina faced a growing credibility problem as the international community worried about its capacity to exercise effective democratic governance.

In an attempt to solve the problem, the UN and UNMIK adopted a policy titled "Standards before Status," first developed in 2002 by Michael Steiner, the head of UNMIK. Under this initiative, Kosovar Albanian officials would have to demonstrate to the international community improvement across eight broad areas of governance in harmony with European values before they would be allowed to enter into final status arrangements.[53] International working committees would monitor Ko-

---

[49] Chesterman 2004, 79.

[50] King and Mason 2006, 93–136.

[51] Ibid., 160.

[52] See, for example, the critiques leveled in Human Rights Watch 2004; International Crisis Group 2004.

[53] See King and Mason 2006, 173–75, 234–39.

sovo's compliance and would issue quarterly evaluations of progress toward meeting these benchmarks.

However, events on the ground undercut the standards efforts.[54] For example, after a period of violence in March 2004, a Human Rights Watch Report suggested that UNMIK and the Kosovo Police Service had "failed catastrophically in their mandate to protect minority communities."[55] In 2005, the standards process was officially interrupted when a report by Norwegian diplomat Kai Eide declared that Kosovo's leadership and governance had failed to meet these targets. The report observed that progress in improving standards would be impossible until Kosovo's future status could be clarified, thereby seemingly reversing the original rationale for the standards requirement.[56] In this state of uncertain residual rights apportioned between the international community and Kosovo's transitional state, both UNMIK and Pristina failed to make their commitments credible—the Kosovar authorities failed to improve local governance while UNMIK proceeded to call for final status talks without insisting on demonstrated improvement in standards.

In March 2007, after fifteen rounds of direct negotiations between Belgrade and Pristina, special UN envoy Martti Ahtisaari declared deadlock between the parties and submitted his recommendation for a final settlement to the UN Security Council. The report recommended that Kosovo be granted "supervised independence," or the right of self-government and international recognition subject to a transitional period over which the Pristina government would have to demonstrate its commitment to uphold democratic practices and protect minority rights. The international supervision role would include the participation of an International Civilian Representative, a European Security and Defense Policy mission, a continued NATO military presence to provide security, and an Organization for Security and Co-operation in Europe (OSCE) mission to monitor implementation.[57] From our theoretical perspective, the plan for "supervised independence" amounted to host country residual rights with third-party supervision. However, the Security Council did not accept the Ahtisaari Plan, given that Serbia refused to accept any type of process that granted "independence" to the province. Russia, which insisted throughout 2007 that granting even conditional independence to Kosovo would constitute a dangerous precedent, backed Belgrade and called for renewed negotiations for a new bilateral solution.[58]

---

[54] See Bardos 2005.

[55] Human Rights Watch 2004, 2–3. Also discussed in Bardos 2005, 17.

[56] On this point and the implications of the report, see Woodward 2007.

[57] Woodward 2007, 17–18.

[58] On Russia's position, see Antonenko 2007.

On February 15, 2008, just a week after the second round of presidential elections in Serbia, the Kosovo Parliament after a special session declared unilateral independence from Serbia. Shortly afterward, the United States, the United Kingdom, France, Germany, and Italy recognized Kosovo's independence, while Russia and Serbia fiercely opposed the move. Several EU countries—including Spain, Romania, and Cyprus—also withheld recognition, fearing that doing so would empower ethnic separatist movements within their own borders. EU-backed teams were dispatched to Pristina to monitor the newly independent state's governance.

Designing Better Institutions for International Administration

Our theory of incomplete contracting illuminates many of the analytical and practical problems confronted by international administrators. As the evolution of the Kosovo case suggests, the various stages of transitional administration correspond to various configurations of hybrid sovereignty arrangements and allocations of residual rights. Immediately following NATO military action, UNMIK effectively governed Kosovo as an imperial authority—its decisions were final and its rule was unchecked. Two years later, UNMIK transferred some governance functions in domestic policy to the newly created institutions of the Kosovar government and its elected officials. Beginning in 2003, UNMIK gradually began to transfer other residual rights to these local authorities in preparation for final status negotiations, effectively creating two competing sets of governing institutions, one at the level of UNMIK and the other local.

With these transfers, however, came the problem of credible commitment. As the Kosovo side built up the institutions for self-governance, its bargaining leverage improved and its need to demonstrate commitment to international standards diminished. In a fixed-term contract with residual rights, local actors have few incentives to invest in the relationship with a third party if they are certain that they subsequently will appropriate complete control at the point of independence. This observation is firmly grounded in the logic of incomplete contracting and the expectation that bargaining leverage will accrue to holders of residual rights.[59] The UN established a "standards before status" process that was designed to assure Belgrade and the international community that a Kosovar Albanian government would be able to credibly guarantee its commitments to the Serbian minority. But rather than smooth the way for a final status negotiation, events on the ground undercut the standards benchmarks.

The imposition of international administration over post-conflict territories has been criticized from a variety of perspectives. Some have criti-

[59] Krasner 2004, 115.

cized the near-colonial powers and lack of accountability that international managers have exhibited in missions such as Bosnia and Kosovo.[60] Others have argued that transitional governments or international trusteeships, such as in Bosnia and Kosovo, seldom work efficiently given that local leaders and elites look to further the interests of their indigenous power base or local ethnic group rather than to cooperate to forge stable institutions that will promote integrated state-building.[61] We would add, however, that the logic of incomplete contracting suggests that institutional design, not just its duration, is potentially critical. The Kosovo case suggests that the staggered transfer of sovereignty from UNMIK to the Kosovar government created institutional uncertainty regarding where power truly rested. Moreover, the international community itself failed to enforce its own standards, thereby undermining its own future credibility for dealing with both Pristina and Belgrade. The Kosovo experience suggests that international administrators must more clearly delineate the sequencing for the transfer of residual rights and, perhaps even more important, not introduce subsequent phases of transfer unless they are certain that a target government has clearly met its obligations. Otherwise, the international community's ability to improve governance after the transfer of residual rights to the host will be limited or even negligible.

A World of Partially Incomplete Contracts

Together with our more in-depth chapter case studies, these three mini-cases suggest a wide variety of potential applications of the incomplete contracting approach. The sketches of ethnofederalism, Middle Eastern water rights, and international transitional administration add to our more detailed examination of decolonization, U.S. basing rights, and regional economic integration. In conclusion, our study suggests three important findings for political scientists, institutional economists, and sociologists interested in sovereignty and governance.

First, we believe that we can no longer treat the institution of sovereignty as zero-sum, either conceptually or practically. Exclusive sovereignty, in both its anarchical and hierarchical forms, is a possible but not a necessary state of affairs. Underlying property rights can be split between two (or more) states and/or with third parties such as a supranational body or an international administrative organization. Indeed, as our decolonization case suggests, brokering incomplete contracts may

---

[60] See Chandler 2006, 2000; Knaus and Martin 2003.

[61] Krasner 2004, 99–105; also see the discussion of the problems of "liberal peace-building" in Paris 2004.

well be a precondition to successfully transferring sovereignty from the exclusive domain of one polity to another. The variety of sovereign forms of governance in international politics is significant and mirrors the variety of organizational forms found in the private sector. Just as firms can organize themselves as joint ventures, public-private partnerships, consortia, and/or subsidiaries, states can use foreign residual rights and national residual rights to configure and govern their sovereign rights.

Some scholars may remain skeptical of the significance of these alternate governance forms. For example, realists might dismiss territorial leasing arrangements as "neocolonial" or regional supranational institutions as irrelevant. Yet, we have taken care to show within our decolonization and basing cases that neo-imperial outcomes actually differed from these incomplete contracts such as territorial leasing. Nor do we accept the premise that incomplete contracting is limited to "marginal" issues in international relations. Some of these issues and their governance may be routine, while others may be related to more fundamental matters concerning peace and security. Regardless, they are now part of the range of institutions that govern international interactions among sovereign states.

Second, our theory and cases highlight the critical importance of credible commitments in contractual design. We have seen that making credible commitments is particularly important for states that retain residual rights of control during renegotiation. States and supranational organizations with residual rights can certainly exploit their bargaining advantage by appropriating surpluses and additional jurisdictional authority. However, there may be a trade-off between expanding sovereign authority and retaining credibility. The failed referenda in 2005 on the EU Constitution in France and the Netherlands demonstrate that such credibility problems can even stall or halt momentum for sovereign transfers. Thus, resolving credibility problems needs to be of paramount importance when contracts are drawn up to enact sovereign transfers.

Third, we believe that our theory and cases suggest that negotiations and renegotiations over sovereign rights can never be truly independent bargains or one-time political acts. Sovereign transfers usually are not akin to the "prisoner's dilemma." Renegotiations will necessarily be conditioned by previous configurations of assets and bargaining power, as well as by states' concerns over future distributional consequences. As long as contracts remain incomplete, transfers of sovereignty are continuous and iterated, even when not explicitly legally codified.

Beyond these analytical lessons, studying sovereign transfers as incomplete contracts provides an important analytical lens for understanding the current state of international politics. For example, we believe that the common proposition that the twin forces of internationalization and globalization are eroding state sovereignty is a clumsy conceptual approach to the topic. Some state functions are indeed being delegated to other international actors such as international organizations, NGOs, the private sector, and even other states. However, others remain firmly within the scope of state autonomy.[62] Yet, what is more important for us is to understand *how* traditionally sovereign functions and assets are being transferred, what types of contracts now govern them, and which party retains the residual rights of control. Indeed, we hope that the growing study of global governance will pay more attention to the mechanisms of governance in addition to identifying the new private and public actors who now perform these governance tasks.

Our analysis also has important policy ramifications. As a practical matter we have become accustomed to think of exclusive sovereignty as a right and even entitlement of modern states and aspiring separatist movements. Yet, as we have shown, several forms of intermediary sovereignty have governed the transfer of state functions and assets. Various states and political actors have managed to share and split sovereignty, and by so doing have averted violent conflict. Finding stable and non-conflictual resolution to territorial disputes and extrication may require actors to adopt creative solutions such as unbundling and reapportioning sovereign rights.

Moreover, in an era in which territorial conquest and colonialism have become less normatively accepted modes of sovereign acquisition by the international community, understanding the various institutional mechanisms available to states to transfer sovereignty peacefully is critical.[63] Having established that sovereignty is rarely absolute and is regularly violated, the pressing task now for scholars and policymakers is to find more effective ways to manage sovereign transfers into stable, durable, and nonviolent institutional solutions. Successfully designing new institutions to manage two or more international actors' competing and potentially equally legitimate claims on a territory or asset remains a central concern in international politics. But we have theoretical guidance and historical precedent for meeting these challenges.

[62] On economic integration and changing state borders, see Alesina and Spolaore 2003.

[63] On anticolonial norms, see Crawford 2002; Jackson 1993. On the emergent norm of territorial integrity, see Fazal 2007; Zacher 2001.

Bibliography

Abbott, Frederick. 2000. NAFTA and the Legalization of World Politics: A Case Study. *International Organization* 54 (3):519–47.

Abdelal, Rawi E. 2001. *National Purpose in the World Economy: Post-Soviet States in Comparative Perspective*. Ithaca: Cornell University Press.

Adler, Emanuel, and Michael Barnett, eds. 1998. *Security Communities*. New York: Cambridge University Press.

Ageron, Charles-Robert. 1992. Les accords d'Évian (1962). *Vingtième siècle: Revue d'histoire* 35:3–15.

Akre, Phillip J. 1992. Algeria and the Politics of Energy-Based Industrialization. In *State and Society in Algeria*, ed. John P. Entelis and Phillip C. Naylor. Boulder, CO: Westview Press.

Alesina, Alberto, and Enrico Spolaore. 2003. *The Size of Nations*. Cambridge, MA: MIT Press.

Alexander, M. S., and John Keiger. 2002. France and the Algerian War, 1954–62: Strategy Operations and Diplomacy. *Journal of Strategic Studies* 25 (2):1–32.

Alter, Karen J. 1998. Who Are the "Masters of the Treaty"?: European Governments and the European Court of Justice. *International Organization* 52 (1):121–47.

———. 2000. The European Union's Legal System and Domestic Policy: Spillover or Backlash? *International Organization* 54 (3):489–518.

Alter, Karen, and David Steinberg. 2007. The Theory and Reality of the European Coal and Steel Community. In *Making History: European Integration and Institutional Change at Fifty*, ed. Sophie Meunier and Kathleen McNamara. New York: Oxford University Press.

Amoretti, Ugo, and Nancy Bermeo, eds. 2003. *Federalism and Territorial Cleavages*. Baltimore: Johns Hopkins University Press.

Antonenko, Oksana. 2007. Russia and the Deadlock over Kosovo. *Survival* 49 (3):91–106.

Antunes, José Freire. 1999. Kennedy, Portugal, and the Azores Base, 1961. In *John F. Kennedy and Europe*, ed. Douglas Brinkley and Richard T. Griffiths. Baton Rouge: Louisiana State University Press.

Archer, Clive. 1990. *Organizing Western Europe*. London: Edward Arnold.

———. 2003. Greenland, U.S. Bases and Missile Defense: New Two-Level Negotiations? *Cooperation and Conflict* 38 (2):125–47.

Arkin, William M., and Richard W. Fieldhouse. 1985. *Nuclear Battlefields: Global Links in the Arms Race*. Cambridge, MA: Ballinger.

Arsenault, David. 2006. The Effects of the Separation Barrier on the Viability of the Future Palestinian State. In *Water for Life in the Middle East*, ed. Hillel Shuval and Hasan Dwiek. Jerusalem: Israel/Palestine Center for Research and Information.

Axelrod, Robert. 1984. *The Evolution of Cooperation*. New York: Basic Books.

Baev, Pavel. 2008. *Russian Energy Policy and Military Power: Putin's Quest for Greatness*. New York: Taylor and Francis.

Bain, William. 2003. *Between Anarchy and Society: Trusteeship and Obligations of Power*. Oxford: Oxford University Press.

Baker-Fox, Annette. 1995. Environment and Trade: The NAFTA Case. *Political Science Quarterly* 110:49–68.

Baldwin, David A. 1989. *Paradoxes of Power*. Oxford: Blackwell.

———, ed. 1993. *Neorealism and Neoliberalism: The Contemporary Debate*. New York: Columbia University Press.

Baldwin, Richard, Perti Haaparanta, and Jaakko Kiander. 1995. *Expanding Membership of the European Union*. Cambridge: Cambridge University Press.

Balencie, Jean-Marc. 1991/92. Le renforcement de la presence navale française en Ocean Indien au debut des années 70. Institut de Stratégie Comparée. *Strate-gique* no. 54. Available at http://www.stratisc.org/strat_054_Balenci.html.

Bardos, Gordon N. 2005. Containing Kosovo. *Mediterranean Quarterly* 16 (3):17–43.

Barnett, Michael. 2005. Humanitarianism Transformed. *Perspectives on Politics* 3 (4):723–40.

Barnett, Thomas P. M. 2004. *The Pentagon's New Map: War and Peace in the 21st Century*. New York: G. P. Putnam's Sons.

Bates, Robert, Avner Greif, Margaret Levi, and Jean-Laurent Rosenthal. 1998. *Analytic Narratives*. Princeton: Princeton University Press.

Beissinger, Mark R. 2002. *Nationalist Mobilization and the Collapse of the Soviet State*. New York: Cambridge University Press.

Bellamy, Alex J. 2002. *Kosovo and International Society*. New York: Palgrave MacMillan.

Bengzon, Alfredo. 1997. *A Matter of Honor: The Story of the 1990–91 RP-US Bases Treaty*. Manila: Anvil Books.

Bernheim, B. Douglas, and Michael D. Whinston. 1998. Incomplete Contracts and Strategic Ambiguity. *American Economic Review* 88 (4):902–32.

Berry, William Jr. 1989. *U.S. Bases in the Philippines: The Evolution of the Special Relationship*. Boulder, CO: Westview Press.

Berstein, Serge. 1986. French Power as Seen by the Political Parties after World War II. In *Power in Europe?: Great Britain, France, Italy, and Germany in a Postwar World, 1945–1950*, ed. Josef Becker and Franz Knipping. New York: W. de Gruyter.

———. 1993. *The Republic of de Gaulle, 1958–1969*. New York: Cambridge University Press.

Bhagwati, Jagdish. 1993. Beyond NAFTA: Clinton's Trading Choices. *Foreign Policy* 91:155–62.

Blaker, James. 1990. *United States Overseas Basing: The Anatomy of the Dilemma*. Westport, CT: Praeger.

Bonner, Raymond. 1987. *Waltzing with a Dictator: The Marcoses and the Making of American Policy*. New York: New York Times Books.

Bowen, Alva Jr. 1988. US Facilities in the Philippines. In *The Philippine Bases: Negotiating for the Future*, ed. Fred Greene. New York: Council on Foreign Relations.

Boycko, Maxim, Andrei Shleiffer, and Robert Vishny. 1995. *Privatizing Russia.* Cambridge, MA: MIT Press.

Brancati, Dawn. 2006. Decentralization: Fueling the Fire or Dampening the Flames of Ethnic Conflict and Secessionism. *International Organization* 60 (3):651–85.

Broad, Robin. 1988. *Unequal Alliance: The World Bank, the International Monetary Fund, and the Philippines.* Berkeley: University of California Press.

Brubaker, Rogers. 1996. *Nationalism Reframed: Nationhood and the National Question in the New Europe.* New York: Cambridge University Press.

Bueno, Gerardo. 1988. A Mexican View. In *Bilateralism, Multilateralism and Canada in U.S. Trade Policy,* ed. William Diebold. Cambridge, MA: Ballinger.

Bueno de Mesquita, Bruce, Alistair Smith, Randolph M. Siverson, and James D. Morrow. 2003. *The Logic of Political Survival.* Cambridge, MA: MIT Press.

Buesst, Tristan. 1932. The Naval Base at Singapore. *Pacific Affairs* 5 (4):306–18.

Bunce, Valerie. 1985. The Empire Strikes Back: The Transformation of the Eastern Bloc from a Soviet Asset to a Soviet Liability. *International Organization* 39 (1):1–46.

———. 1999. *Subversive Institutions: The Design and Destruction of Socialism and the State.* New York: Cambridge University Press.

Burley, Anne-Marie, and Walter Mattli. 1993. Europe before the Court: A Political Theory of Legal Integration. *International Organization* 47 (1):41–76.

Butt, Ronald. 1966. The Common Market and Conservative Party Politics, 1961–62. *Government and Opposition* 2:372–86.

Calder. Kent. 2007. *Embattled Garrisons: Comparative Base Politics and American Globalism.* Princeton: Princeton University Press.

Calvet de Magalhães, José. 1993. U.S. Forces in Portugal, 1943–1962. In *U.S. Military Forces in Europe: The Early Years, 1945–1970,* ed. Simon Duke and Wolfgang Krieger. Boulder, CO: Westview Press.

Cameron, Maxwell A., and Brian Tomlin. 2000. *The Making of NAFTA: How the Deal Was Done.* Ithaca: Cornell University Press.

Camp, Roderic. 1990. Camarillas in Mexican Politics: The Case of the Salinas Cabinet. *Mexican Studies* 6 (1):85–107.

Campbell, Kurt M., and Celeste Johnson Ward. 2003. New Battle Stations? *Foreign Affairs* 82, no. 5 (September–October):95–103.

Caplan, Richard. 2002. *A New Trusteeship? The International Administration of War-Torn Territories.* New York: Oxford University Press.

Carver, Michael. 1992. *Tightrope Walking: British Defence Policy since 1945.* London: Hutchinson.

Castro, A., ed. 1983. *Agreements on United States Military Facilities in Philippine Military Bases.* Manila: Foreign Service Institute.

Chandler, David. 2000. *Bosnia: Faking Democracy after Dayton.* London: Pluto.

———. 2006. *Empire in Denial: The Politics of State-Building.* London: Pluto.

Chandrasekaran, Rajiv. 2006. *Imperial Life in the Emerald City: Inside Iraq's Green Zone.* New York: Knopf.

Chesterman, Simon. 2004. *You, the People: The United Nations, Transitional Administration, and State-Building.* New York: Oxford University Press.

Clarke, Duncan L., and Daniel O'Connor. 1993. U.S. Base Rights Payments after the Cold War. *Orbis* 37:441–57.

Clayton, Anthony. 1988. *France, Soldiers, and Africa*. London: Brassey's Defence Publishers.

———. 1999. Deceptive Might: Imperial Defence and Security, 1900–1968. In *The Oxford History of the British Empire: The Twentieth Century*, ed. Judith Brown and Wm. Roger Louis. Oxford: Oxford University Press.

Cohen, Benjamin J. 2003. *The Future of Money*. Princeton: Princeton University Press.

Cohen-Tanugi, Laurent. 2005. The End of Europe? *Foreign Affairs* 84 (6):55–67.

Cooley, Alexander. 2000–2001. Imperial Wreckage: Property Rights, Sovereignty and Security in the Post-Soviet Space. *International Security* 26 (3):100–127.

———. 2005a. *Logics of Hierarchy: The Organization of Empires, States and Military Occupations*. Ithaca: Cornell University Press.

———. 2005b. Base Politics. *Foreign Affairs* 84 (6):79–92.

———. 2008. *Base Politics: Democratic Change and the U.S. Military Overseas*. Ithaca: Cornell University Press.

Cooley, Alexander, and James Ron. 2002. The NGO Scramble: Organizational Insecurity and the Political Economy of Transnational Action. *International Security* 27 (1):5–39.

Cooley, John K. 1984. The War over Water. *Foreign Policy* no. 54 (Spring):3–26.

Cornell, Svante E. 2002. Autonomy as a Source of Conflict: Caucasian Conflicts in Theoretical Perspective. *World Politics* 54 (January):245--76.

———. 2004. The United States and Central Asia: In the Steppes to Stay? *Cambridge Review of International Affairs* 17, no. 2 (July):239–54.

Cotrell, A., and A. Moorer. 1977. U.S. Bases Overseas. Washington Paper No. 47. Beverly Hills, CA: Sage.

Cowhey, Peter F. 1993. Domestic Institutions and the Credibility of International Commitments: Japan and the United States. *International Organization* 47 (2):299–326.

Cox, Michael. 2004. Empire, Imperialism and the Bush Doctrine. *Review of International Studies* 30 (4):49–63.

Crawford, Neta C. 2002. *Argument and Change: Ethics, Decolonization and Humanitarian Intervention*. New York: Cambridge University Press.

Cribb, R. B., and Colin Brown. 1995. *Modern Indonesia: A History since 1945*. New York: Longman.

Cullather, Nick, ed. 1992. *Managing Nationalism: United States National Security Council Documents on the Philippines, 1953–1960*. Quezon City, Philippines: New Day Publishers.

———. 1994. *Illusions of Influence: The Political Economy of United States–Philippine Relations, 1942–1960*. Palo Alto, CA: Stanford University Press.

Darby, Philip. 1973. *British Defence Policy East of Suez, 1947–68*. Oxford: Oxford University Press.

Darwin, John. 1999. A Third British Empire? The Dominion Idea in Imperial Politics. In *The Oxford History of the British Empire: The Twentieth Century*, ed. Judith Brown and Wm. Roger Louis. Oxford: Oxford University Press.

de Gaulle, Charles. 1971. *Memoirs of Hope: Renewal and Endeavor.* New York: Simon and Schuster.

Delaporte, Isabelle. 2002. La base française de Mers-el-Kébir de l'après-Second Guerre mondiale à l'évacuation (1945–1968). In *Les bases et les arsenaux français d'Outre-Mer.* Paris: Charles-Lavauzelle.

Delbrück, Jost. 1993. International Law and Military Forces Abroad: U.S. Military Presence in Europe, 1945–1965. In *U.S. Military Forces in Europe: The Early Years, 1945–1970,* ed. Simon W. Duke and Wolfgang Krieger. Boulder, CO: Westview Press.

Desch, Michael. 1989. The Keys That Lock Up the World: Identifying American Interests in the Periphery. *International Security* 14 (1):86–121.

———. 1993. Bases for the Future: U.S. Post–Cold War Military Base Requirements in the Third World. *Security Studies* 2 (2):201–24.

Detter, Ingrid. 1966. The Problem of Unequal Treaties. *International and Comparative Law Quarterly* 15 (4):1069–89.

Diamond, Larry. 2006. *Squandered Victory: The American Occupation and the Bungled Effort to Bring Democracy to Iraq.* New York: Henry Holt.

Diebold, William. 1959. *The Schuman Plan.* New York: Frederick Praeger.

———, ed. 1988. *Bilateralism, Multilateralism and Canada in U.S. Trade Policy.* Cambridge, MA: Ballinger.

Dinan, Desmond. 1999. *Ever Closer Union.* Boulder, CO: Lynne Rienner.

Doleys, Thomas J. 2000. Member States and the European Commission: Theoretical Insights from the New Economics of Organization. *Journal of European Public Policy* 7 (4):532–53.

Dow, Gregory K. 1987. The Function of Authority in Transaction Costs Economics. *Journal of Economic Behavior and Organization* 8 (1):13–38.Doyle, Michael. 1986. *Empires.* Ithaca: Cornell University Press.

Dragsdahl, Jørgen. 2001. The Danish Dilemma. *Bulletin of the Atomic Scientists* 57 (5):45–51.

Drezner, Daniel W. 1999. *The Sanctions Paradox: Economic Statecraft and International Relations.* New York: Cambridge University Press.

———. 2007. *All Politics Is Global: Explaining International Regulatory Regimes.* Princeton: Princeton University Press.

Dufey, Gunter, and Michael Ryan. 1994. *NAFTA: Honda Motor Company or Free Trade in the Real World.* Washington, DC: Institute for the Study of Diplomacy, Georgetown University.

Duke, Simon. 1987. *U.S. Defence Bases in the United Kingdom: A Matter for Joint Decision?* Basingstoke, UK: Macmillan.

———. 1989. *United States Forces and Military Installations in Europe.* Stockholm: SIPRI and Oxford University Press.

Dunlop, John B. 1993. *The Rise of Russia and the Fall of the Soviet Empire.* Princeton: Princeton University Press.

Du Plessis, Anton 1979. *Die Maritiem-Strategiese Betekenis van die Simonstad-Vlootbasis.* Pretoria: Universiteit van Pretoria, Instituut vir Strategiese Studies.

Easter, Gerald. 1997. Preference for Presidentialism: Postcommunist Regime Change in Russia and the NIS. *World Politics* 49 (2):184–211.

Ebel, Robert, and Rajan Menon. 2000. *Energy and Conflict in Central Asia and the Caucasus*. Lanham, MD: Rowman and Littlefield.

Egan, John W. 2006. The Future of Criminal Jurisdiction over the Deployed American Soldier: Four Major Trends in Bilateral U.S. Status of Forces Agreements. *Emory International Law Review* 20 (Spring): 291–344.

Eggertsson, Thráinn. 1990. *Economic Behavior and Institutions*. New York: Cambridge University Press.

Eisenhardt, Kathleen M. 1989. Agency Theory: An Assessment and Review. *Academy of Management Review* 14 (1):57–74.

Eldridge, Richard. 2001. *The Origins of the Bilateral Okinawa Problem: Okinawa in Postwar U.S.-Japan Relations, 1945–1952*. New York: Garland.

Emerson, Michael, Michel Aujean, Michel Catinat, Philippe Goybet, and Alexis Jacquemin. 1988. *The Economics of 1992*. Oxford: Oxford University Press.

Encarnación, Omer G. 2004. Democracy and Federalism in Spain. *Mediterranean Quarterly* 15 (1):59–74.

Enloe, Cynthia. 1989. *Bananas, Beaches & Bases*. London: Pandora.

Entelis, John P., and Phillip C. Naylor, eds. 1992. *State and Society in Algeria*. Boulder, CO: Westview Press.

Epstein, David, and Sharyn O'Halloran. 1999. *Delegating Powers: A Transaction Costs Politics Approach to Policy Making under Separate Powers*. New York: Cambridge University Press.

Evans, Graham. 1990. Walvis Bay: South Africa, Namibia and the Question of Sovereignty. *International Affairs* 66 (3):559–68.

Fazal, Tanisha. 2007. *State Death: The Politics and Geography of Conquest, Occupation, and Annexation*. Princeton: Princeton University Press.

Fearon, James. 1994. Domestic Political Audiences and the Escalation of International Disputes. *American Political Science Review* 88 (3):577–92.

Fearon, James D., and David D. Laitin. 2004. Neotrusteeship and the Problem of Weak States. *International Security* 28 (4):5–43.

Fieldhouse, D. K. 1999. The Metropolitan Economics of Empire. In *The Oxford History of the British Empire: The Twentieth Century*, ed. Judith Brown and Wm. Roger Louis. Oxford: Oxford University Press.

Friedberg, Aaron. 1988. *The Weary Titan*. Princeton: Princeton University Press.

Frieden, Jeffry A. 1994. International Investment and Colonial Control: A New Interpretation. *International Organization* 48 (4):559–93.

Gallagher, Tom. 1979. Portugal's Atlantic Territories: The Separatist Challenge. *The World Today* 35 (9):353–59.

Garrett, Geoffrey. 1995. The Politics of Legal Integration in the European Union. *International Organization* 49 (1):171–81.

Garrett, Geoffrey, Daniel Keleman, and Heiner Schulz. 1998. The European Court of Justice, National Governments, and Legal Integration in the European Union. *International Organization* 52 (1):149–76.

Gat, Joel. 2006. Planning and Management of a Sustainable and Equitable Water Supply under Stress of Water Scarcity and Quality Deterioration and the Constraints of Societal and Political Divisions. In *Water for Life in the Middle East*, ed. Hillel Shuval and Hasan Dwiek. Jerusalem: Israel/Palestine Center for Research and Information.

Gehrels, Franz, and Bruce Johnston. 1955. The Economic Gains of European Integration. *Journal of Political Economy* 63 (4):275–92.

George, Alexander L. 1979. Case Studies and Theory Development: The Method of Structured, Focused Comparison. In *Diplomacy: New Approaches in History, Theory, and Policy*, ed. Paul Gordon Lauren. New York: Free Press.

George, Stephen. 1985. *Politics and Policy in the European Community*. Oxford: Clarendon.

Gerson, Joseph, and Bruce Birchard, eds. 1991. *The Sun Never Sets: Confronting the Network of Foreign U.S. Military Bases*. Boston: South End Press.

Girault, René. 1986. The French Decision Makers and Their Perception of French Power in 1948. In *Power in Europe?: Great Britain, France, Italy, and Germany in a Postwar World, 1945–1950*, ed. Josef Becker and Franz Knipping. New York: W. de Gruyter.

Glassburner, Bruce, ed. 1971. *The Economy of Indonesia*. Ithaca: Cornell University Press.

Goddard, Stacie E. 2006. Uncommon Ground: Indivisible Territory and the Politics of Legitimacy. *International Organization* 60 (1):35–68.

Gold, Peter. 2004. Sovereignty Negotiations and Gibraltar's Military Facilities: How Two "Red-Line" Issues Became Three. *Diplomacy and Statecraft* 15 (2):375–84.

Goldstein, Judith. 1996. International Law and Domestic Institutions: Reconciling North American "Unfair" Trade Laws. *International Organization* 50 (4):541–64.

Golob, Stephanie. 2003. Beyond the Policy Frontier: Canada, Mexico, and the Ideological Origins of NAFTA. *World Politics* 55 (3):361–98.

Gordon, Daniel A. 2000. World Reactions to the 1961 Paris Program. *University of Sussex Journal of Contemporary History* 1:1–6.

Gordon, Donald C. 1965. *The Dominion Partnership in Imperial Defense, 1870–1914*. Baltimore: Johns Hopkins University Press.

Gordon, Richard L. 1962. Coal Price Regulation in the European Community, 1946–1961. *Journal of Industrial Economics* 10 (3):188–203.

Gow, James 1992. *Legitimacy and the Military: The Yugoslav Crisis*. New York: St. Martin's Press.

Gray, Alan. 1962. Quarterly Chronicle. *African Affairs* 61 (244):178–82.

Greene, Fred, ed. 1988. *The Philippine Bases: Negotiating for the Future American and Philippine Perspectives*. New York: Council on Foreign Relations.

Gregory, Paul, and Robert Stuart. 1994. *Soviet and Post-Soviet Economic Structure and Performance*. New York: Harper Collins.

Grieco, Joseph. 1990. *Cooperation among Nations: Europe, America, and Non-Tariff Barriers to Trade*. Ithaca: Cornell University Press.

———. 1994. Variation in Regional Economic Institutions in Western Europe, East Asia, and the Americas: Magnitude and Sources. Karl W. Deutsch Professorship, Discussion Paper. Wissenschaftszentrum Berlin.

———. 1995. The Maastricht Treaty, Economic and Monetary Union, and the Neo-Realist Research Programme. *Review of International Studies* 21:21–40.

Grimmett, Richard. 1986. *U.S. Military Installations in NATO's Southern Region*. Report prepared for the U.S. Congress. Washington, DC.

Grossman, Sanford, and Oliver Hart. 1986. The Costs and Benefits of Ownership: A Theory of Vertical and Lateral Integration. *Journal of Political Economy* 94 (4):691–719.

Grove, Eric. 1987. *Vanguard to Trident: British Naval Policy since World War II*. London: Bodley Head.

Haas, Ernst B. 2004 [1958]. *The Uniting of Europe*. Notre Dame, IN: Notre Dame University Press.

Hancock, Kathleen. 2001. Surrendering Sovereignty: Hierarchy in the International System and the Former Soviet Union. Ph.D. diss., University of California–San Diego.

Hanning, Hugh. 1966. Britain East of Suez—Facts and Figures. *International Affairs* 42 (2):253–60.

Hale, Henry E. 2004. Divided We Stand: Institutional Sources of Ethnofederal State Survival and Collapse. *World Politics* 56 (2):165–93.

Hargreaves, John. 1996. *Decolonization in Africa*. New York: Longman.

Harkavy, Robert. 1989. *Bases Abroad: The Global Foreign Military Presence*. New York: Oxford University Press and SIPRI.

———. 1993. The Changing Strategic and Technological Bases. In *United States Military Forces in Europe: The Early Years*, ed. Simon Duke and Wolfgang Krieger. Boulder, CO: Westview Press.

Harrison, Christopher. 1983. French Attitudes to Empire and the Algerian War. *African Affairs* 82 (326):75–95.

Harrop, Jeffrey. 1989. *The Political Economy of Integration in the European Community*. Aldershot, UK: Edward Alger.

Hart, Oliver. 1995. *Firms, Contracts and Financial Structure*. New York: Oxford University Press.

Hart, Oliver, and Bengt Holström. 1987. The Theory of Contracts. In *Advances in Economic Theory: Fifth World Congress*, ed. Truman F. Bewley. Cambridge: Cambridge University Press.

Hart, Oliver, and John Moore. 1990. Property Rights and the Nature of the Firm. *Journal of Political Economy* 98 (6):1119–58.

Hawkins, David. 1969. Britain and Malaysia—Another View: Was the Decision to Withdraw Entirely Voluntary or Was Britain Pushed a Little? *Asian Survey* 9 (7):546–62.

Hechter, Michael. 2006. Alien Rule and Its Discontents. Paper presented at the Rationalist Approaches to Empire, February 9, Columbia University.

Helleiner, Eric. 2002. *The Making of National Money: Territorial Currencies in Historical Perspective*. Ithaca: Cornell University Press.

Henshaw, Peter. 1992. Transfer of Simonstown: Afrikaner Nationalism, South African Strategic Dependence and British Global Power. *Journal of Imperial and Commonwealth History* 20 (3):419–44.

Herz, John. 1976. *The Nation-State and the Crisis of World Politics*. New York: David McKay.

Herz, Norman. 2004. *Operation Alacrity: The Azores and the War in the Atlantic*. Annapolis: Naval Institute Press.

Hill, J. R., ed. 1995. *The Oxford Illustrated History of the Royal Navy*. New York: Oxford University Press.

Hix, Simon. 2002. Constitutional Agenda-Setting through Discretion in Rule-Interpretation: Why the European Parliament Won at Amsterdam. *British Journal of Political Science* 32 (2):259–80.

Horne, Alistair. 1978. *A Savage War of Peace: Algeria, 1954–1962*. New York: Viking.

Howard, Michael. 1966. Britain's Strategic Problem East of Suez. *International Affairs* 42 (2):179–83.

Hufbauer, Gary, and Jeffrey Schott. 1992. *North American Free Trade*. Washington, DC: Institute for International Economics.

———. 1993. *NAFTA: An Assessment*. Washington, DC: Institute for International Economics.

Human Rights Watch. 2004. Failure to Protect: Anti-Minority Violence in Kosovo. New York, March 2004. http://www.hrw.org/reports/2004/kosovo0704.

Hurtig, Serge. 1958. The European Common Market. *International Conciliation* 517:321–81.

Hyam, Ronald, ed. 1992. The Labour Government and the End of Empire, 1945–1951. *British Documents on the End of Empire. Parts I–IV* (Series A). London: HMSO.

Hyam, Ronald, and Wm. Rogers Louis, eds. 2000. The Conservative Government and the End of Empire, 1957–1964. *British Documents on the End of Empire, Parts I, II*. London: The Stationary Office.

Ikenberry, John. 2001. *After Victory: Institutions, Strategic Restraint, and the Rebuilding of Order after Major Wars*. Princeton: Princeton University Press.

Immergut, Helen. 1992. The Rules of the Game: The Logic of Health Policy-Making in France, Switzerland, and Sweden. In *Structuring Politics: Historical Institutionalism in Comparative Analysis*, ed. Kathleen Thelen, Sven Steinmo, and Frank Longstreth. New York: Cambridge University Press.

International Crisis Group. 2004. Collapse in Kosovo. Europe Report No. 155. Pristina/Belgrade/Brussels, April 22.

———. 2005. Unmaking Iraq: A Constitutional Process Gone Awry. Middle East Briefing No. 19. Available at http://www.crisisgroup.org/home/index .cfm?id=3703.

Isaac, Jad. 1999. The Palestinian Water Crisis. The Palestine Center. Available at http://www.palestinecenter.org/cpap/pubs/19990818ib.html.

Jabko, Nicolas. 2006. *Playing the Market: Political Strategy for Unifying Europe, 1985–2005*. Ithaca: Cornell University Press.

Jackson, Robert H. 1993. The Weight of Ideas in Decolonization: Normative Change in International Relations. In *Ideas and Foreign Policy*, ed. Judith Goldstein and Robert Keohane. Ithaca: Cornell University Press.

James, Lawrence. 1994. *The Rise and Fall of the British Empire*. New York: St. Martin's Press.

Janis, Mark W. 1993. *An Introduction to International Law*. Boston: Little, Brown.

Jerozolimski, Ana. 2003. Development-Mideast: Water Divides, But Can It Unite? In *Inter Press Service News*. Available at http://ipsnews.net/interna.asp ?idnews=17755.

Johnson, Chalmers, ed. 1999. *Okinawa: Cold War Island*. Cardiff, CA: Japan Policy Research Institute.

———. 2000. *Blowback: The Costs and Consequences of American Empire*. New York: Henry Holt.

———. 2004. *The Sorrows of Empire*. New York: Metropolitan.

———. 2007. *Nemesis: The Last Days of the American Republic*. New York: Henry Holt.

Joskow, Paul. 1985. Vertical Integration and Long-Term Contracts: The Case of Coal-Burning Electric Generating Plants. *Journal of Law, Economics and Organization* 1 (1):33–80.

Katzenstein, Peter J., ed. 1996. *The Culture of National Security: Norms and Identity in World Politics*. Ithaca: Cornell University Press.

Kay, N. M. 1992. Markets, False Hierarchies, and the Evolution of the Modern Corporation. *Journal of Economic Behavior and Organization* 17 (3):315–33.

Kennedy, Raymond, W. L. Holland, and Hsu Yung-ying. 1943. Notes and Comment: Dutch Charter for the Indies. *Pacific Affairs* 16 (2):216–23.

Keohane, Robert O. 1984. *After Hegemony: Cooperation and Discord in the World Political Economy*. Princeton: Princeton University Press.

———, ed. 1986. *Neorealism and Its Critics*. New York: Columbia University Press.

King, Gary, Robert O. Keohane, and Sidney Verba. 1994. *Designing Social Inquiry*. Princeton: Princeton University Press.

King, Iain, and Whit Mason. 2006. *Peace at Any Price: How the World Failed Kosovo*. Ithaca: Cornell University Press.

Klein, Benjamin. 1988. Vertical Integration as Organizational Ownership: The Fisher Body–General Motors Relationship Revisited. *Journal of Law, Economics, and Organization* 4 (1):199–213.

Knaus, Gerald, and Felix Martin. 2003. Travails of the European Raj: Lessons from Bosnia and Herzegovina. *Journal of Democracy* 14 (3):60–74.

Kogut, Bruce. 1988. Joint Ventures: Theoretical and Empirical Perspectives. *Strategic Management Journal* 9 (4):319–32.

Kohl, Wilfrid. 1971. *French Nuclear Diplomacy*. Princeton: Princeton University Press.

Koremenos, Barbara. 2001. Loosening the Ties That Bind: A Learning Model of Flexibility. *International Organization* 55 (2):289–325.

Koremenos, Barbara, Charles Lipson, and Duncan Snidal. 2001. The Rational Design of International Institutions. *International Organization* 55 (4): 761–800.

Kornai, Janos. 1992. *The Socialist System: The Political Economy of Communism*. Princeton: Princeton University Press.

Krasner, Stephen D. 1978. *Defending the National Interest: Raw Materials Investment and American Foreign Policy*. Princeton: Princeton University Press.

———. 1999. *Sovereignty: Organized Hypocrisy*. Princeton: Princeton University Press.

———. 2004. Sharing Sovereignty: New Institutions for Collapsed and Failing States. *International Security* 29 (2):85–120.

————. 2005. The Case for Shared Sovereignty. *Journal of Democracy* 16 (1):69–83.

Kriesberg, Louis. 1959. German Public Opinion and the European Coal and Steel Community. *Public Opinion Quarterly* 23 (1):28–42.

Krysiek, Timothy F. 2007. Agreements from Another Era: Production Sharing Agreements in Putin's Russia, 2000–2007. Oxford Institute for Energy Studies, Working Paper 34.

Kupchan, Charles. 1994. *The Vulnerability of Empire*. Ithaca: Cornell University Press.

Laitin, David D. 1999. National Revivals and Violence. In *Critical Comparisons in Politics and Culture*, ed. John Bowen and Roger Petersen. New York: Cambridge University Press.

Lake, David A. 1996. Anarchy, Hierarchy, and the Variety of International Relations. *International Organization* 50 (1):1–33.

————. 1997. The Rise, Fall, and Future of the Russian Empire: A Theoretical Interpretation. In *The End of Empire? The Transformation of the USSR in Comparative Perspective*, ed. Karen Dawisha and Bruce Parrott. Armonk, NY: M. E. Sharpe.

————. 1999. *Entangling Relations: American Foreign Policy in Its Century*. Princeton: Princeton University Press.

Lapidus, Gail, Victor Zaslavsky, and Philip Goldman, eds. 1992. *From Union to Commonwealth: Nationalism and Separatism in the Soviet Republics*. New York: Cambridge University Press.

Leff, Carol Skalnik. 1999. Democratization and Disintegration in Multinational States: The Breakup of the Communist Federations. *World Politics* 51 (2):205–35.

LeVine, Steve. 2007. *The Oil and the Glory: The Pursuit of Empire and Fortune on the Caspian Sea*. New York: Random House.

Lijphart, Arend. 1971. Comparative Politics and the Comparative Method *American Political Science Review* 65 (3):682–93.

————. 1977. *Democracy in Plural Societies: A Comparative Exploration*. New Haven: Yale University Press.

Lipson, Charles. 1985. *Standing Guard: Protecting Foreign Capital in the Nineteenth and Twentieth Centuries*. Berkeley: University of California Press.

————. 2003. *Reliable Partners: How Democracies Have Made a Separate Peace*. Princeton: Princeton University Press.

Lloyd, Selwyn. 1978. *Suez 1956*. New York: Mayflower.

Loehman, Edna, and Nir Becke. 2006. Groundwater Management in a Cross Boundary Case: Application to Israel and the Palestinian Authority. In *Water for Life in the Middle East*, ed. Hillel Shuval and Hasan Dwiek. Jerusalem: Israel/Palestine Center for Research and Information.

Losada, Anton, and Ramon Maiz. 2005. Devolution and Involution: De-Federalization Politics through Educational Policies in Spain (1996–2004). *Regional and Federal Studies* 14 (4):437–51.

Lowi, Miriam. 1999. Water and Conflict in the Middle East and South Asia: Are Environmental Issues and Security Issues Linked? *Journal of Environment and Development* 8 (4):376–96.

Luft, Gal. 2002. The Wazzani Water Dispute. Washington, DC: Washington Institute for Near East Policy.

Lukauskas, Arvid John. 1997. *Regulating Finance: The Political Economy of Spanish Financial Policy from Franco to Democracy*. Ann Arbor: University of Michigan Press.

Lustick, Ian S. 1993. *Unsettled States, Disputed Lands: Britain and Ireland, France and Algeria, Israel and the West Bank–Gaza*. Ithaca: Cornell University Press.

Maddison, Angus. 1990. Dutch Colonialism in Indonesia: A Comparative Perspective. In *Indonesian Economic History in the Dutch Colonial Era*, ed. Anne Booth, W. J. O'Malley, and Anna Weidemann. New Haven: Yale University South East Asian Studies.

Mahant, Edelgard. 2004. *Birthmarks of Europe: The Origins of the European Community Reconsidered*. Aldershot, UK: Ashgate.

Majone, Giandomenico. 2005. *Dilemmas of European Integration*. Oxford: Oxford University Press.

Marseille, Jacques. 1976. Commerce international et termes de l'échange. *Revue française d'histoire d'Outre-Mer* 63 (232):529–37.

———. 1984. *Empire coloniale et capitalisme français*. Paris: Albin Michel.

Marten, Kimberly. 2004. *Enforcing the Peace: Learning from the Imperial Past*. New York: Columbia University Press.

———. 2007. Russian Efforts to Control Kazakhstan's Oil: The Kumkol Case. *Post-Soviet Affairs* 23 (1):18–37.

Martin, Lisa L. 2000. *Democratic Commitments: Legislatures and International Cooperation*. Princeton: Princeton University Press.

Matlock, Jack F. 1995. *Autopsy on an Empire: The American Ambassador's Account of the Collapse of the Soviet Union*. New York: Random House.

Mattli, Walter. 1999. *The Logic of Regional Integration*. New York: Cambridge University Press.

———. 2001. Private Justice in a Global Economy: From Litigation to Arbitration. *International Organization* 55 (4):919–48.

Mattli, Walter, and Anne-Marie Slaughter. 1998. Revisiting the European Court of Justice. *International Organization* 52 (1):177–209.

Maxwell, Kenneth. 1997. *The Making of Portuguese Democracy*. New York: Cambridge University Press.

McDonald, John W., and Diane B. Bendahmane. 1990. *US Bases Overseas: Negotiations with Spain, Greece, and the Philippines*. Boulder, CO: Westview Press.

Meadows, Martin. 1965. Recent Developments in Philippine-American Relations. *Asian Survey* 5 (6):305–18.

Mearsheimer, John J. 1994–95. The False Promise of International Institutions. *International Security* 19 (3):5–49.

———. 2001. *The Tragedy of Great Power Politics*. New York: W. W. Norton.

Menon, Rajan, and Hendrik Spruyt. 1997. Possibilities for Conflict and Conflict Resolution in Post-Soviet Central Asia. In *Post-Soviet Political Order*, ed. Barnett Rubin and Jack Snyder. New York: Routledge.

———. 1999. The Limits of Neorealism: Understanding Security in Central Asia. *Review of International Studies* 25 (1):87–105.

Mikesell, Raymond F. 1958. The Lessons of Benelux and the European Coal and Steel Community for the European Economic Community. *American Economic Review* 48 (2):428–41.

Milgrom, Paul, and John Roberts. 1992. *Economics, Organizations and Management*. Englewood Cliffs, NJ: Prentice-Hall.

Miller, Gary J. 1992. *Managerial Dilemmas: The Political Economy of Hierarchy*. New York: Cambridge University Press.

Milner, Helen V. 1997. *Interests, Institutions, and Information: Domestic Politics and International Relations*. Princeton: Princeton University Press.

Milward, Alan. 1992. *The European Rescue of the Nation-State*. Berkeley: University of California Press.

Monje, Scott C. 1992. The Azores in the Atlantic World: Geostrategic Aspects. *Camões Center Quarterly* 3 (3–4):2–12.

Monteleone, Carla. 2007. The Evolution of American Military Bases in Italy. Available at http://foreignpolicy.it/file_adon/monteleone.rtf (accessed March 15, 2008).

Montinola, Gabriella, Yingyi Qian, and Barry R. Weingast. 1995. Federalism, Chinese Style: The Political Basis for Economic Success in China. *World Politics* 48 (1):50–81.

Moran, Theodore H. 1974. *Multinational Corporations and the Politics of Dependence: Copper in Chile*. Princeton: Princeton University Press.

Moravcsik, Andrew. 1991. Negotiating the Single European Act: National Interests and Conventional Statecraft. *International Organization* 45 (1):19–56.

———. 1998. *The Choice for Europe*. Ithaca: Cornell University Press.

Motyl, Alexander. 2006. Empire Falls. *Foreign Affairs* 85 (4):190–94.

Murfett, Malcolm. 1995. *In Jeopardy: The Royal Navy and British Far Eastern Defence Policy, 1945–1951*. Oxford: Oxford University Press.

Nailor, Peter. 1996. The Ministry of Defence, 1959–1979. In *Government and the Armed Forces*, ed. Paul Smith. Rio Grande, OH: Hambledon Press.

Nash, Frank. 1957. *United States Overseas Military Bases*. White House Report. Washington, DC. December 1. Declassified February 7, 1990.

Nassar, Yasser. 2006. Virtual Water Trade as a Policy Instrument for Achieving Water Security in Palestine. In *Water for Life in the Middle East*, ed. Hillel Shuval and Hasan Dwiek. Jerusalem: Israel/Palestine Center for Research and Information.

Navias, Martin. 1996. Vested Interests and Vanished Dreams: Duncan Sandys, the Chiefs of Staff, and the 1957 White Paper. In *Government and the Armed Forces*, ed. Paul Smith. Rio Grande, OH: Hambledon Press.

Naylor, Phillip C. 1992. French-Algerian Relations, 1980–1990. In *State and Society in Algeria*, ed. John P. Entelis and Phillip C. Naylor. Boulder, CO: Westview Press.

———. 2000. *France and Algeria: A History of Decolonization and Transformation*. Gainesville: University of Florida Press.

Nexon, Daniel, and Thomas Wright. 2007. What's at Stake in the American Empire Debate. *American Political Science Review* 101 (2):253–71.

North, Douglass. 1990. *Institutions, Institutional Change and Economic Performance*. New York: Cambridge.

Odell, John, and Margit Matzinger-Tchakerian. 1988. European Community Enlargement and the United States. Washington, DC: Institute for the Study of Diplomacy, Georgetown University.

Ohmae, Kenichi. 1995. *The End of the Nation-State: The Rise of Regional Economies*. New York: Simon and Schuster.

Ostrom, Elinor. 2005. *Understanding Institutional Diversity*. Princeton: Princeton University Press.

Overseas Basing Commission (OBC). 2005. *Report of the Commission on Review of the Overseas Military Facility Structure of the United States*. Washington, DC. August.

Panglaykim, J. 1978. Economic Cooperation: Indonesian-Japanese Joint Ventures. *Asian Survey* 18 (3):247–60.

Paris, Roland. 2004. *At War's End: Building Peace after Civil Conflict*. New York: Cambridge University Press.

Parsons, Craig. 2003. *A Certain Idea of Europe*. Ithaca: Cornell University Press.

Pearce, Fred. 2004. Israel Lays Claim to Palestine's Water. *New Scientist*, May 27, 2004.

Pfeifer, Karen. 1992. Economic Liberalization in the 1980s. In *State and Society in Algeria*, ed. John P. Entelis and Phillip C. Naylor. Boulder, CO: Westview Press.

Pierson, Paul. 2000. Increasing Returns, Path Dependence, and the Study of Politics. *American Political Science Review* 94 (2):251–67.

Pollack, Mark. 1997. Delegation, Agency, and Agenda Setting in the European Community. *International Organization* 51 (1):99–134.

Pugh, Mark. 1989. *The ANZUS Crisis, Nuclear Visiting and Deterrence*. New York: Cambridge University Press.

Rector, Chad. 2003. Federations in International Politics. Ph.D. diss., University of California–San Diego.

Risse-Kappen, Thomas. 1996. Collective Identity in a Democratic Community: The Case of NATO. In *The Culture of National Security: Norms and Identity in World Politics*, ed. Peter Katzenstein. New York: Columbia University Press.

Robison, Richard. 1986. *Indonesia: The Rise of Capital*. North Sydney: Allen and Unwin.

Rodrigues, Luís Nuno. 2002. *Salazar-Kennedy: Crisis of an Alliance*. Lisbon: Noticias Editorial.

———. 2004. About-Face: The United States and Portuguese Colonialism in 1961. *Electronic Journal of Portuguese History* 2 (1).

Roeder, Phillip G. 1991. Soviet Federalism and Ethnic Mobilization. *World Politics* 43 (2):196–232.

———. 1993. *Red Sunset: The Failure of Soviet Politics*. Princeton: Princeton University Press.

Rooth, Tim. 1992. *British Protectionism and the International Economy: Overseas Commercial Policy in the 1930s*. Cambridge: Cambridge University Press.

Ross, Michael L. 2001. Does Oil Hinder Democracy? *World Politics* 53 (1): 325–61.

Rouse, Joseph H. 1957. The Exercise of Criminal Jurisdiction under the NATO Status of Forces Agreement. *American Journal of International Law* 51 (1):46–52.

Rouyer, Alwyn. 1999. The Water Accords of Oslo II: Averting a Looming Disaster. *Middle East Policy* 7 (1):113–35.

Rubin, Barnett. 1994. Tajikistan: From Soviet Republic to Russian-Uzbek Protectorate. In *Central Asia and the World*, ed. Michael Mandelbaum. New York: Council on Foreign Relations.

Rubin, Barnett, and Jack Snyder, eds. 1998. *Post-Soviet Political Order*. New York: Routledge.

Ruf, Werner. 1971. The Bizerta Crisis: A Bourguibist Attempt to Resolve Tunisia's Border Problems. *Middle East Journal* 25 (2):201–11.

Ruggie, John. 1986. Continuity and Transformation in the World Polity. In *Neorealism and Its Critics*, ed. Robert Keohane. New York: Columbia University Press.

———, ed. 1998. *Multilateralism Matters: The Theory and Praxis of an Institutional Form*. New York: Columbia University Press.

Rumer, Boris. 1990. *Soviet Central Asia: A Tragic Experiment*. Boston: Unwin Hyman.

Ruseckas, Laurent, and Hendrik Spruyt. 1999. Economic Development and Energy as Security Concerns in the Southern Tier. In *Russia's New Security Environment*, ed. Rajan Menon, Yuri Fedorov, and Ghia Nodia. Armonk, NY: M. E. Sharpe.

Said, Edward. 2000. *The End of the Peace Process*. New York: Pantheon.

Sandars, C. T. 2000. *America's Overseas Garrisons: The Leasehold Empire*. New York: Oxford University Press.

Sartori, Anne. 2005. *Deterrence by Diplomacy*. Princeton: Princeton University Press.

Sbragia, Alberta, ed. 1992. *Europolitics*. Washington, DC: Brookings Institution.

Schenk, Catherine. 1996. Decolonization and European Economic Integration: The Free Trade Area Negotiations, 1956–58. *Journal of Imperial and Commonwealth History* 24 (3):444–63.

Schmitz, Patrick W. 2001. The Hold-Up Problem and Incomplete Contracts: A Survey of Recent Topics in Contract Theory. *Bulletin of Economic Research* 53 (1):1–17.

Schweller, Randall. 1998. *Deadly Imbalances: Tripolarity and Hitler's Strategy of World Conquest*. New York: Columbia University Press.

Selby, Jan. 2003. Dressing up Domination as "Cooperation": The Case of Israeli-Palestinian Water Relations. *Review of International Studies* 29:121–38.

———. 2006. Joint Mismanagement: Reappraising the Oslo Water Regime. In *Water for Life in the Middle East*, ed. Hillel Shuval and Hasan Dwiek. Jerusalem: Israel/Palestine Center for Research and Information.

Shikaki, Khalil. 2002. Palestinians Divided. *Foreign Affairs* 81 (January–February):89–105.

Simmons, Beth A. 2002. Capacity, Commitment, and Compliance: International Institutions and Territorial Disputes. *Journal of Conflict Resolution* 46 (6):829–56.

Smith, David, and Louis Wells. 1975. Mineral Agreements in Developing Countries: Structures and Substance. *American Journal of International Law* 69 (3):560–90.

Snyder, Jack L. 2000. *From Voting to Violence: Democratization and Nationalist Conflict*. New York: W. W. Norton.

Solnick, Steven L. 1998. *Stealing the State: Control and Collapse in Soviet Institutions*. Cambridge, MA: Harvard University Press.

Spruyt, Hendrik. 1994. *The Sovereign State and Its Competitors*. Princeton: Princeton University Press.

———. 2005. *Ending Empire: Contested Sovereignty and Territorial Partition*. Ithaca: Cornell University Press.

Stepan, Alfred. 1999. Federalism and Democracy: Beyond the U.S. Model. *Journal of Democracy* 10 (4):19–34.

Stephan, Raya. 2006. The Legal Framework of Groundwater Management in the Middle East (Israel, Jordan, Lebanon, Syria and the Palestinian Territories). In *Water for Life in the Middle East*, ed. Hillel Shuval and Hasan Dwiek. Jerusalem: Israel/Palestine Center for Research and Information.

Stevenson, Matthew. 2000. Bias and the NAFTA Dispute Panels: Controversies and Counter-Evidence. *American Review of Canadian Studies* 30 (1):19–33.

Stone Sweet, Alec, and Thomas Brunell. 1998. Constructing a Supranational Constitution: Dispute Resolution and Governance in the European Community. *American Political Science Review* 92 (1):63–81.

Suny, Ronald Grigor. 1997. *The Soviet Experiment: Russia, the USSR, and the Successor States*. New York: Oxford University Press.

Thacker, Strom. 1999. NAFTA Coalitions and the Political Viability of Neoliberalism in Mexico. *Journal of Interamerican Studies and World Affairs* 41 (2):57–89.

Thelen, Kathleen. 2004. *How Institutions Evolve: The Political Economy of Skills in Germany, Britain, the United States, and Japan*. Cambridge: Cambridge University Press.

Tirole, Jean. 1999. Incomplete Contracts: Where Do We Stand? *Econometrica* 67 (4):741–82.

Tsebelis, George. 1995. Decision Making in Political Systems: Veto Players in Presidentialism, Parliamentarism, Multicameralism and Multipartyism. *British Journal of Political Science* 25:289–325.

———. 1999. Veto Players and Law Production in Parliamentary Democracies: An Empirical Analysis. *American Political Science Review* 93 (3):591–608.

Vachudova, Milada. 2005. *Europe Undivided: Democracy, Leverage & Integration after Communism*. New York: Oxford University Press.

van de Kerkhof, J. P. 2005. Onmisbaar maar onbemind: De Koninklijke Paketvaart Maatschappij en de Billiton Maatschappij in het onafhankelijke Indonesië (1945–1958). *Tijdschrift voor Sociale en Economische Geschiedenis* 4:122–46.

van den Doel, H. W. 1996. *Het Rijk van Insulinde*. Amsterdam: Prometheus.

van der Kroef, Justus. 1955. Indonesia's Economic Difficulties. *Far Eastern Survey* 24 (2):17–24.

van Doorn, J. A. 1990. De Verwerking van het Einde van Indie. In *De Politionele Acties: Afwikkeling en Verwerking*, ed. Gerke Teitler and J. Hoffenaar. Amsterdam: Bataafsche Leeuw.

———. 1995. The Past Is a Strong Present: The Dutch-Indonesian Conflict and the Persistence of the Colonial Pattern. *Netherlands Journal of Social Sciences* 31 (2):153–71.

Van Evera, Stephen. 1997. *Guide to Methods for Students of Political Science.* Ithaca: Cornell University Press.

Van Harten, Gus. 2007. *Investment Treaty Arbitration and Public Law.* Oxford: Oxford University Press.

Vernon, Raymond. 1971. *Sovereignty at Bay: The Multinational Spread of U.S. Enterprises.* New York: Basic Books.

Vial, Philippe. 2002. Un impossible renouveau: Bases et arsenaux d'Outre-mer, 1945–1975. In *Les bases et les arsenaux français d'Outre-mer.* Paris: Charles-Lavauzelle.

Vintras, R. E. 1974. *The Portuguese Connection: The Secret History of the Azores Base.* London: Bachman and Turner.

Wallander, Celeste A. 2000. Institutional Assets and Adaptability: NATO After the Cold War. *International Organization* 54 (4):705–35.

Walt, Stephen. 1987. *The Origins of Alliances.* Ithaca: Cornell University Press.

Waltz, Kenneth N. 1979. *Theory of International Politics.* Reading, MA: Addison-Wesley.

Weber, Katja. 2000. *Hierarchy amidst Anarchy: Transaction Costs and Institutional Choice.* Albany: State University of New York Press.

Weber, Katja, and Mark Hallerberg. 2001. Explaining Variation in Institutional Integration in the European Union: Why Firms May Prefer European Solutions. *Journal of European Public Policy* 8 (2):171–91.

Wendt, Alexander. 1999. *Social Theory of International Politics.* New York: Cambridge University Press.

White, Nicholas. 1998. Capitalism and Counter-Insurgency? Business and Government in the Malayan Emergency, 1948–57. *Modern Asian Studies* 32 (1):149–77.

Williamson, John. 2003. Dollarization Does Not Make Sense Everywhere. In *The Dollarization Debate*, ed. Dominick Salvatore, James W. Dean, and Thomas Willett. New York: Oxford University Press.

Williamson, Oliver E. 1975. *Markets and Hierarchies: Analysis and Antitrust Implications.* New York: Free Press.

———. 1985. *The Economic Institutions of Capitalism.* New York: Free Press.

———. 1986. *Economic Organization.* New York: New York University Press.

Winham, Gilbert. 1988. Why Canada Acted. In *Multilateralism and Canada in U.S. Trade Policy*, ed. William Diebold. Cambridge, MA: Ballinger.

Wolf, Aaron T. 1995. *Hydropolitics along the Jordan River.* New York: United Nations University Press.

Woodliffe, J. C. 1971. White Paper on the Legal Obligations of the British Government Arising out of the Simonstown Agreements. *International and Comparative Law Quarterly* 20 (4):753–61.

Woodliffe, John. 1992. *The Peacetime Use of Foreign Military Installations under Modern International Law*. Boston: Kluwer.

Woodward, Susan L. 1995. *Socialist Unemployment: The Political Economy of Yugoslavia, 1945–1990*. Princeton: Princeton University Press.

———. 2007. Does Kosovo's Status Matter? Criteria and Consequences in the International Management of Statehood. Paper presented to the Harriman Institute's seminar series Soft Borders and Limited Sovereignty in Southeast Europe and the Former Soviet States. Columbia University, March 22.

Worrall, Richard John. 2007. The Strategic Limitations of a Middle East Client State by the Mid-1950s: Britain, Libya and the Suez Crisis. *Journal of Strategic Studies* 30 (2):309–47.

Yarbrough, Beth V., and Robert M. Yarbrough. 1992. *Cooperation and Governance in International Trade: The Strategic Organizational Approach*. Princeton: Princeton University Press.

Zacher, Mark W. 2001. The Territorial Integrity Norm: International Boundaries and the Use of Force. *International Organization* 55 (2):215–50.

Zeckhauser, Richard J., and John W. Pratt. 1985. *Principals and Agents: The Structure of Business*. Cambridge, MA: Harvard University Press.

Index

Pages numbers with an *f* indicate figures; those with a *t* indicate tables

Ho Chi Minh, 71
Hong Kong, 76, 79, 81, 94, 97*t*
Horne, Alistair, 62n24
Human Rights Watch, 202
Hungarian uprising (1956), 159
hybrid sovereignty arrangements, 1–7,
    142; Algerian, 30, 43, 58–66; British,
    74–84, 92, 94; choice of, 52; conse-
    quences of, 42, 57*f*; incomplete contracts
    and, 1–5, 10–12, 13*t*, 34–35, 42–44; In-
    donesian, 70–74; international transi-
    tional administrations and, 199–204;
    Russian, 87–90; transaction-specific
    assets and, 23, 112; Tunisian, 66–68;
    United States and, 110–12. *See also*
    sovereign transfers

Iceland, 108, 110, 126
Ikenberry, John, 5n16
incomplete contracting, 24–28, 40–44,
    204–6; complete versus, 11–15, 13*t*, 19,
    25–26, 33–35; consequences of, 11, 42,
    54–56, 57*f*; disengagement and, 50–51,
    51*f*; European Court of Justice and,
    181–82; Evian Accords as, 58–61; feder-
    alism and, 188–91; Global Defense Pos-
    ture Review and, 137–39; hybrid sover-
    eignty arrangements and, 1–5, 10–12,
    13*t*, 34–35, 42–44; importance of, 5–8;
    Kosovo conflict and, 199–204; logic of,
    8–10; neo-imperialism and, 53; proposi-
    tions on, 33–39, 40*t*; regional integra-
    tion and, 142–47, 149–55, 152*f*, 178–
    82; sovereign transfers and, 1–7, 10–12,
    13*t*, 37–39, 48–58, 57*f*, 204–5; U.S.
    basing agreements as, 107–9; U.S.
    Constitution as, 156n30
India, 76n76, 78, 79, 96
Indonesia, 11, 16, 45, 54, 69–74, 92–93;
    communist purge in, 81; foreign invest-
    ment in, 12, 73, 74; Japan and, 73n68,
    74; Vietnam and, 71
Inouye, Daniel, 119
integration. *See* regional integration
intergovernmentality, 143, 145, 149–51
International Crisis Group, 191
International Monetary Fund (IMF), 189
international regimes theory, 20
international transitional administration,
    199–204

Iraq, 106; federalism of, 191–92; Gulf War
    and, 125, 133, 195; interim government
    of, 1–5
Ireland, 2, 166
Israel, 132; Six-Day War and, 64, 192;
    water rights of, 48n1, 192–98; Yom Kip-
    pur War and, 110, 125, 130
Issar, Arie, 196
Italy, 66, 78, 161, 167; GDP of, 162*t*; U.S.
    bases in, 103

Jabko, Nicolas, 171
Japan: Canadian trade agreement with,
    177; GATT and, 172, 173; Indonesia
    and, 73n68, 74; Philippines and, 113;
    United Kingdom and, 76–78; United
    States bases in, 101, 104, 107, 110,
    111, 137
John Hay Air Station (Philippines), 120
"joint decision trap," 168
Jordan, 64, 192–98

Karimov, Islam A., 139
Karshi-Khanabad ("K2") airbase
    (Uzbekistan), 138–39
Kay, N. M., 23n16
Kazakhstan, 86–88, 142
Kennedy, John F., 127–29
Kenya, 80
Keohane, Robert, 20, 43n47
Kissinger, Henry, 119
Korea, 104, 107, 137
Koremenos, Barbara, 5n14, 10, 32,
    154n24
Kosovo, 125, 133, 198–204
Krasner, Stephen, 3, 6, 24n22
Kyrgyzstan, 84, 138–40

Laitin, David D., 142n1
Lajes military bases (Azores), 125–26, 132,
    133, 135*t*
Lake, David A., 4n11, 5, 21, 53n5
Latvia, 86
Lebanon, 192
Liberia, 53n4
Libya, 56, 67, 110
Linggadjati Agreement (1947), 71
Lipson, Charles, 10, 21, 32, 50n2
Lisbon Agreement (2007), 2, 179
Loehman, Edna, 193
López Portillo, José, 173
Lukoil company, 88